The Art of Printing

www.royalcollins.com

GREAT CHINESE INVENTIONS

The Art of Printing

Edited by
Hua Jueming and Feng Lisheng

By Li Ying

Translated by
Chen Wei
(Jiangnan University)

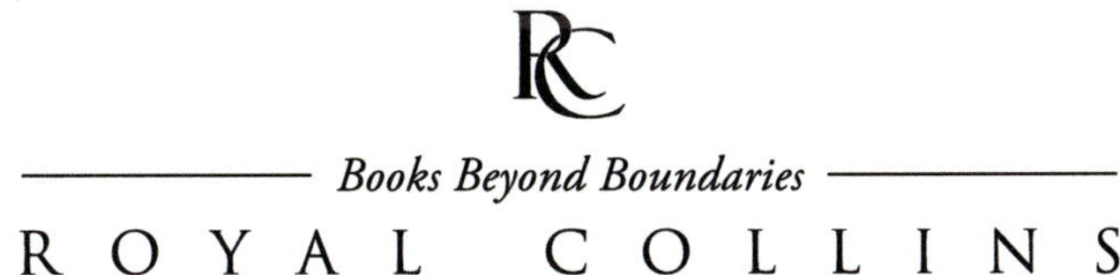

Great Chinese Inventions:
The Art of Printing

Edited by Hua Jueming and Feng Lisheng
By Li Ying
Translated by Chen Wei (Jiangnan University)

Project Coordinator: Zhang Shaowen and Wang Xiaoyuan

First published in 2025 by Royal Collins Publishing Group Inc.
Groupe Publication Royal Collins Inc.
550-555 boul. René-Lévesque O Montréal (Québec) H2Z1B1 Canada

10 9 8 7 6 5 4 3 2 1

ISBN: 978-1-4878-1285-0

To find out more about our publications,
please visit www.royalcollins.com.

Contents

Preface

The "Four Great Inventions" of China have attracted significant attention from the Chinese people due to their profound impact on the course of modern world history. The term "Four Great Inventions" is widely known, but it originated from Western scholars. While this term holds classical significance, it carries a specific background and meaning. However, it fails to comprehensively reflect the significant inventions and technological cultural traditions of China. Throughout its five-thousand-year history of civilization, China's major inventions far exceed these four great inventions. Since the 20th century, especially in recent decades, China's science and technology have undergone rapid development, playing an increasingly important role in social and economic development. The question of what great inventions and creations exist in Chinese history has become a matter of concern not only for the academic community but also for the public. To answer this question truthfully, objectively, and scientifically, further exploration and sorting are needed based on the study of the history of science and technology in China. This involves selecting major inventions that are original, distinct in character, and have made outstanding contributions and significant impacts on both Chinese and world civilizations and discussing their background and evolutionary processes. To this end, we invited experts in the history of science and related fields to compile the book *Thirty Great Inventions of China*, which was published in May 2017. The book received praise from academia and readers, gaining widespread attention. It was awarded the 13th Wenjin Book Award and the National Excellent Popular Science Works Award by the Ministry of Science and Technology in 2018. It was also selected as one of the "Good Books of China" for 2017 and one of the "40 Most Influential Popular Science Books in China in 40 Years of Reform and Opening Up."

To further promote the research on the history of inventions in China and disseminate knowledge of Chinese science and technology culture, we have organized and compiled the Great Chinese Inventions series based on the book *Thirty Great Inventions of China*. The aim is to provide a more comprehensive and detailed exposition of the significance of major technological inventions in China, to understand their origins and developments, and to enable readers to better comprehend and appreciate the historical and modern value of important ancient Chinese technological inventions and creations. Each book in this series is relatively concise, focusing on knowledge dissemination with rich illustrations, aiming to allow readers to obtain relevant information and knowledge about each invention from the narratives of historians of science and technology in a relatively short period of time.

China boasts a profound history and culture, with the Chinese nation having made numerous great inventions and creations that not only propelled the advancement of Chinese civilization but also exerted significant influence on the progress of world civilization. Every Chinese individual should strive to understand history as accurately as possible. Chinese affairs should be clarified by the Chinese themselves, and Chinese people should have a say in matters of invention and creation. This series of books aims to embody the concept of cultural consciousness and comprehensively summarize the significant contributions of the Chinese nation to human technological civilization as much as possible. In the selection of great inventions, adjustments and expansions have been made, expanding the original thirty inventions to more than forty items, particularly adding significant inventions of modern and contemporary China. This series of books examines Chinese great inventions from both cultural tradition and a global perspective. For instance, Chinese characters and traditional Chinese cooking techniques were previously less regarded as major inventions. Still, they serve as important symbols of Chinese civilization and hold significant positions in Chinese cultural and technological traditions, qualifying as great Chinese inventions. Particularly, Chinese characters, as tools for recording information and expressing thoughts for Chinese people, remain vibrant to this day. They not only play an irreplaceable role in the formation, dissemination, and inheritance of Chinese culture but also have had a significant influence on neighboring countries and regions such as Japan, Korea, and Vietnam. Traditional Chinese cooking techniques have played a crucial role in improving the quality of people's lives and enhancing physical health. With the strengthening of China's comprehensive national strength and international influence, Chinese cooking techniques have spread to various parts of the world and are playing an increasingly important role. Traditional Chinese medicine also embodies some pioneering achievements in modern science and technology, such as the practice of variolation, which is a pioneering immunological achievement with global impact.

We also pay attention to significant inventions in modern and contemporary China. For example, Tu Youyou, representing a group of Chinese scientists, extracted artemisinin, a highly effective and low-toxicity antimalarial drug, based on the inheritance of traditional clinical experience in Chinese medicine and the application of modern scientific methods. After its clinical application, artemisinin has saved the lives of thousands of patients, making a tremendous contribution to human health. Rice is one of the world's major food crops, serving as the staple food for about half the global population. The super hybrid rice cultivation technology invented by Yuan Longping is considered a world-class original and significant invention. Hanzi laser typesetting technology, founded by Wang Xuan, is a great invention in the history of modern printing technology in China. It has played an important role in promoting the dissemination of science and culture. Cultural consciousness is a challenging process. On one hand, we need to understand our technological and cultural traditions to enhance cultural identity and confidence. On the other hand, we need to update and transform our cultural traditions and technology, integrating traditional techniques with modern and foreign technologies and enabling modern technology to take root and develop vigorously in China.

Invention and discovery are inherent drivers of the development of human social civilization. Ancient Chinese science and technology have achieved remarkable success, with our ancestors making significant contributions to the progress of world civilization. Over the past century, China has undergone drastic social changes and cultural transformations, so it is understandable that there haven't been many great inventions and creations during this time. While cherishing and valuing our national cultural traditions and historical experiences, we should also take the initiative in cultural transformation and technological development, continuously enhancing our capacity for independent innovation and making greater contributions to the development of human technology and civilization. Looking at the long-term trend of historical development, Chinese science and technology have entered a new period of accelerated development. The innovation consciousness and capability of the Chinese people have been activated, and we can expect more and more original inventions and creations in the future. The prosperity of Chinese science and technology is something to look forward to.

The question of how many great inventions there have been in Chinese history is subjective, and opinions or disputes are inevitable. We hope that the publication of this series of books will attract more attention and participation from experts and readers, stimulating further discussion and exchanges and contributing to the improvement of related research. We also welcome corrections and feedback from colleagues in the academic community and readers on our work.

Hua Jueming and Feng Lisheng
July 28, 2021

Introduction

On May 15, 2019, at the opening ceremony of the Conference on Dialogue of Asian Civilizations, Xi Jinping mentioned printing techniques twice in his speech, "In building civilizations over the course of several millennia, we, the people of Asia, have made brilliant achievements. Literary classics such as *Book of Songs*, *The Analects*, *Talmud*, *Thousand and One Nights*, *Rig-veda*, *The Tale of Genji*, and inventions such as cuneiform script, maps, glass, Arabic numerals, papermaking, and printing techniques. They are all invaluable assets of human civilization." "Chinese inventions such as papermaking, gunpowder, printing, and the compass, as well as China's astronomical knowledge, calendar system, philosophy, and the people-centered doctrine, have all had a global impact and propelled the development of human civilizations."

It is well known that through the development of over 5,000 years, the Chinese nation has created a highly advanced civilization. Our ancestors not only invented papermaking, gunpowder, printing, and the compass, but also contributed countless other technological innovations to the world. Among them, printing is hailed as the "mother of civilization." The printing technology invented by the Chinese has led and inspired the development of printing in other parts of the world, greatly advancing the progress of human civilization. Chronologically, printing technology has evolved gradually as people accumulate experience through continuous exploration. Globally, the printing techniques of the East and the West have not only exchanged and learned from each other, but also have their own unique characteristics, jointly carrying forward printing techniques.

As a comprehensive craft technology, printing is an inevitable fruit of the development of politics, economy, culture, and other aspects to a certain stage and level. The invention of printing has gone through a long process of accumulation, including cultural foundation represented by letters, material premise represented by paper, technical preparation represented by rubbing, social demands represented by mass reading, and so on.

China was not only the first to invent block printing technology but also the earliest in the world to apply movable type printing in clay, wood, and metal. Starting from the Song Dynasty (960–1279), China introduced the technique of two-color overprinting, and by the Yuan Dynasty (1206–1368), this technique was officially used for printing books, with the overprinting technique developed from two colors to three colors, four colors. The woodblock overprinting technique pioneered in the Ming Dynasty (1368–1644) was the earliest printing approach in the world that could print editions with a similar gradient level to the original paintings. Copperplate printing was invented in the Song Dynasty, indicating that the ink technology suitable for metal plates had been basically mastered as early as the Song Dynasty. In the Yuan Dynasty, the Chinese invented mechanical equipment for typesetting and picking characters.

The community of a shared future for humankind tightly connects people of various countries living on the same planet. From its birthplace, printing technology has spread to all corners of the world, becoming the "most powerful lever" underlying the progress of human civilization, exchanges and mutual learning, and cultural diversity. Chinese printing technology was introduced to Europe through the maritime and overland Silk Road. Around 1450, the German Johannes Gutenberg invented mechanical printing, which was centered around the invention of the printing press. Within decades, mechanical printing spread throughout Europe.

In the 1980s, a scientific team led by a Chinese researcher named Wang Xuan successfully developed a Chinese character laser phototypesetting system, which was hailed as the "second invention of Chinese character printing." Wang Xuan's invention marked the beginning of the digitalization process in the field of Chinese character printing, pushing for the informatization of Chinese characters. The Internet has completely upended many traditional industries, including the printing industry. With the development and application of digital technology and material technology, the application of printing has expanded from the reproduction of images and text to functional printing in product manufacturing.

Imagine, if the invention of printing had not occurred, could Chinese civilization have been passed down through generations? Could the West have ended the "Dark Ages"? The answer is certainly negative. However, there are still many doubts about our brilliant cultural treasures:

Who proposed the concept of the "Four Great Inventions"? Why was printing not invented by the United States, the United Kingdom, Egypt, or India? Why is it said that Gutenberg was not the inventor of movable type? What is the form of printing in contemporary times?... These questions can all be found in this book.

CHAPTER I

The Origin and Invention of Printing

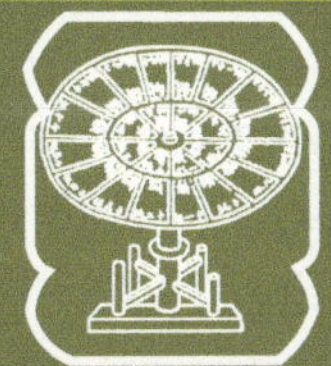

For the Chinese nation, the term "printing" boasts both cultural and technical attributes, containing special ethnic emotions. It is not only one of the well-known Four Great Inventions in ancient China, but also known as the "mother of civilization." Marx pointed out that printing is the "tool of Protestantism," "the means of scientific rejuvenation," and "the most powerful lever for creating necessary prerequisites for spiritual development." According to Engels, printing was both an "enlightener" and a "noble deity." As the first nation to invent engraved block printing, in order to meet various needs, the Chinese people have successively invented clay movable type printing, wood movable type printing, metal movable type printing, process printing, woodblock overprint, Gong Hua printing, magnetic block printing, and clay block printing through adopting new printing techniques and methods. These constantly advancing and innovative printing techniques have been brilliant in history. In terms of printing materials, the ink printing technique is advancing step by step in addition to continuously optimizing plate materials. In short, in the ancient history of printing, the Chinese people, creators of a series of rich inventions, have made breakthroughs, significantly fostering human civilization and social progress.

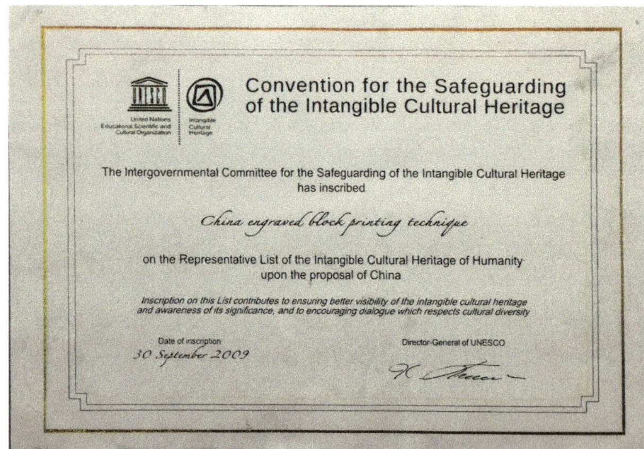

UNESCO

United Nations Educational, Scientific and Cultural Organization

Intangible Cultural Heritage

Convention for the Safeguarding of the Intangible Cultural Heritage

The Intergovernmental Committee for the Safeguarding of the Intangible Cultural Heritage has inscribed

China engraved block printing technique

on the Representative List of the Intangible Cultural Heritage of Humanity upon the proposal of China

Inscription on this List contributes to ensuring better visibility of the intangible cultural heritage and awareness of its significance, and to encouraging dialogue which respects cultural diversity

Date of inscription

30 September 2009

Director-General of UNESCO

In 2009, UNESCO issued the World Intangible Cultural Heritage Certificate for China's engraved block printing technique.

1. The Four Great Inventions and Printing

Papermaking, printing, gunpowder, and compass are the Four Great Inventions of ancient China, which are also the glory and pride of the Chinese people. However, why are they called the Four Great Inventions? Who first proposed the concept? When did it come up? The answers to these questions are rarely known.

In fact, the "Four Great Inventions" was not the concept that was first put forward, but the "Three Great Inventions" without papermaking. Besides, the "Three Great Inventions" was not first proposed by the Chinese people. Mr. Cang Xiaohe, former director of the Institute of the History of Natural Science of the Chinese Academy of Sciences and former vice president of the Chinese Society for the History of Science and Technology, wrote in his *Compendium of the History of Natural Science* that in 1550, Italian mathematician Jerome Cardan (1501–1576) pointed out for the first time that the magnetic compass, printing, and gunpowder were China's three great inventions, and "there was no comparable invention in the whole ancient times."

Since the 16th century, Western scholars have regarded printing as an important invention for academic research, generously awarding various honors to it. British philosopher Francis Bacon (1561–1626) not only exclaimed that "knowledge is power," but also wrote that printing, gunpowder, and magnets (compass) had changed the looks and situation of the entire world, "and thus caused countless changes. It seemed that no empire, religion, or star had more influence on human affairs than these mechanical discoveries."

In the 19th century, the study of printing history reached its peak in the Western academic community. Great scholars such as Marx and Engels highly praised the important contributions of printing. In 1838, British missionary and sinologist Walter Henry Medhurst (1796–1857) gave high praise to the three great inventions of the Chinese people in his epic work *The Current Situation and Missionary Prospects of China*, "The genius of the Chinese people in invention has long been manifested in various aspects. The three great inventions of the Chinese people (compass, printing, and gunpowder) provided an extraordinary driving force for the development of European civilization."In 1884, British missionary and sinologist Joseph Edkins (1823–1905) first added papermaking to the three great inventions mentioned above. In his book *Religions in China*, Joseph pointed out after carefully comparing the civilizations of China and Japan, "We must always remember that they (referring to Japan) did not have outstanding inventions like printing, papermaking, compass, and gunpowder."

American scholar Thomas Francis Carter (1882–1925) wrote in his book *The Invention of Printing in China and Its Spread Westward*, published in 1925, "The introduction and dissemination of the Four Great Inventions during the early European Renaissance played a significant role in shaping the modern world... Among Chinese inventions, papermaking and printing were the most famous in terms of their impact on Eurasian culture.

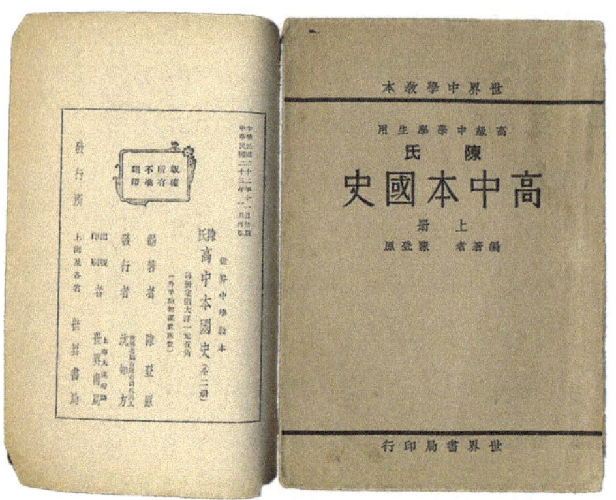

The Chen's High School Chinese History, edited by Chen Dengyuan and published by World Books in 1933

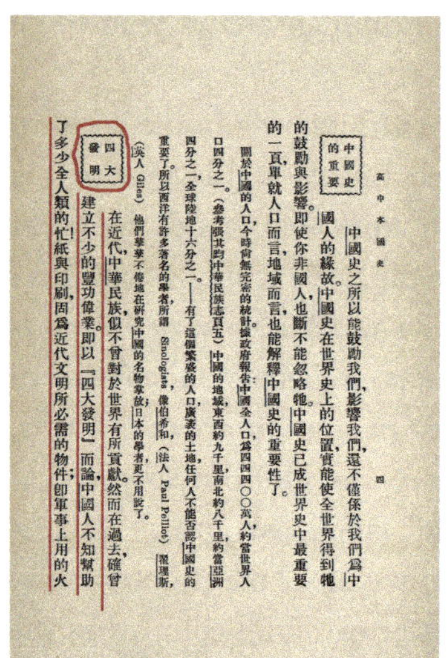

高中本國史 四

中國史的重要

中國史之所以能鼓勵我們，影響我們，還不僅係於我們爲中國人的緣故。中國史在世界史上的位置，實能使全世界得到牠的鼓勵與影響。即使你非國人，也斷不能忽略牠。中國史已成世界史中最重要的一頁，單就人口而言，地域而言，也能解釋中國史的重要性了。

關於中國的人口，今時尙無完密的統計。據政府報告：中國全人口爲四四四〇〇萬人，約當世界人口四分之一。（參考張其昀中華民族志頁五）中國的地域，東西約九千里，南北約八千里，約當亞洲四分之一，全球陸地十六分之一。——有了這個繁庶的人口廣袤的土地，任何人不能否認中國史的重要了。所以西洋有許多著名的學者所謂 Sinologists，像伯希和，（法人 Paul Pelliot）翟理斯，（英人 Giles）他們孳孳不倦地在研究中國的名物掌故；日本的學者更不用說了。

四大發明

在近代，中華民族，似不曾對於世界有所貢獻。然而在過去，確曾建立不少的豐功偉業。即以「四大發明」而論，中國人不知幫助了多少全人類的忙！紙與印刷，固爲近代文明所必需的物件；卽軍事上用的火

The entry "Four Great Inventions" listed separately in Chen Dengyuan's book *The Chen's High School Chinese History*

It was the Chinese who first fully described the "Four Great Inventions." In Chinese history textbooks published in the 1930s, the concept of the "Three Great Inventions" began to appear frequently. In 1933, Chen Dengyuan, a Chinese scholar, edited *The Chen's High School Chinese History*, published by World Books, which specifically explained the "Four Great Inventions" as an entry. He pointed out, "In modern times, it seems that the Chinese nation has barely contributed to the world. However, in the past, we indeed made many great achievements. Regarding the 'Four Great Inventions,' countless things have been made easier thanks to the Chinese people. Paper and printing, which are necessary for modern civilization; gunpowder, used in military affairs; and compass needle, used in navigation, are of huge use. Indeed, these inventions have just unleashed the curtain of China's inventions in history." Since then, the expression of the "Four Great Inventions" has officially entered the knowledge system of Chinese textbooks and gradually spread. In 1940, the *High and Primary History Textbook* written by the then General Administration of Education Editorial Board demonstrated the emergence and spread of the "Four Great Inventions." In this way, through the efforts of textbook compilers over several generations, the theory of the "Four Great Inventions" has gradually become common sense in China, which the public can understand and remember.

In 1954, Joseph Needham's (1900–1995) masterpiece *Science and Civilisation in China* was grandly published by the Cambridge University Press. Its publication has aroused widespread attention in the world history of the science and technology community, making the brilliant achievements of ancient China known to Westerners and the "Four Great Inventions" famous around the world. Many people regard Joseph

Needham as the first person to propose the concept of the "Four Great Inventions," which is a total misunderstanding.

2. *The Definition of Printing*

When it comes to printing, printed books will come to people's minds. Why do we have such an impression? Because we often hear the saying, "Printing is the mother of human civilization." Specifically speaking, printing here refers to the book printing technique. Book publishing was one of the most important printing applications in ancient times. However, even in ancient times, its application was not limited to the field of news, publishing, and culture. It has also made significant contributions to beautifying people's lives, promoting commerce, and other aspects, such as printed fabrics, cards, wallpaper, New Year paintings, and tickets.

So, although we are familiar with printing, it is not easy to define it accurately. The reason is that any technique must go through the development process of invention, improvement, and innovation. Ancient printing is prominently featured by continuous innovation through its process of invention and development. In this connection, the definition of printing needs to be viewed historically and dialectically, which is not fixed, but should keep up with the times.

Printing, as a term, first appeared nearly a thousand years ago in *Dream Pool Essays · Craftsmanship*, "One plate has printed while another one has been typeset." Printing has the following definitions for today's reference books and relevant national standards.

Ci Yuan (*Sources of Words*) writes, "To publish books, make a printing plate based on the original text and pictures, use a brown brush to apply ink to the board, lay paper, and then wipe it with a clean brush before removing it. This repeated process is called printing."

Dictionary of Modern Science and Technology (1980 edition) gives such a definition, "Any method of transferring ink from the surface of a printing plate to paper (or other materials) to replicate images or text."

Although the descriptions of printing above are slightly different, we can still summarize the three elements of printing: first, images and texts; second, printing plates; and third, impress.

However, with the development of our times, we increasingly feel the limitations of this definition. Since printing is a technique that belongs to the category of science and technology, the continuous innovation of science and technology will inevitably lead to the updating of the definition of printing. Its traditional definition has been upended by the integration of digital technology, internet technology, and printing technologies in modern society. In the *Terminology of Printing Technology Part 1: Basic Terminology* (GB/T 9851.1-2008), printing is defined as "the replication process of using analog or digital image carriers to transfer colorants/pigments (such as ink) to the substrate." Therefore, with rapidly advancing technologies, it is difficult to describe this highly technical and long-standing term with a fixed definition. We can look at printing from a different perspective in this new era. As technology never stops advancing, if defined from a cultural perspective, printing can be said to be a technique for expressing and disseminating human ideas.

If we ask people today: Do decorative paintings count as printed works? Is the image on the T-shirt printed? Are the pictures on the plastic packaging printed? It's believed that the answers should be consistent and affirmative. Printed objects can not only be text, but also patterns; materials used for printing can be either paper, fabric, metal, plastic... or even "everything except water and air which cannot be printed." Printing not only deals with white paper and black letters, but also presents readers with a millennium-long brilliant picture of its history in a broad sense.

So, what is the earliest printing technique?

When printing is applied to beautifying people's daily lives, it is no more than a common technique that has no connection with the "cultural god." Nevertheless, it is not until the technique is applied to printing letters and serves in the field of cultural communication that it shines brightly on the stage of history, receiving the highest praise generously from both Chinese and Western scholars.

The earliest letter printing technique is engraved block printing, which refers to the process of engraving characters and images reversely onto a wooden board, then brushing ink, laying paper, and pressing the printing plate to transfer the images and texts on the paper. The word "engraved block" is added, so as to distinguish between different techniques, such as "movable type" and "stone slabs," which are attributes added before "printing." The term "home computer" initially refers to desktop computers, but after the development of lightweight laptops, in order to distinguish them from the lightweight ones, the attribute "desktop" was added before "computer." In ancient times, the woodblock used in engraved block printing was also known as "Louban," "Keban," "Qianban," "Ziban," "Kanban," etc., with engraved block printing also known as "Fuzi," "Zixing" (publishing). In ancient literature, two Chinese characters, "ban" (版 and 板), have the same meaning: woodblock in English.

3. Fundamentals of the Invention

Regarding the invention of printing, first, there are some questions that are worth considering: Why did China invent printing? Why wasn't the United States or Europe the first to invent printing?

Only by clarifying how engraved block printing was invented can people understand how great this technique is, admire how intelligent our ancestors are, and take pride in this "Chinese intellectual creation." Overall, there are five indispensable prerequisites for the invention of printing: firstly, the basic one—characters; the second is basic skills—stamping and seals; the third is China's unique invention—papermaking technology; the fourth is China's unique pioneering technique—stone rubbing; the fifth is the driving force of invention—social needs.

3.1 Basic Element: Characters

Among various elements of civilization, the emergence of characters is the most important symbol. Before characters emerged, tying ropes was a commonly used method for recording events in the early days. Larger knots represent major events, while smaller knots stand for minor events. According to the *Book of Changes · Xi Ci II*, "In ancient times, people used knotting as a way to manage affairs. Later, emperors replaced this method with written documents, on which officials relied to make decisions on government affairs, and people relied to decide how to act. All these activities are based on the Hexagram Menace." People regarded Cang Jie ("仓颉," also known as "苍颉"), the legendary historiographer of the Yellow Emperor, as the creator of Chinese characters. The legend of "Cang Jie creating characters" has been passed down for a long time. During the Warring States period, it was recorded in the *Huai Nan Zi · Ben Jing Xun* that "When Cang Jie created characters, suddenly

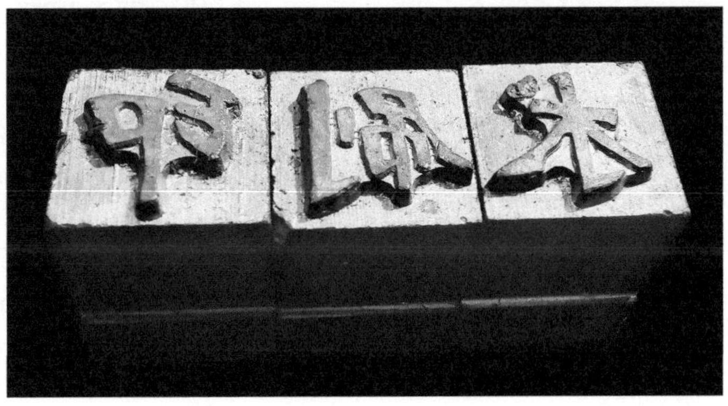

The lead movable type

there was a rain of millet in the sky during the day, while ghosts were crying at night." The ancients believed that Cang Jie's creation of characters was a "heavenly" thing, enough to startle the world and move ghosts and gods to tears.

With increasing archaeological discoveries, the origin of Chinese characters can be traced back to about 8,000 years ago. It is widely believed that Chinese characters have gradually evolved from pictographic symbols to achieve maturity. Modern archaeology discoveries have found inscriptions with textual characteristics dating back to approximately 8,000 years at the Jiahu site in Wuyang, Henan Province. Inscriptions dating back approximately 7,000 years have been discovered at the Shuangdun site in Bengbu, Anhui Province. Painted pottery inscriptions dating back to approximately 6,000 years have been discovered at the Banpo site in Xi'an, Shaanxi Province, in the Yangshao culture. Inscriptions dating back to approximately 5,000 years have been discovered at the Zhuangqiao tomb site in Jiaxing, Zhejiang Province, in the Liangzhu culture. Mr. Li Boqian believes that these characters in Liangzhu culture can already be connected into sentences. Modern archaeology has also discovered inscriptions dating back to over 4,500 years at the Dawenkou site in Shandong Province, with cinnabar scripts dating back to approximately 4,000 years unearthed at the Taosi site in Xiangfen, Shanxi Province.

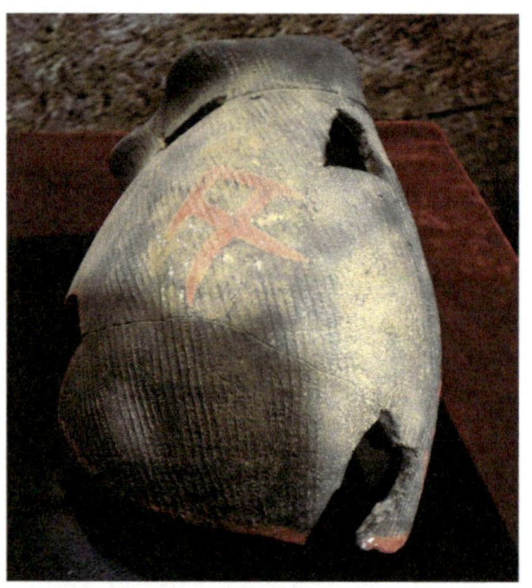

Cinnabar inscribed on a flat bottle, unearthed from the Taosi site in Shanxi (late Neolithic period), on which the symbol carved in cinnabar is the character "文" verified by scholars.

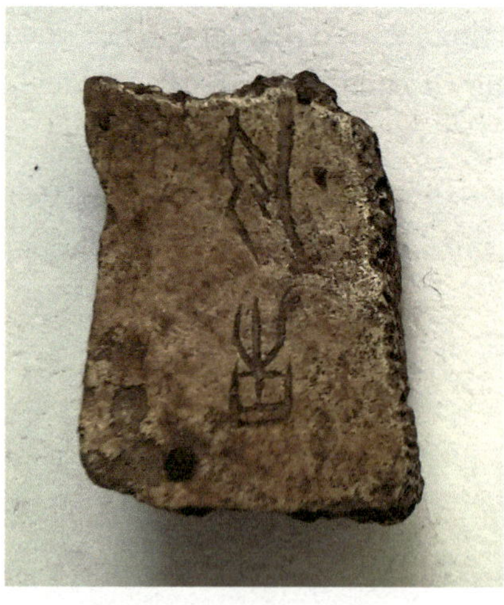

A fragment of oracle bone script

The characters engraved on turtle shells or animal bones by the Shang Dynasty people over 3,000 years ago are known as "oracle bone inscriptions." Merchants performed divination on turtle shells almost every day. There is a legend about the discovery of oracle bone inscriptions: "A piece of oracle bone startled the world." In 1899, Wang Yirong, a scholar and epigrapher of the late Qing Dynasty, first discovered oracle bone inscriptions in the traditional Chinese medicine "dragon bone." Since then, a total of approximately 160,000 oracle bones with characters have been discovered in the Yin Ruins. More than 4,500 single characters have been used, and more than 2,000 characters can be recognized. They already possess the basic form of Chinese character structure.

Chinese characters, a unique spiritual symbol, are the genetic code of our Chinese nation. However, Chinese characters are not the oldest characters in the world. Other ancient civilizations also have their own unique scripts, such as the hieroglyphs of ancient Egypt, the cuneiform script of ancient Babylon, and the hieroglyphs of ancient India. But they disappeared long ago. Only Chinese characters, after oracle bone inscriptions, have undergone the evolution of different fonts, such as bronze inscriptions, large seal scripts, small seal scripts, clerical scripts, regular scripts, and semi-cursive scripts, before becoming basically fixed. So only we Chinese people in the world have no obstacles in reading the words of our ancestors two or three thousand years ago.

3.2 Basic Skills: Stamping and Seals

The engraving technique used in the process of making seals has always been considered the technological precursor to the invention of printing. Seals appeared very early in ancient civilization, and they were found not only in the Chinese civilization but also in other ancient civilizations around the world, such as ancient Egypt and India. Seals are usually engraved with reverse characters in relief or intaglio on metal, stone, or wood. In ancient China, seals were not only used as symbols of power, but also had some practical functions before the invention of paper, such as branding (which means burning a mark onto the skin of people, livestock, or the surface of utensils), printing, or stamping words on gold coins during the Warring States period. It was also used as a seal on ancient documents such as bamboo slips and wooden tablets, serving as a proof of closure for both official and private purposes. Usually, documents were bound with a rope, and the knot was covered with clay. Sealing on the knot can prevent documents from being disclosed. After the invention of papermaking, seals were commonly used to make copies of texts quickly by pressing seals with pigments on paper. The imprints are divided into "relief inscription" and "intaglio inscriptions," with "relief inscription" being imprinted by seals carved in relief and "intaglio inscriptions" being imprinted by seals carved in intaglio. Generally, ancient seals had fewer words and smaller printing surfaces, but there were also some ones with more words and larger printing surfaces. According to the *Inner Chapter of Master Embracing Simplicity* written by Ge Hong (c. AD

281–341) of the Eastern Jin Dynasty, when a Taoist entered a mountain, in order to avoid the invasion of tigers, wolves, and ghosts, he must wear a seal with 120 words engraved on it. This type of seal was stamped on top of the sealing mud, and if placed on paper, it was equivalent to a small printed work. After the Southern and Northern Dynasties, many Buddha statues with seals appeared, as well as many physical relics in Dunhuang literature.

In China, the art of textile printing has a long history. Well before the early Western Han Dynasty (202 BC–AD 8), relief printing had already been mature, which is a

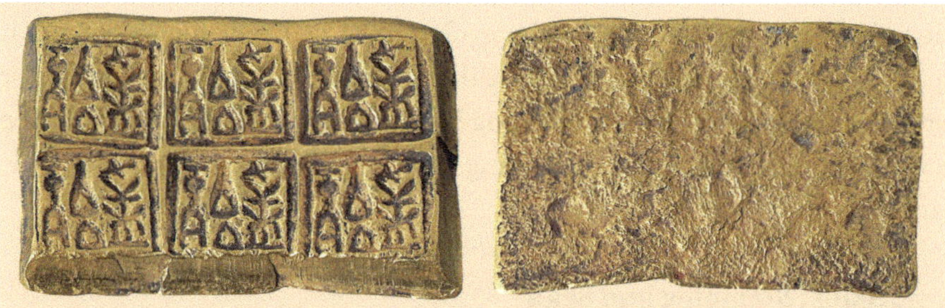

The six-Yingyuan plate in the Warring States period, on which seal symbols and text are engraved by chisels. Yingyuan was a gold currency of the Chu State in the pre-Qin period, "Ying" was the name of the Chu capital city, and "yuan" was the unit of currency weight.

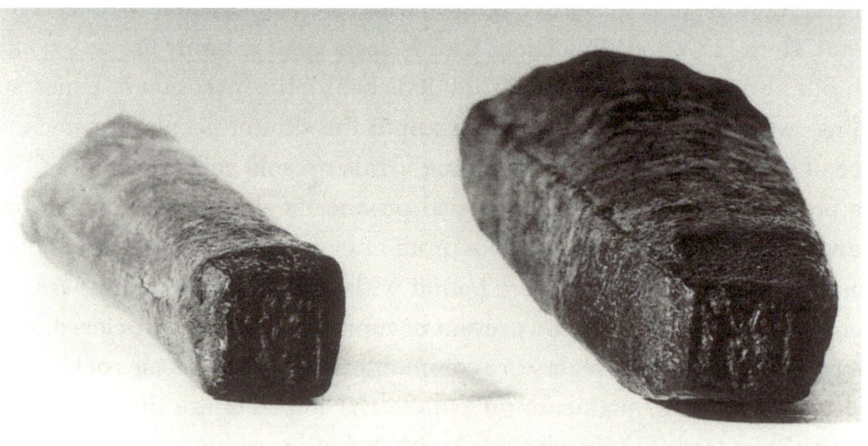

Bronze seal in the Warring States period, unearthed in Shouxian County, Anhui Province. It has a larger upper part and a smaller lower part, with a square shape at the lower end. The smaller end side has the reverse relief inscription "Yingyuan." Due to its long-time use, there are obvious hammer marks on the top, indicating that it is a copper seal used to hammer Yingyuan sheet metal.

process of engraving protruding patterns on wooden boards or other materials and pressing them onto textiles. In 1972, several pieces of printed gauze were unearthed from the No. 1 Han Tomb in Mawangdui, Changsha, Hunan Province. They are divided into two categories: one is printed and painted floss silk padded gauze, and the other is gold and silver-colored printed gauze.

In terms of the technique itself, stamping and printing are similar, but their main differences are reflected in three aspects: content, substrate, and function.

3.3 Unique Chinese Element: Papermaking Technology

Since the emergence of characters, humans have been searching for inexpensive and lightweight writing materials that are easy to obtain and can be produced in large quantities. People around the world have used clay boards and sheepskins to record events. The ancient Egyptians made papyrus paper by slicing and arranging papyrus stems and then pressing them heavily. The ancient Indians wrote with palmyra tree leaves. The Chinese once used silk, wooden slips, and bamboo slips to write. However, all these writing materials have many limitations.

In AD 105, Cai Lun (c. AD 62–121) reported to the imperial court and subsequently promoted paper in the true sense among the public, which was affordable, simple in craftsmanship, practical, and convenient. The *Book of Later Han · Biography of Cai Lun* records, "Since ancient times, characters have been written or carved on bamboo pieces and then compiled into books. The silk used for writing was called paper. Silk was expensive, and bamboo slips were too cumbersome to use. So, Cai Lun came up with a solution, which was to use bark, hemp waste, rags, and fishnets to make paper. From then on, people began to use the paper invented by Cai Lun, thus commonly known as 'Cai Hou paper.'" Therefore, paper has become an ideal carrier of writing and has gradually been promoted. It has revolutionized the tools for recording and disseminating knowledge. Paper is not only an important material for printing, but has also triggered cultural demands, which are a vital driving force for the invention of printing.

Cai Lun, as well as his invention, has deeply influenced the advancement of human civilization. In the book *The 100: A Ranking of the Most Influential Persons in History*, edited by American scholar Michael H. Hart, Cai Lun ranks 6th.

Among the Four Great Inventions in ancient China, papermaking was the first to spread to other countries. In AD 751, after the Battle of Taros, Chinese craftsmen began to teach the Arabs papermaking techniques. In AD 794, under the guidance of Chinese craftsmen, the Arab Empire established a paper mill in the capital city of Baghdad. In 1276, the Montefano region in the central part of the Italian peninsula

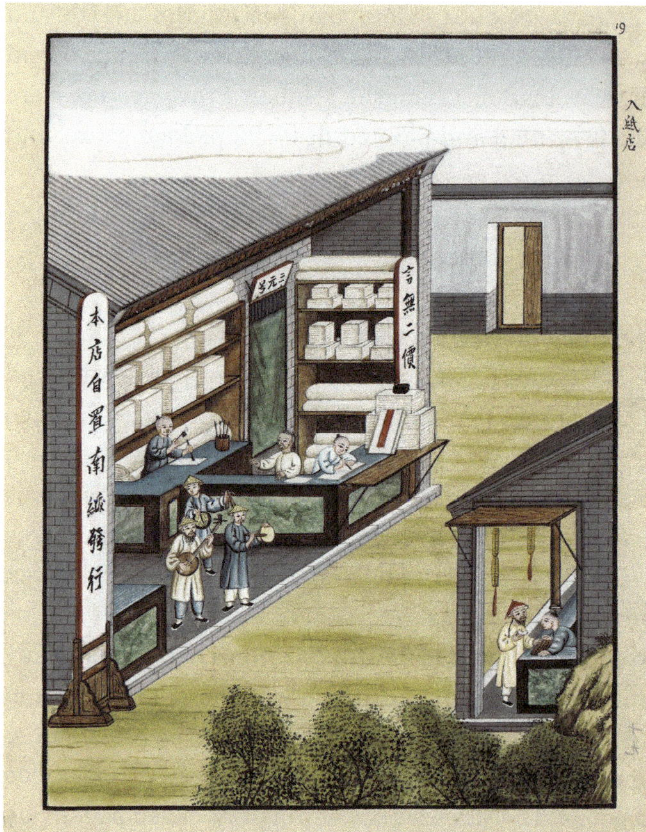

"The Picture of a Paper Shop," excerpted from *The Illustrated Handbook of Chinese Papermaking Art*. The handbook was edited based on the materials recorded by Michel Benoist, a Jesuit missionary from France, who lived in China during the reign of Emperor Qianlong of the Qing Dynasty. It was published in France in 1775 and depicts the process of making bamboo paper through 27 watercolor paintings.

established Italy's first paper mill that produced hemp paper. Afterward, Europeans began to improve papermaking techniques. In 1797, Louis Robert (1761–1828), a Frenchman, invented the method of making paper by machine.

3.4 China's Unique Technological Leader: Stone Rubbing

The stone rubbing technique was a unique invention in ancient China, which is the embryonic form of engraved block printing. The word "unique" emphasizes that this skill was not only invented by the Chinese people, but also widely used in ancient China. Other ancient civilizations in the world had a tradition of engraving stones to record events, but only the Chinese invented the art of stone rubbing. The main reasons include: firstly, other ancient civilizations could not produce thin and tough paper, and secondly, other ancient civilizations did not have the fanatical pursuit of Chinese calligraphy art as the Chinese did.

Rubbing is also known as stone rubbing. The process mainly consists of four steps: the first step is to fold and soak the paper to make it evenly hydrated for later use; the second step is to spread the soaked Xuan paper onto the printing plate and repeatedly brush it with a brown brush to make the paper closely adhere to the concave and convex edges of the image and text; the third step is to wait for the paper to dry, and adopt techniques such as rubbing and brushing to evenly apply ink from shallow to deep, finally displaying a clear distinction between black and white with clear characters; The fourth step is to remove the paper, complete rubbings and finally organize or mount it uniformly.

Currently, there is no definitive answer to when the rubbing technique was invented. However, some clues in this regard can be found in the *Sui Shu · Jing Ji Zhi*. The 32nd volume records the 1st volume of the *Qin Huang Dong Xun Kuaiji Stone Inscription*, the 34th volume of the *Yi Zi Stone Classics* (namely the *Stone Classics of the Xiping Regin* of the Eastern Han Dynasty), and the 17th volume of the *San Zi Stone Classics*. The annotation reads, "In the Later Han Dynasty, the *Seven Classics* were engraved on stone tablets, all written by Cai Yong. In the fifth year of the Cao Wei government, 'San Zi Stone Classics' were made, which were inherited as the standard form of 'Seven Classics.'... At the beginning of the Zhengguan Period, the Palace Library officer Wei Zheng began to collect them with less than one in ten volumes left. The original rubbing edition was still housed in the imperial secret repository." Here, the "original rubbing edition" refers to rubbing.

Demand is the "mother of invention." The earliest event stimulating rubbing may have been the establishment of the *Stone Classics of the Xiping Regin* in front of the Imperial Academy Lecture Hall in the south of Luoyang during the Eastern Han Dynasty. In the *Book of Later Han · Biography of Cai Yong*, it is recorded that "Cai Yong felt that the ancient classics written by the sages a long time ago contained many errors, which misled the students. Therefore, he, along with General Tang Xidian, Yang Ci, Glorious Grand Master (honorific title), Ma Midi, Adviser to the Emperor, Zhang Xun, Han Shuo, court counselors, and Shan Yang, Imperial Astronomer, requested to proofread *Six Classics*, which was approved by Emperor Ling." In AD 175, Cai Yong submitted a request to Emperor Ling of the Han Dynasty to proofread scriptures and engrave them on stones, which was approved. At this time, papermaking technology happened to undergo a revolution, which gradually matured, thus nurturing the birth of the rubbing technique. It can be imagined that in order to cope with exams and not be misled by incorrect versions, the literati at that time had to accurately record the *Six Classics*, so relying on manual copying was obviously unreliable. Under this urgent need, people finally invented rubbing, which can replicate the original quickly and completely.

Chinese people's love for calligraphy is deeply ingrained in their bones. Especially in ancient times, calligraphy was a part of the ancient literati's life. Therefore, the works of calligraphers and the calligraphy templates for study became a specialized category of books, initially known as "calligraphy." Due to the uniqueness of a calligraphy work, it is necessary to replicate it for dissemination, copying, and learning, which makes rubbing the most accurate means of replication. So, in ancient China, there was a tradition of rubbing calligraphy works on stones, which was later replaced with wood. The process is to first engrave the calligraphy work on a stone or wooden board to make a printing plate, then lay the paper for rubbing, and finally mount it to make a calligraphy. Du Fu wrote a poem titled "Song for Li Chao's Bafen Small Seal Script": "Cang Jie's unfathomable character-creation modeled after bird tracks; the forms of characters vary like drifting clouds in the sky. Even the Stone Drums at Chencang had changed, after the seal scripts, large and small, the bafen was born. In Qin, there was Li Si; in Han, there was Cai Yong; between those two, practitioners are not heard of at all. The stele on Mount Yi has been burned by wildfire, carvings on date-wood are distorted to become too wide." Due to the fact that "the stele on Mount Yi has been burned by wildfire" and the shortcomings of steles such as bulkiness and difficulty in engraving, later generations replaced stones with wood, continuing to copy and engrave classics. As stated in the annotation to the *Rhapsodies on Calligraphers through the Ages* by scholar Dou Ji of the Tang Dynasty, "'Yi Shan Stele' was engraved in small seal script by (Li Si), whose name was later added to the stone tablet. After the stele was destroyed, scholars engraved with wood to replace it, similar to the original version." The time of "engraving wood" here should have been before the prosperous Tang Dynasty as described in Du Fu's "Song for Li Chao's Bafen Small Seal Script," referring to the Sui Dynasty and the early Tang Dynasty.

The practice of "carvings on date-wood are distorted to become too wide" is no longer the original flavor, but the method of using wood instead of stone solves the problems of bulky and difficult carving of stone tablets.

Until the early Tang Dynasty, before the widespread application of printing, the profession of rubbing calligraphy existed. Each of them was a calligrapher responsible for both tracing and rubbing the calligraphy of famous masters. According to Volume 8 of the *Six Classics of the Tang Dynasty*, there were three staff members who were rubbing calligraphy in the Hongwen Hall. Li Linfu noted, "The rubbing started in the 23rd year of the Zhenguan era (AD 649). In the third year of the Longshuo era (AD

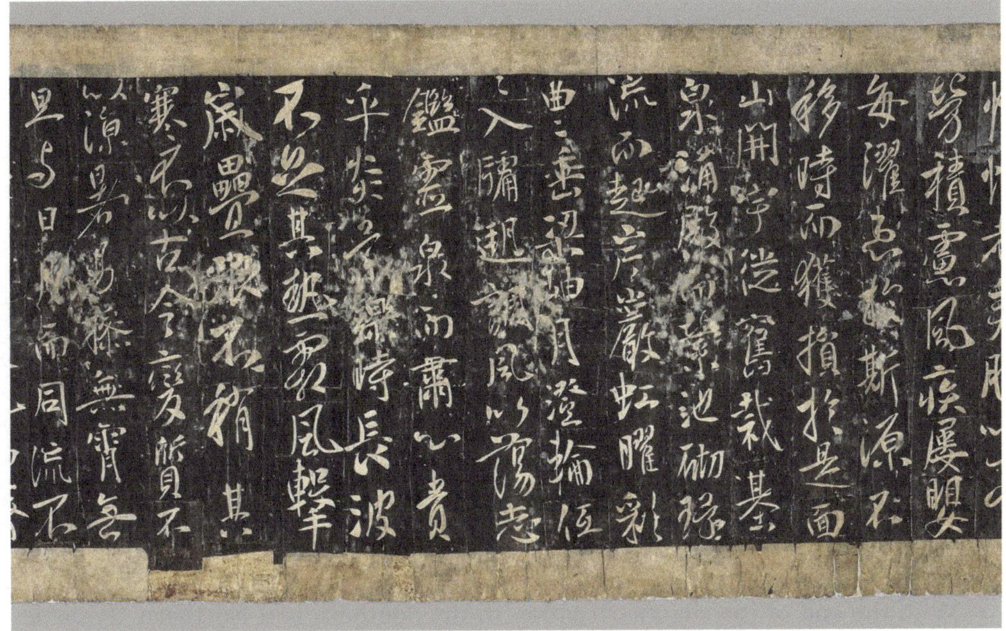

The partial rubbing of the *Hot Spring Inscription*, unearthed from the Dunhuang Cave Library. It was created before the fourth year of the Tang Yonghui era (AD 653) and is currently housed in the National Library of France.

663), three staff completed their work with 949 volumes of Dharma scriptures all bound. In the first year of the Shenlong era (AD 705), the rubbing started again." The Chongwen Hall, in charge of the Eastern Palace, also had two staff. According to the *New Book of Tang*, in the sixth year of the Kaiyuan era (AD 718), there were six people who specialized in rubbing at the Jixian Academy.

In short, rubbing is the earliest printing technique, with books made from rubbing the earliest printed copies. Compared with the printing technique later known as the "mother of civilization," it has two main drawbacks: firstly, white characters on a black background are not conducive to reading long texts and are also quite ink intensive; the second is time-consuming and labor-intensive, with relatively slow output speed and numerous processes. Since the application of the rubbing technique, the birth of printing has been brewing and is only awaiting a favorable opportunity.

3.5 The Driving Force of Invention: Social Needs

All inventions are born out of necessity. Without the "east wind" of social demands, the fruits of invention cannot be produced even if everything is ready.

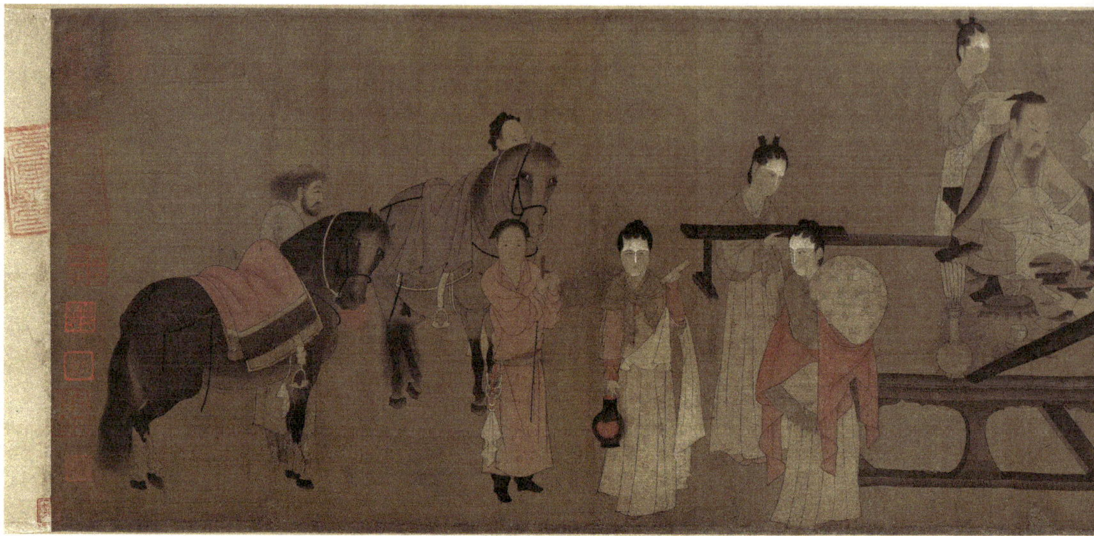

With the end of the chaotic situation in the Southern and Northern Dynasties and the unification of the Sui and Tang dynasties, China entered a period of long-term and sustained development. With the rapid development of cities, there has been great progress in industry and commerce. People's demand for reading was gradually formed. The demand for public reading during the Sui and Tang dynasties mainly came from three aspects.

Folk demands

Based on implementing the equal land system in the early Tang Dynasty, the Zuyongdiao tax and corvee system[1] was promulgated, which stabilized Chinese farmers' lives, enabling them to have more time to engage in agricultural production, which was conducive to the development of the social economy. Furthermore, since the improvement of agricultural production requires professional guidance, demands for daily reading materials such as almanacs increased. After ensuring basic living standards, people sought entertainment; thus, demands for reading materials such as lyrics and divination also increased. According to the *Old Book of Tang · Wenzong II*, "In the Dingchou year (the 14th year of the Sexagenary Cycle), local governments were warned that they were not allowed to promulgate calendars privately."

1. The Zuyongdiao consists of Zu (租), the tax paid in grains, Yong (庸) that was paid in corvee, and Diao (調) which was paid in textiles.

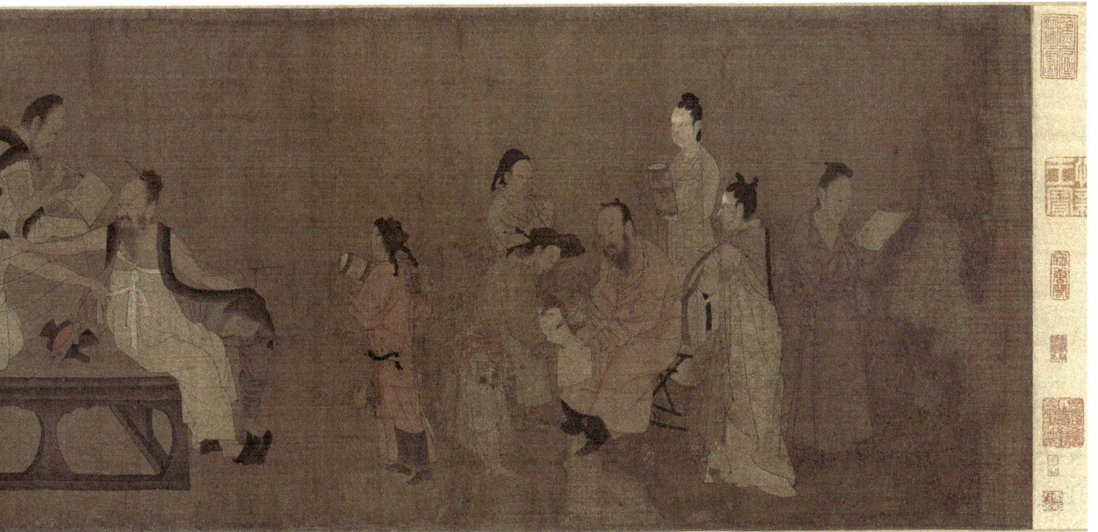

The painting *Northern Qi Scholars Collating Classic Texts* depicts the story of Fan Xun, Gao Qian, and others collating the *Five Classics* and other various historical texts stored in the imperial court during the seventh year (556) of the Tianbao reign of Emperor Wenxuan of the Northern Qi Dynasty (550-577). In the painting, there are three groups of persons, with four scholars sitting on a couch in the center. They are either deep in thought while unrolling scrolls, writing with a brush, about to leave their seats, or trying to hold others back by grabbing their clothes.

Reading needs

The imperial examination system was implemented in the Sui Dynasty and abolished in the 31st year of the reign of Emperor Guangxu in the Qing Dynasty (1905), with a history of over 1,000 years. The imperial examination system enabled the lower class to achieve upward mobility, greatly stimulating society's enthusiasm for reading. Since then, the farming-reading idea has been anchored among the common Chinese families.

In addition, the invention of printing is closely related to the needs of collectors. The means by which collectors obtain books, in addition to borrowing and giving away, are mostly purchased. Ouyang Xiu's *Collection of Ancient Records* has the following writing, "Items often gather around those who love them, but they are often obtained by capable individuals. Those who are capable but do not love them, or those who love them but lack capability, even if they are close and easily accessible, cannot obtain them." Before the invention of printing, the reproduction of books relied mainly on manual copying, which lasted for years and months. The variety and copies of books were extremely limited, failing to meet the needs of collectors. The more book collectors there were, the greater the demand for books, the more difficult it was to collect books, and the stronger people's desire to invent printing.

Belief needs

Generally speaking, the development of the Silk Road reached its peak during the early Tang Dynasty (7th century), with unprecedented prosperity in political, economic, and cultural exchanges between the East and the West. The boom of cultural exchange has promoted the dissemination of religions such as Buddhism and Taoism. As a local religion in China, Taoism was designated as the national religion in the early Tang Dynasty. Since ancient times, Taoism has demanded the dissemination of spells and so on. As early as the Eastern Jin Dynasty, Daoists wore seals of spells. A considerable number of people had a demand for Taoist paper spells and talismans. Beyond Taoism, the invention of printing was closely related to diplomacy and Buddhism. China has maintained friendly exchanges with countries around the world since ancient times, especially in terms of communication with India. Chinese and Indian monks went to each other's countries to go on a pilgrimage for scriptures, which led to numerous Indian works related to scriptures, medicine, astronomy, and

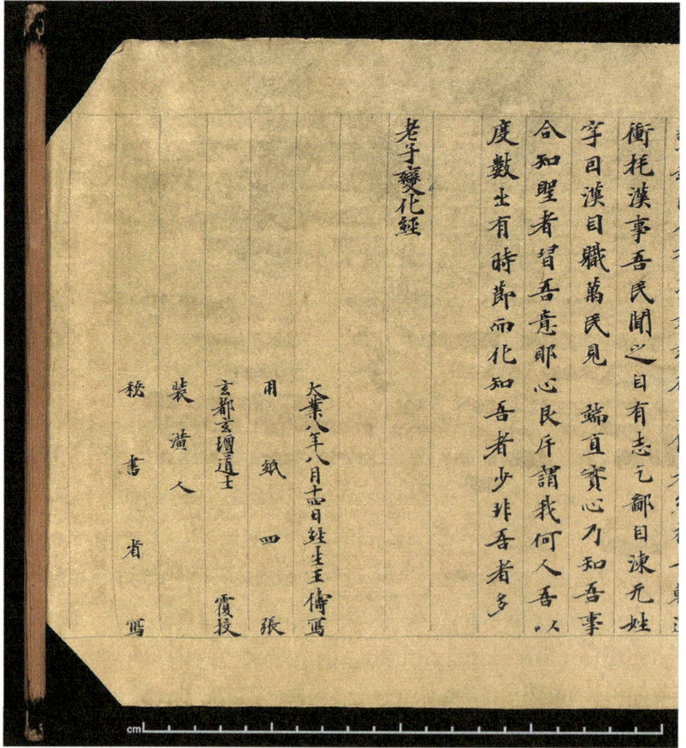
老子變化經

大業八年八月十四日經生王儔寫

用紙四張

玄都玄壇道士 覆校

裝潢人

秘書省 寫

The *Laozi Transformation Scripture*, unearthed in Dunhuang, was copied in the eighth year of the Daye era (AD 612) by Wang Chou, a professional scribe. The book was published by the Palace Library.

calendars entering the Chinese market. Similarly, a large number of Chinese works also entered the Indian book market. Buddhist believers consider praying to Buddha, reciting scriptures, creating statues, and giving alms as "merits." The more prosperous Taoism and Buddhism were, the more scriptures they wrote, the higher the call for the invention of printing. In this sense, it can be seen that cultural exchanges and religious dissemination required books. The invention of printing was just born in the camel bells along the Silk Road and the blessings of Buddhist and Taoist temples.

After cultural foundation, materials, and craftsmanship became mature and complete, engraved block printing was invented, stimulated by the general public's need for reading during the Sui and Tang dynasties. The engraved block printing pioneered the development of paper-printed books, gradually phasing out bulky bamboo slips and expensive silk books, bidding farewell to handwritten books, and ushering in the era of standardized, lightweight, and fast printing of books.

4. Time of the Invention

Combing through history, culture, and craftsmanship, it can be concluded that the accumulation of Chinese stamping and rubbing techniques, the application of pen, ink, and paper, as well as the reading needs of the public, all provided necessary prerequisites for the invention of engraved block printing.

Therefore, during the prosperous Sui and Tang dynasties, the invention of printing came naturally, thus shedding light on the time of invention. It was not invented by someone on a certain day, but rather a masterpiece of ancient Chinese culture. Regarding its origin and development, most people agree with the summary made in *Shaoshi Shanfang Bicong* written by scholar Hu Yinglin of the Ming Dynasty: "The engraved blocking printing emerged in the Sui Dynasty, became popular in the Tang Dynasty, expanded during the Five Dynasties and became professional in the Song Dynasty."

In January 2015, the Research Group on "Important Inventions and Creations" of the Institute for the History of Natural Sciences at the Chinese Academy of Sciences organized relevant experts to conduct collective research for nearly a year and a half. They selected 85 items from "Important Ancient Technological Inventions and Creations in China," which were divided into three categories: scientific discoveries and creations, technological inventions, and engineering achievements. Engraved block printing, as one of the technological inventions, was listed 61st. The 7th century AD was identified by the research group as the birth of engraved block printing.

In summary, printing, as mentioned by people, refers to engraved block printing rather than movable type printing. Engraved block printing has unlocked the standardization process of the inheritance and dissemination of Chinese characters, books, and even culture. From then on, the dissemination and inheritance of knowledge have been relatively standardized and uniform. The invention and promotion of engraved block printing techniques have reduced the cost of books, improved the efficiency of book production, accelerated the dissemination of knowledge, and promoted the advancement of civilization. After the invention of engraved block printing, a complete industrial chain of book engraving, printing, and sales emerged, contributing to the development of the ink and papermaking industries. The printing and publishing industry has ever since become a new point of economic growth in society. In human history, engraved block printing has been widely used for over 1,000 years. Therefore, it is the technique that has occupied the mainstream position for the longest time and has the strongest vitality among the techniques for human cultural communication to date.

CHAPTER II

The Historical Development of Engraved Block Printing

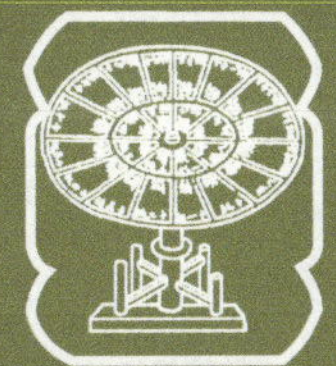

From the 7th century until the introduction of Western mechanical printing technology to China in the 19th century, engraved block printing remained the dominant form of publishing in China for about 1,200 years. movable type printing, process printing, and other printing techniques were invented on the basis of block printing. The invention of engraved block printing has made China the only country in the world that can widely replicate written texts, boasting the richest collection of books for up to six centuries.

In the 9th century, engraved block printing was widely used in China. During the Song Dynasty, woodblock printing became even more advanced, and the technique approached perfection. According to *The World Book*, from the Five Dynasties to the Ming Dynasty, China published a total of approximately 32,283 books (including 407,589 volumes). During the Song Dynasty alone, over 11,000 books and over 124,000 volumes were published. During the Yuan, Ming, and Qing dynasties, academies, bookstores, individuals, and officials at all levels were engaged in engraving books. The books they engraved covered the Confucian classics, history, philosophy, and literature.

After the invention of Chinese engraved block printing, it gradually spread to all directions. As early as 1294, the capital city of Ilkhanate, Tabriz, had already printed and issued banknotes in imitation of the Chinese government in the Yuan Dynasty. In 1310, the politician and historian Rashid al-Din Fadl Allah (1247–1318) elaborated on China's engraved printing calligraphy in his complied work, *Jami' al-Tawarikh*. The Italian Marco Polo (c. 1254–1324) traveled to China, promoting cultural exchanges

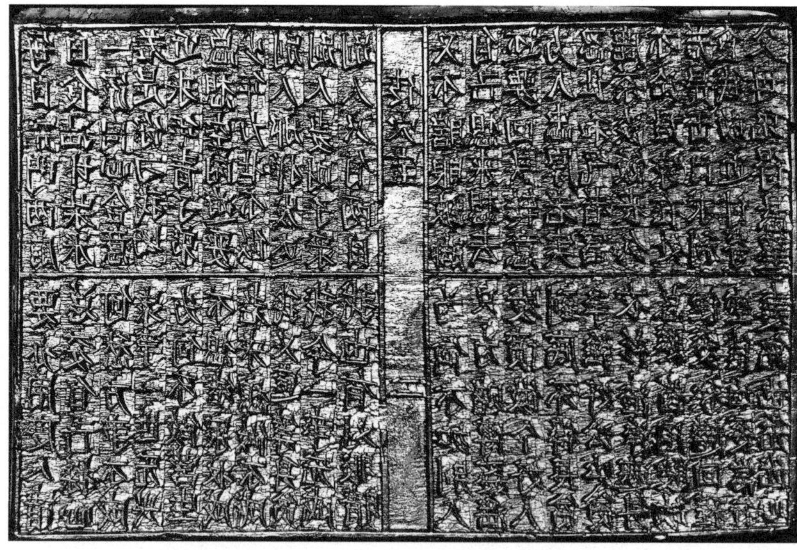

The Family Heirloom, a double-sided wood engraved work in the Qing Dynasty

between the East and the West. At the end of the 14th century, Europe began to use wooden and copper plates to engrave holy images and cards. The earliest extant woodblock print in Europe is the *St. Christopher and Christ Crossing the Water*, printed in 1423. In the mid-15th century, Europe adopted block printing to publish the grammar textbook written by Aelius Donatus (?–c. AD 355), which had profound impacts.

1. *The Process of Engraved Block Printing*

The process of engraved block printing mainly encompasses the following four steps, each of which includes several processes.

1.1 Material Preparation

(1) Material selection: Generally, fine-grained woods such as jujube wood, pear wood, catalpa wood, and boxwood are selected.
(2) Plate making: The wood is crafted into smooth and appropriately sized blank plates and treated to prevent cracking and deformation.
(3) Paper preparation: Prepare corresponding sizes and quantities of paper.
(4) Ink preparation: Prepare the ink required for printing.
(5) Tool preparation: Prepare tools such as engraving knives, ink brushes, brown brushes, and stamp pads.

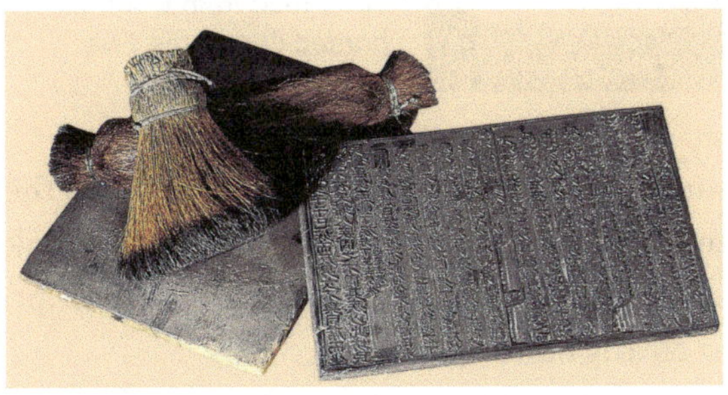

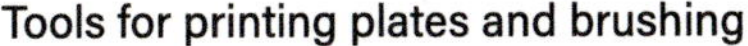

Tools for printing plates and brushing

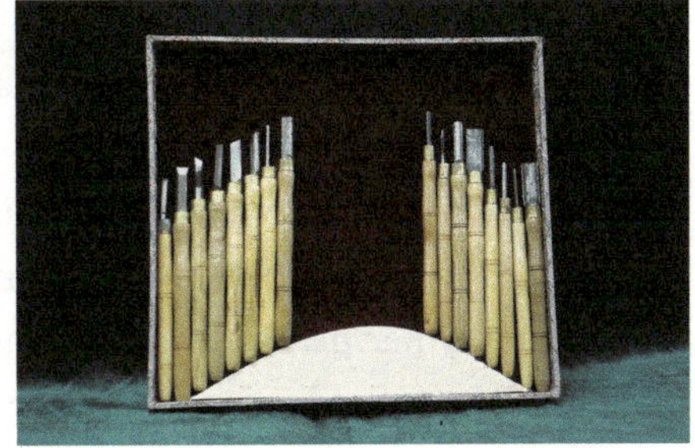

Tools for engraving plates

1.2 Plate Engraving

(1) Copying: Generally, a person with good calligraphy writes the manuscript on paper according to the format.
(2) Correction: Proofread the written manuscript and repair any typos.

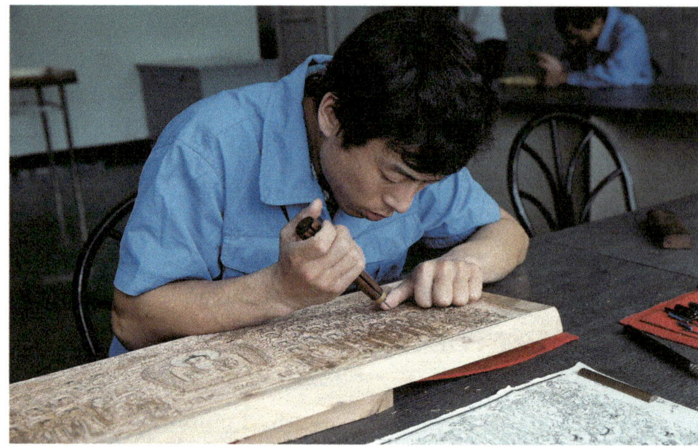

The staff of the Capital Tripitaka Protection Base are carving printing plates.

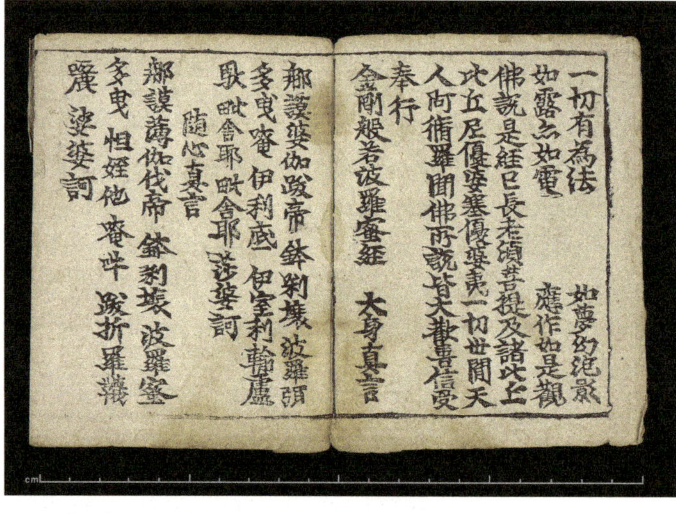

一切有為法　如夢幻泡影
如露亦如電　應作如是觀
佛說是經已長老須菩提及諸比丘
比丘尼優婆塞優婆夷一切世間天
人阿脩羅聞佛所說皆大歡喜信受
奉行
金剛般若波羅蜜經　大身真言
那謨婆伽跋帝　鉢剌壤　波羅弭
多曳　唵　伊利底　伊室利輸盧
馱　毗舍耶　毗舍耶　莎婆訶
隨心真言
那謨薄伽伐帝　鉢剌壤　波羅蜜
多曳　怛姪他　唵　[illegible]　[illegible]折羅[illegible]
麗　娑婆訶

The Diamond Sutra, the sutra binding version unearthed from Dunhuang, printed during the Five Dynasties period

(3) Pasting: Also known as plate adjusting, it is the process of applying paste to the back of a well-written or drawn manuscript and sticking it onto the plate. The ink gradually permeates into the plate. After drying, gently remove the manuscript, and the reversed imprint will appear clearly on the plate.

(4) Engraving: Engravers adopt different cutting techniques and select different engraving tools to carve the reversed elevated characters or images along the ink imprint.

1.3 Brushing

(1) Ink brushing: Fix the printing plate on the table and evenly apply ink on the surface of the plate with a brush.

(2) Printing: Cover a piece of paper on the inked surface of the printing plate, gently rub the back of the paper with a printing brush until the ink is evenly distributed, then remove the paper to complete one printing.

1.4 Binding

Printed paper is called a printed page or sheet, usually bound according to the usage requirements. Different binding methods have different techniques. The main binding forms for engraved block printing include sutra binding, scroll binding, butterfly-like binding, wrapped-back binding, thread-stitching, etc.

2. *Printing in the Tang and the Five Dynasties and Ten Kingdoms Period*

Very few early printed works in China have been passed down to now. However, in the early 20th century, a great number of block printing works were unearthed from the Dunhuang Sutra Cave. They were mainly printed during the 9th to 10th

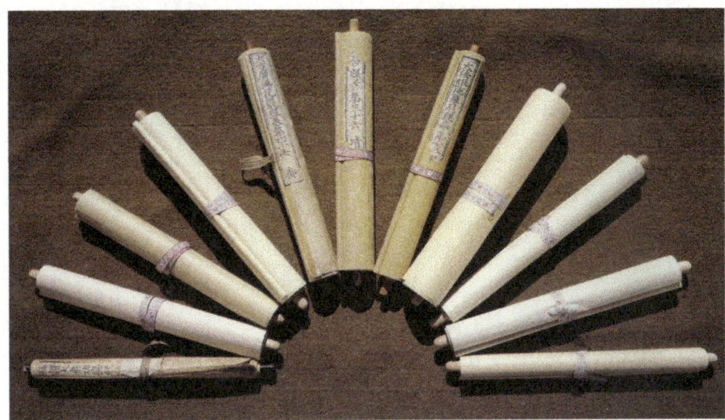

Buddhist scriptures with scroll binding

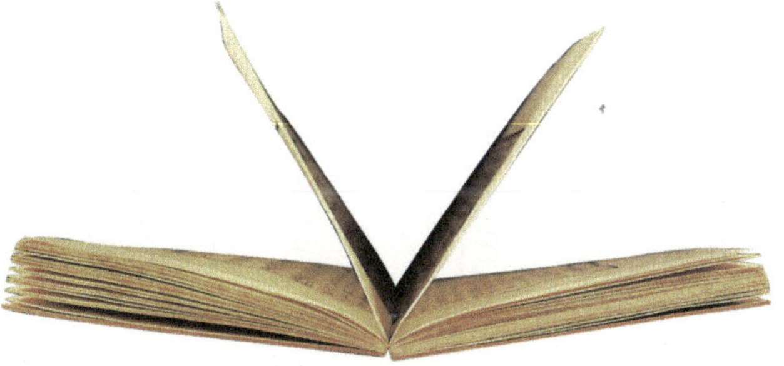

Butterfly-like bound book

centuries, namely the late Tang, Five Dynasties, and early Song in Chinese history. These discoveries include religious prints such as woodcut and Buddhist scriptures and printed works such as almanacs, rhyme dictionaries, and folk literature closely related to people's daily lives.

2.1 Printing Industry in the Tang Dynasty

At the end of the Tang Dynasty, Feng Zhi recorded in his *Miscellaneous Notes of Unzen* something since the 19th year of the Zhenguan reign (AD 645), Xuan Zang "printed the images of Buddha on the Huifeng paper and handed them out. Every year, five loads of prints were all given away with no one left." This is the earliest record of Buddhist printing in China. The printed work is about the images of Buddha, and despite a large annual printing volume, unfortunately, it has not been passed down.

In 1974, the Sanskrit *Dharani Sutra* was unearthed in the suburbs of Xi'an. Archaeologists have identified it as a 7th-century print, maybe the earliest surviving printed work. Other early copies with clear printing dates include a Chinese volume of the *Great Dhāraṇī Scripture of Immaculate Radiance* discovered in the Sakya Pagoda

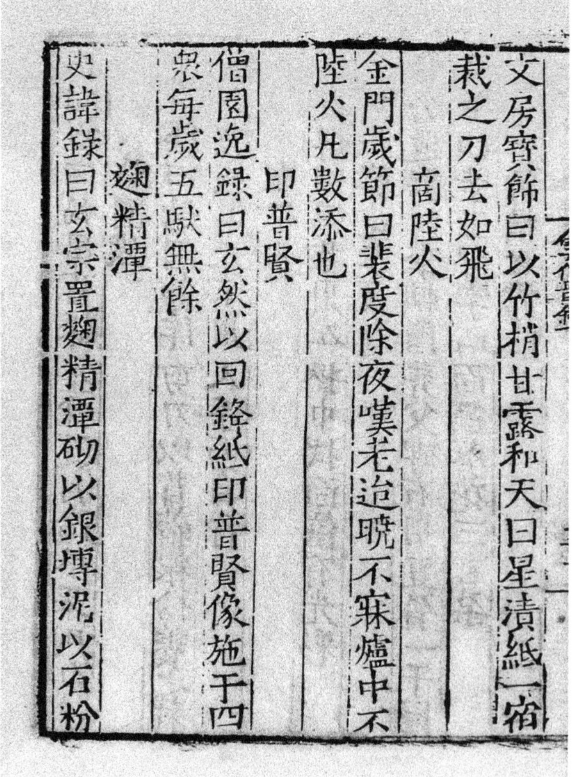
文房寶飾曰以竹精甘露和天曰星漬紙一宿
裁之刀去如飛
啇陸火
金門歲節曰裴度除夜嘆老迨曉不寐爐中不
陸火凡數添也
印普賢
僧園逸錄曰玄奘以回鋒紙印普賢像施于四
衆每歲五馱無餘
麴精潭
史諱錄曰玄宗置麴精潭砌以銀塼泥以石粉

According to the records of *Seng Yuan Yi Lu* cited by Feng Zhi in his work *Miscellaneous Notes of Unzen* in the late Tang Dynasty, Xuan Zang "printed the images of Buddha on the Huifeng paper and handed them out. Every year, five loads of prints were all given away with no one left."

of the Gyeongju Buddhist Temple in South Korea in 1966. After repeated research by experts from various countries, it is believed that it was engraved between AD 704 and AD 751 years, possibly in the eastern capital of the Tang Dynasty, Luoyang.

Japan now houses *Hyakumanto Darani*, engraved from AD 764 to AD 770 by the then Empress Kōken. According to records, they were stored in one million small wooden pagodas. Dozens of prints created from the Tang Dynasty to the Five Dynasties were unearthed from the Mogao Caves in Dunhuang, Gansu Province, including Buddhist scriptures, Buddha statues, almanacs, and miscellaneous stone carvings. Unfortunately, although created in China, most of them are now preserved in museums in countries such as the United Kingdom, France, Germany, and Japan. One example of the block prints passed down from the Tang Dynasty is the block-printed edition *Maha Pratisara Dharani* by the Bian family in Longchifang, Chengdu County, Chengdu Prefecture, which was unearthed from a Tang tomb in Chengdu, Sichuan, in 1944. Research shows that it was engraved between AD 850 and AD 900. The spread of these written records and physical artifacts proves that engraved block printing was a great invention of ancient China, giving credit to the claim that this technique originated in the Sui Dynasty and flourished in the Tang Dynasty.

In the late Tang Dynasty, block printing workshops gradually spread widely throughout present-day Shaanxi, Henan, Sichuan, Jiangsu, Zhejiang, and Jiangxi, with Chang'an, Luoyang, and Chengdu as the centers of the printing industry at that time. In the east market of Chang'an City, there were folk bookstores housing, for example, the almanac printed by the Dadiao family and the famous medical books printed by the Li family. The *New Organized Moxibustion Classic for Emergency*, a block-printed edition by the Li family, was unearthed from Dunhuang and is the earliest existing medical book.

In the Tang Dynasty, Chengdu, a powerhouse of the block printing industry, was home to various types of printing and printing workshops. For example, some remaining pages of the almanac printed by the Fan Shang family in AD 882 have been passed down to today. They were printed with the words "The almanac of the Fan Shang family in Chengdu, Xichuan, Jiannan" on them. This almanac and the almanac of Dingyou in AD 877 are the earliest block-printed editions in the world. There were also Buddhist scriptures printed by the "Xichuan Guo family." Today, the National Library of China still houses a fragment of *The Diamond Sutra* that was re-written by an anonymous old man in the late Tang Dynasty based on "the real version printed by the Xichuan Guo family." The National Library of France also has *The Diamond Sutra*, the edition of "the real version printed by the Xichuan Guo family" in AD 943. Research indicates that the Guo family ran a long-established bookstore in Chengdu, printing Buddhist scriptures from the late Tang Dynasty to the Five Dynasties. Xichuan also published reference books that were used in poetry creation, such as rhyme and character books. Shuei (AD 809–884), a monk of Japanese Shingon Buddhism, studied in China from AD 862 to AD 865 of the Tang Dynasty. When he returned to Japan, he brought a total of 134 volumes of scriptures and compiled the *New Book of Buddhist Scriptures and Other Works*. The book recorded that among the foreign books brought back, there were "a five-volume *Tang Yun* and a thirty-volume *Yupian* printed by the Xichuan family." At that time, the printed books in Chengdu covered a wide range of topics. According to the preface of *The Liu Family Precepts* written by a government official named Liu Pin, in the year AD 883 of the Tang Dynasty, he saw various printed books in Chengdu's bookstores, including books on yin and yang, miscellaneous notes, dream interpretation, geomancy practicing, as well as dictionaries and primary school readings. However, the printing quality was not high with blurred ink, making it "not fully understandable."

THE STORY BEHIND CULTURAL RELICS

The national treasure of *The Diamond Sutra* drifting in a foreign land

Most of the original block prints of the Tang Dynasty have been lost. The famous volume of *The Diamond Sutra* preserved in the British Library is the earliest dated engraved block print in the world. With a length of 488 centimeters, the front of the volume is an image of Buddha, showing the mythical story of Sakyamuni speaking to his disciples, surrounded by heavenly gods listening quietly. Everyone looks solemn, and the picture is exquisite, with smooth lines. The image is followed by scriptures in neat fonts, with even ink and skilled engraving techniques. This volume of *The Diamond Sutra* was a Buddhist scripture carved by a man named Wang Jie in the 9th year of Xiantong (AD 868) for his parents to pray for blessings and dispel disasters.

Why did such precious cultural relics end up in a foreign country? This can date back to 1900, the 26th year in the reign of Emperor Guangxu of the Qing Dynasty. Wang Yuanlu, a Taoist who lived in the Mogao Grottoes of Dunhuang, accidentally found a hidden enclosure while cleaning up the sand accumulated in one of the caves. After he opened the enclosure, he found this small cave was densely filled with bundles of scriptures, documents, and other cultural relics, piled from the ground to the roof, which amazed the onlookers and was regarded as a sacred object by the people who heard about

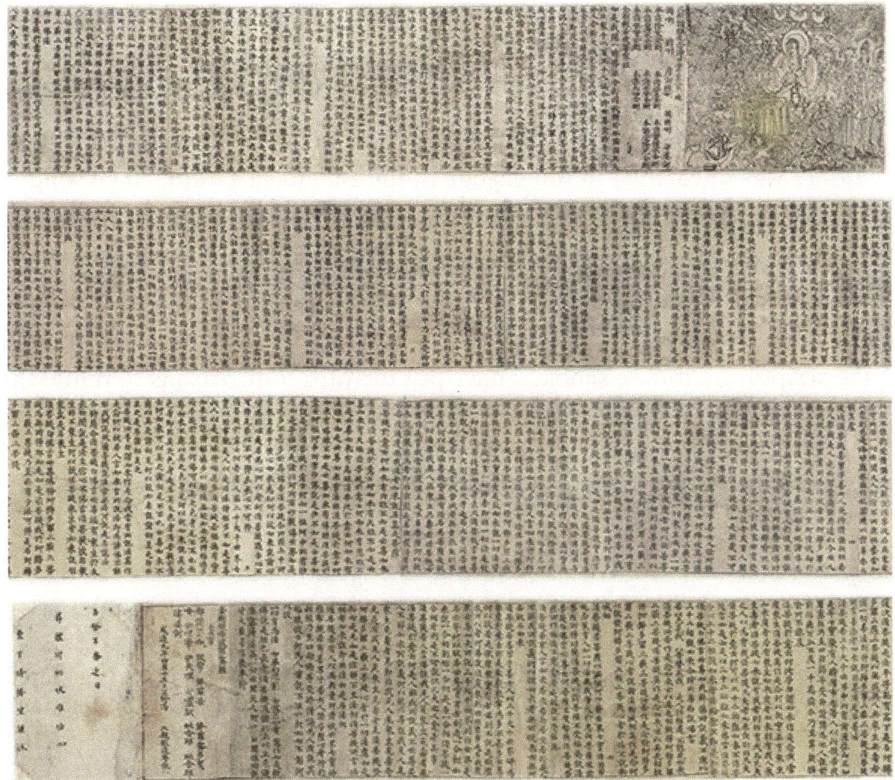

The Diamond Sutra, block printed in the year AD 868, found in Dunhuang Caves

it. This is the famous Dunhuang Cave for storing Buddhist scriptures, now known as Mogao Cave No. 17. The discovery of this treasure house of cultural relics and art soon attracted the attention of the imperialists. In 1907, after hearing about this, the British Hungarian Marc Aurel Stein (1862–1943) immediately came to the cave with his Chinese translator, Jiang Xiaowan. By deceiving Taoist Wang with every means, he selected 24 boxes of ancient manuscripts and five boxes of ancient paintings and silk embroidery, totaling more than 10,000 pieces, all of which were shipped to the British Museum in London, England. But he only paid 200 taels of silver to Taoist Wang and 130 pounds of taxes for these rare treasures. In 1914, Stein swindled five large boxes of Buddhist scriptures with more than 600 volumes. He was a greedy "sinologist" who conducted three raids on cultural relics in the western regions of China over 16 years, stealing and swindling precious cultural relics that could fill up a museum. This was the first cultural relics disaster in China in the 20th century.

THE STORY BEHIND CULTURAL RELICS
The Buddhist scriptures that triggered the "Sino-Korean dispute"

In 1966, the over three-meter-long *Great Dhāraṇī Scripture of Immaculate Radiance* was unearthed in the pagoda of the Bulguksa Temple in Gyeongju, South Korea. According to research, this scripture was inscribed in the 8th century. Based on this discovery unearthed, Korean scholars attempted to prove that the engraved block printing originated in South Korea, which led to the "Sino-Korean dispute" in the history of printing. Since the discovery of the scripture, Chinese scholars have put forward four reasons to refute the claim. First, according to historical documents, the pagoda in South Korea

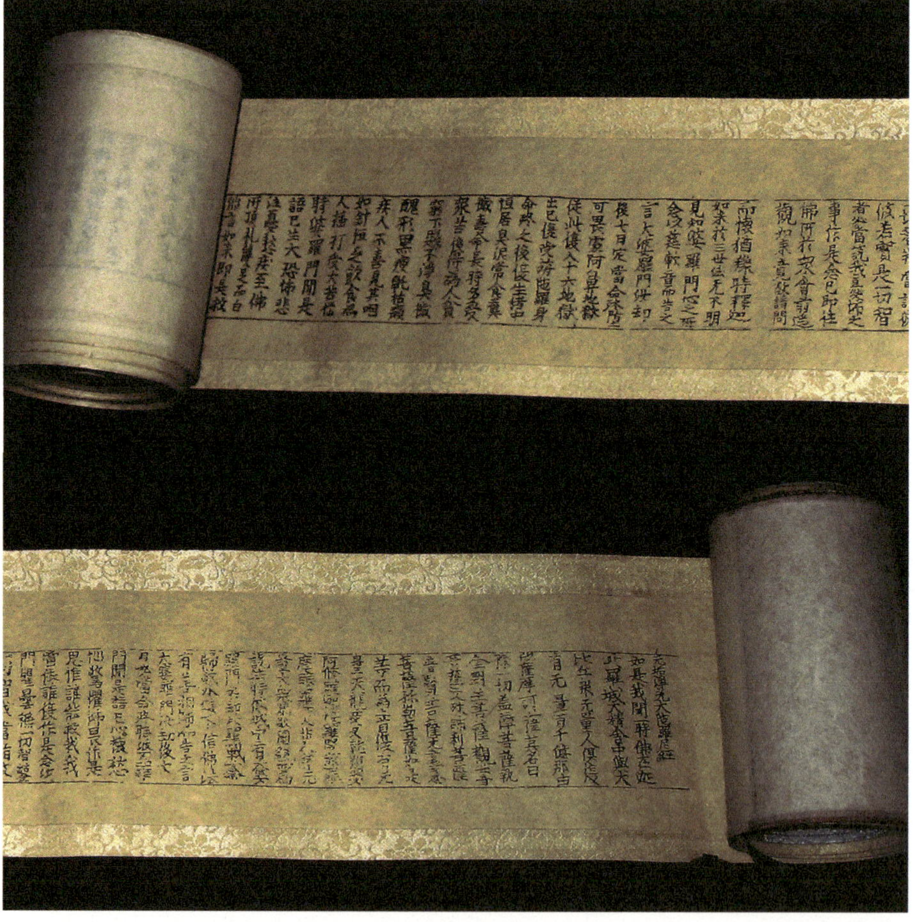

Great Dhāraṇī Scripture of Immaculate Radiance of the Tang Dynasty, unearthed at the Buddhist Temple in Gyeongju, South Korea

was built under the guidance of Chinese monks. Second, there were four characters created during the reign of Empress Wu Zetian in the scripture, which appeared eight times in total, indicating the time when the scripture was printed. Third, the *Great Dhāraṇī Scripture of Immaculate Radiance* was very popular during the reign of Empress Wu Zetian, especially in Luoyang, proving that the scripture was printed in Luoyang. Fourth, there was only one artifact unearthed during this period in South Korea's history that failed to prove that printing originated in Korea in accordance with the principle that "a single discovery cannot serve as evidence" in archaeology. On the contrary, many printed materials about the Tang Dynasty have been unearthed in China. With the unremitting efforts of Chinese scholars and the evidence of many cultural relics, it is an unshakable fact that the engraved block printing originated in China. Now, after disclosure, the Buddhist temple and pagoda where the scripture was unearthed have been renovated by later generations, and the offerings supplemented by later generations have been stored in the renovated pagoda. Therefore, the date when scripture was printed cannot be determined. In fact, the scriptures, printed in Chinese characters, originally came from the Tang Dynasty. Therefore, there is no need for reasons or arguments; the historical status of the Tang Dynasty is beyond doubt or dispute.

2.2 Printing Industry in the Five Dynasties

The Five Dynasties and the Ten Kingdoms were a relatively short and turbulent period. However, during this period, the block printing industry completed a magnificent turn from the folk to the official, from printing miscellaneous books, scriptures, and images to printing Confucian classics. Ever since, block printing has become a dominant publishing technique.

In AD 932, Feng Dao, the prime minister of the Later Tang Dynasty, first advocated the printing of Confucian classics. At that time, although there were many kinds of books printed nationwide, most of them were ordinary reference books for folks, such as *yin* and *yang* miscellaneous notes, character books for primary schools, almanacs, and Buddhist scriptures, with no Confucian classics printed. Therefore, he submitted a petition to the emperor requesting the printing of *Jiu Jing* based on the stone scriptures. After obtaining the emperor's approval, Tian Min, a Confucian scholar, and others convened the experts and disciples of the Imperial Academy to proofread scriptures carefully based on the best official version of *Inscription on Stone*. Then, calligraphy masters were asked to write in regular script, after which craftsmen were organized and required to carve and print the scriptures. In this way, it took 21 years from AD 932 to AD 953 to complete, unlocking the beginning of a large-scale book printing project by the government. Since it was printed by the Imperial Academy, it was later called "*Jiu Jing* of Imperial College edition in the Five Dynasties."

Feng Dao was famous for his recognition and advocacy of block printing. Many scholars have regarded him as the inventor of block printing in history. After the emergence of "*Jiu Jing* of Imperial College edition in the Five Dynasties," thanks to the government's promotion of the printing industry, there have been more privately engraved books by scholars. The prime minister of the Later Shu Dynasty, Wu Zhaoyi, riding on the waves, became the pioneer of large-scale privately engraved books in Chinese history. Historical records show that when Wu Zhaoyi was young, he often borrowed copies of the poetry anthology titled *The Selections of Refined Literature* and the subject-specific reference book named *A Reference for the Primary Learning* from others, and he was enraged by others' refusal. He vowed to himself that if he ever achieved success, he would engrave books and print them to facilitate learners around the world.

With effortless work, he eventually became a prime minister, finally holding the two books he had been seeking for a long time. He fulfilled his vow by printing and distributing the books. He also funded schools and printed a large number of books.

During the Five Dynasties and the Ten Kingdoms period, the printing industry in Hangzhou, the capital of the State of Wuyue, was also quite developed. In particular, King Qian Chu (formerly known as Qian Hongchu), a devout Buddhist, became famous for publishing Buddhist scriptures along with monk Yan Shou. They carved and printed an unprecedented number of Buddhist scriptures, Buddha statues, pagoda maps, and mantras, with 680,000 volumes countable. The prosperity of printing and publishing also enhanced the development of related industries such as paper and ink industries. The printing technique of the State of Wuyue reached a relatively high level, with white paper, black ink, clear and pleasing fonts, and exquisite graphics.

THE STORY BEHIND CULTURAL RELICS
There is no Madam White Snake under the Leifeng Pagoda

Madam White Snake was suppressed under the Leifeng Pagoda at the bank of the West Lake, which is a well-known folklore in China. This folklore and Mr. Lu Xun's article "On the Collapse of the Leifeng Pagoda" make the Leifeng

Pagoda a household name. In fact, the collapse of the former Leifeng Pagoda was closely related to an ancient book.

According to folklore, many "gold hidden bricks," with gold inside, were used to build the pagoda by Qian Chu, the King of Wuyue. As a result, endless "gold seekers" illegally begin digging the pagoda bricks for a long span. Over time, at around 1:40 pm on September 25, 1924, the Leifeng Pagoda, a famous pagoda on the bank of the West Lake in Hangzhou, collapsed with a bang after failing to bear the heavy burden anymore. Its collapse disclosed the secret of the "gold-hidden" pagoda bricks, which turned out that some of the pagoda bricks were hollow ones with treasures inside, though not real gold, but real scriptures.

During the Five Dynasties period, Qian Liu, the first ruler of the southern State of Wuyue, was appointed as king of Wuyue by Zhu Wen, Emperor Taizu of the Liang Dynasty, later awarded the title of Command in chief. The State of Wuyue had been ruled by five kings over three generations for more than 70 years. All kings in the Qian family believed in Buddhism, with the most devout one named Qian Chu, the king of loyalty and righteousness. He had built many temples and pagodas and carved Buddhist scriptures. The Buddhist scripture *Sutra of the Whole-Body Relic Treasure Chest Seal Dharani*, wrapped in yellow silk, was hidden in the hollow bricks of the Leifeng Pagoda.

The scripture has an inscription that reads, "The Command-in-Chief, King Qian Chu of the State of Wuyue, has 84,000 copies of this sutra printed for placement and worship in the Xiguan brick pagoda on August 10, the year of Yihai." Yihai was the eighth year of the reign of Emperor Taizu of the Song Dynasty (AD 975). Still, despite this, the State of Wuyue had not yet been under the control of the Song Dynasty, so the scripture can still be classified as a print in the Five Dynasties period.

Since the 20th century, many Buddhist scriptures engraved and printed by the State of Wuyue have been discovered. In 1917, during the reconstruction of the Tianning Temple in Huzhou, Zhejiang Province, several volumes of the *Treasure Chest Seal Dharani* were found hidden inside the elephant's trunk-shaped stone columns. The front cover of the first volume has the inscription, "Qian Chu, the Commander-in-Chief and King of the State of Wuyue, had 84,000 copies of this sutra printed for placement in the pagoda in AD 956, the third year of Xiande." The time was only slightly later than the completion of the carved and printed Confucian classic *Jiu Jing* in AD 953. In this sense, the State of Wuyue had carried out large-scale projects to print scriptures.

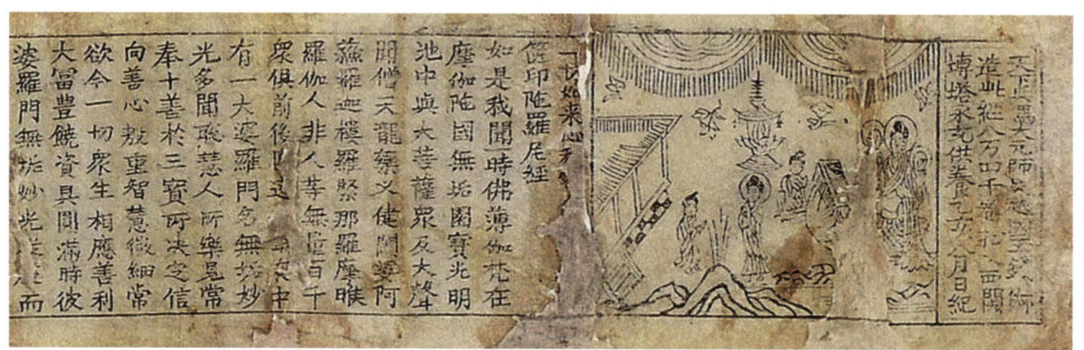

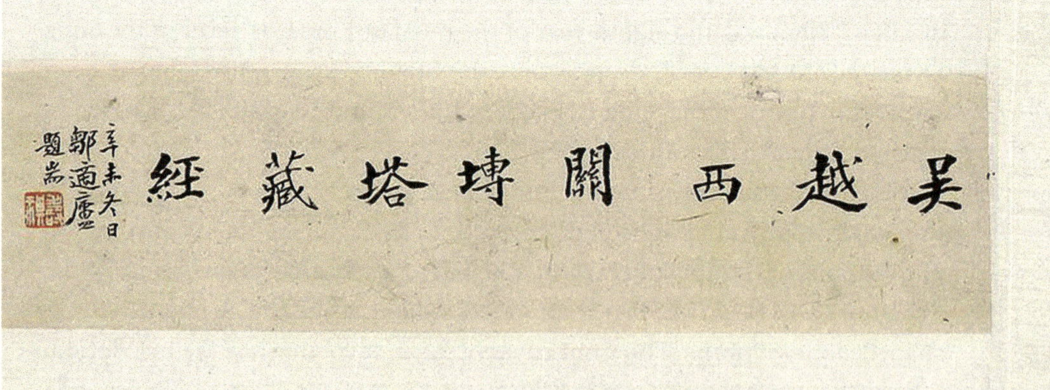

Sutra of the Whole-Body Relic Treasure Chest Seal Dharani, stored in the bricks of the Leifeng Pagoda

塔所尒時塔上[illegible]大光明
赫然熾盛於土聚中出善
哉聲讚言善哉善哉釋迦
牟尼如来今日所行極善
境界又言汝婆羅門汝於
今日獲大善利尒時世尊
礼彼朽塔右遶三匝脫身
上衣用覆其上[illegible]然垂淚
涕血交流泣已微笑當尒
之時十方諸佛皆同觀視
亦皆泣淚俱放光明來照
是塔是時大衆集會皆同
怖異驚佛而住尒時金剛
手菩薩亦皆流淚威焰熾
盛執杵旋轉[illegible]佛所
言世尊此何因緣現是光
相何於如来眼流淚如是
此是佛之大瑞光相現前
唯願如来於此大衆解釋
我疑時薄伽梵告金剛手
大全身舍利聚如来塔一
切如来俱胝如[illegible]麻心陁
羅尼印法要今在其中金
剛手有此法要在是中故
塔即為如胡麻俱胝百千
如来之身亦是如胡麻百
千俱胝如来全身舍利聚
乃至八万四千法蘊亦在
其中即九十九百千俱胝

如来頂相在其中是塔一
切如来之所授記若是塔
所在之處有大功勲具大
威德能滿一切吉慶尒時
大衆聞佛是說遠塵離垢
及隨煩惱得法[illegible][illegible]
即有得須陁洹果者得斯
陁含果者得阿那含果者
得阿羅漢果者或有得辟
支佛道者或有入菩薩位
者或有得阿毗跋致者或
有得菩薩授記者或有得
初地二[illegible][illegible]十[illegible]者或
有滿足六波羅蜜者其婆
羅門遠塵離垢得五神通
尒時金剛手菩薩見此奇
特希有之事白佛言世尊
甚奇特希有但聞此事尚
獲如是殊勝功德何況於
此法要種植善[illegible]獲大福
聚佛言諦聽金剛手若有
善男子善女人比丘比丘
尼優婆塞優婆夷書寫此
經典者即為書寫彼九十
九百千俱胝如胡麻如来
所說經典即[illegible]彼九十九
百千俱胝如胡麻如来種
植善根即為彼等如来護
念攝受若人讀誦即為讀

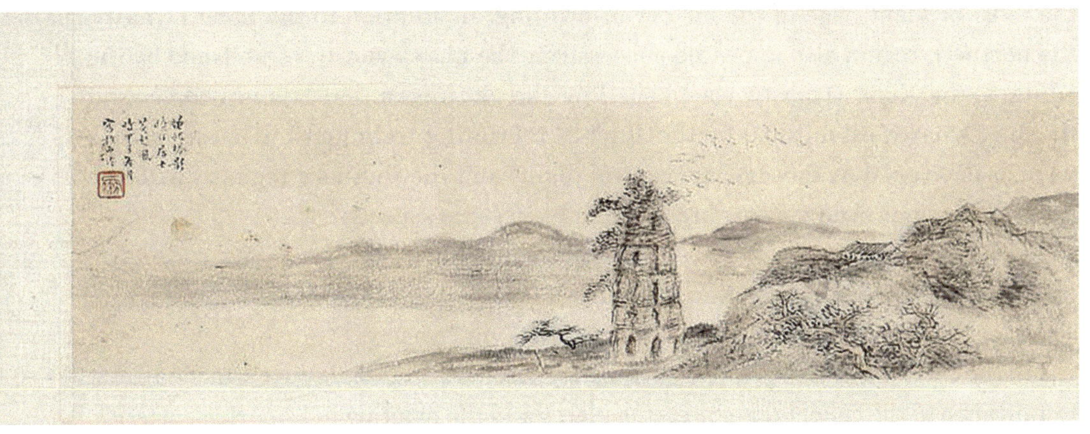

In 1971, a gold-coated pagoda with a square pedestal was unearthed at the construction site of the Materials Company in Chengguan Town, Shaoxing, Zhejiang Province. Now housed in the Zhejiang Provincial Museum, the gold-coated pagoda is completely cast, consisting of a Sumeru platform and a tacha. Inside the pedestal lies a small red wooden cylinder, about 10 centimeters long, which is short and thick, with a wooden sleeve at one end. Hidden in the cylinder is a volume of the *Treasure Chest Seal Dharani* with the inscription "King Qian Chu of the State of Wuyue has 84,000 copies of this sutra printed for placement and worship in the second year of the reign of Emperor Taizu of the Song Dynasty (AD 965). The sutra was clearly printed on white paper with the front cover an invaluable painting showing the Concubine Huang worshiping the Buddha, with a slight difference in composition from the one mentioned before.

So, the truth is that there was no Madam White Snake or real gold under the Leifeng Pagoda, but printed scriptures.

3. Printing in the Song, Liao, Jin, and Xixia Dynasties

After the development throughout the Tang and the Five Dynasties, the block printing technique had become very mature. After entering the Song Dynasty, thanks to the attention and advocacy of the government, the printing industry flourished, opening the most brilliant page in the history of printing. In addition to the Song Dynasty, the northern region also appeared successively the Liao Dynasty, established by the Khitans, the Xixia Dynasty, established by the Northwest Dangxiang people, and the Jin Dynasty, established by the Jurchens. Printing techniques in these regions were as developed as those of the central plains and the southern regions, with the northern regions even making breakthroughs in some aspects.

3.1 Printing Industry in the Song Dynasty

The block printing reached its peak during the Song Dynasty.

In the early years of the Northern Song Dynasty, the imperial court attached great importance to the collection of printing plates and the printing of important classics, engraving books such as the Confucian classics, history, philosophy, and collections with plans and division of labor. In the Song Dynasty, as the main department of the central imperial court to engrave books, the Imperial Academy took charge of national printing. The academy was also the highest learning institution and the national educational management institution. Books engraved by the Imperial Academy were known as the "Imperial College edition." During the Northern Song Dynasty, engraved books by the Imperial Academy represented the peak of the block printing history, reflected in outstanding achievements in papermaking, ink making, layout design, printing fonts, bookbinding, and other crafts, which became a model for the printing industry in later generations. These progresses with far-reaching influence were highly respected and imitated by later generations, playing an important role in the history of ancient printing.

The Song Dynasty witnessed widespread development of woodblock printing, with book engraving and printing activities taking place throughout the country. Due to different geographical, natural, and cultural conditions, several book engraving centers at different levels of prosperity emerged in the Song Dynasty, with the books engraved in each area boasting their own characteristics. In the early Northern Song Dynasty, books engraved in today's Sichuan Province were the most prosperous, which was inherited from the Tang and Five Dynasties. By the late Northern Song Dynasty, Zhejiang engraved the most exquisite books. In the Southern Song Dynasty, Fujian had the highest number of book engravings in the whole country. Therefore, these places produced three famous centers of book engraving in the Song Dynasty.

The books printed by folks in the Song Dynasty were divided into home-made editions, private schools-made editions, and workshop-made editions. Home-made editions, also known as "private-made editions," refer to books that were printed by craftsmen hired by individuals or by book-printing workshops with financial contributions. Most of these books were written by individuals or by their ancestors. Printing these books was mainly to spread and promote their reputation or commemorate their ancestors. Therefore, these books were often given as gifts and sometimes sold to cover the costs.

The printing of Buddhist scriptures was also well-developed during the Song Dynasty. The most influential work was *The Kaibao Tripitaka*, completed between 971 and 983. After 12 years of work, 130,000 woodblocks were carved to create the edition, based on the *Kaiyuan Catalogue of Buddhist Scriptures* as the main source for the collection of Buddhist scriptures, consisting of 480 volumes and 5,048 scrolls. The format is scroll-binding, with 23 lines and 14 characters per line. The beginning of each edition includes the title of the scripture, edition number, and volume number, with the end of each scroll marked with the year and month of the carving. This magnificent project holds great sway in the history of ancient printing and publishing, marking the beginning of the complete collection of Buddhist scriptures in China. It also directly influences the development of woodblock printing in countries such as Japan, Korea, and Vietnam.

The Song-edition books were exquisitely carved, with superior paper quality and rich ink color. In terms of the craftsmanship of bookbinding, the butterfly-like binding technique was widely used, thus creating a rectangular format for book pages. Throughout the ages, all collectors have taken pride in housing Song-edition books. There is a saying that goes, "One page of the Song-edition book is worth a tael of gold." American scholar Carter once said, "In terms of the exquisiteness of woodblock printing, there is hardly any period in Chinese history that can surpass the Song Dynasty." In summary, there are three main reasons why Song-edition books are precious. The first is their scarcity. Dating back to approximately 1,000 years, Song-edition books have become increasingly rare, making them highly sought after by collectors. The second is their lingering charm. The concept of "exquisite edition" just originated in the Song Dynasty. These kinds of books have been regarded as the most beautiful ones in the eyes of Chinese scholars. The Song people pursued aesthetic "charm" in terms of calligraphy, typography, and bookbinding, resulting in a distinct appeal. Gu Qianli, a book collector in the Qing Dynasty, even believed that the blank spaces in Song-edition books were also beautiful. The third reason is their craftsmanship. In the history of Chinese books, the skilled craftsmen of the Song Dynasty demonstrated unique creativity and thoughtfulness in areas such as collation, engraving, paper quality, and bookbinding.

During the Northern Song Dynasty, regulations on copyright protection were established to safeguard the authority of imperial publications, pioneering copyright protection in China. In the Southern Song Dynasty, individuals who privately printed books would seek the protection of the government to enforce copyright protection, ensuring the economic interests of publishers and the rights of authors. Punishments for copyright infringement included "tracking down and destroying engraved plates" or "cleaving printing plates," which were quite severe.

THE STORY BEHIND CULTURAL RELICS

Please recognize the trademark of Bai Tu'er

China has a long history of using commodity marks associated with commodity exchange. During the Northern Song Dynasty, competition became increasingly fierce with the development of private business. Many shops, in addition to decorating their storefronts, also printed advertisements with their

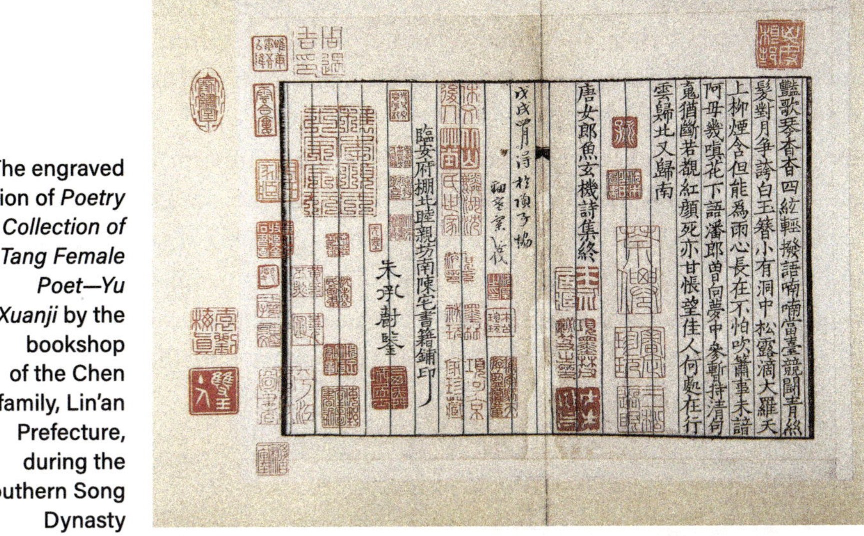
豔歌琴杳四絃輕撥語喃喃當臺競鬪青絲
髮對月爭誇白玉簪小有洞中松露滴大羅天
上柳煙含但能為雨心長在不怕吹簫事未諳
阿母幾嗔花下語潘郎曾向夢中參暫持清句
魂猶斷若覩紅顏死亦甘悵望佳人何處在行
雲歸北又歸南

唐女郎魚玄機詩集終

臨安府棚北睦親坊南陳宅書籍鋪印

朱承爵鑒

The engraved edition of *Poetry Collection of Tang Female Poet—Yu Xuanji* by the bookshop of the Chen family, Lin'an Prefecture, during the Southern Song Dynasty

shop marks. The National Museum of China preserves a copper printing plate from the Northern Song Dynasty, measuring 13.2 centimeters in length and 12.4 centimeters in width. The top of the plate bears the name of the shop—"Ji'nan Liu Family's Kung Fu Needle Shop" and in the center is the shop mark—"A white rabbit pounding medicine," as well as the annotation "Recognizing the white rabbit in front of the door as the mark." The bottom of the plate features an advertising text that says, "We buy high-quality steel bars to make fine needles that are suitable for household use. Moderate discounts can be offered if purchased wholesale. Please remember the logo of a white rabbit." At that time, self-production and self-sales were the main modes of commodity operation, under which these shop marks had become specific identifiers for goods. This copper plate with "Ji'nan Liu Family's Kung Fu Needle Shop" is the earliest known physical evidence of a trademark advertisement in the world.

The design of the white rabbit trademark registered by this needle shop in Ji'nan is rich in cultural connotation, embodying a beautiful and auspicious legend. Why is the white rabbit holding a sewing needle to pound medicine? In fact, this white rabbit is the embodiment of Chang'e, and this trademark pattern is based on the legendary story of "Chang'e Flying to the Moon." The myth of "Chang'e running to the moon," from the article "Yi sought the elixir of immortality from the Queen Mother of the West, and Chang'e stole it to run to the moon" in *Huai Nan Zi · Lanming Xun*, has been passed down among the folks for over 2,000 years.

Chang'e, also known as Heng'e, was a fairy in ancient mythology. She was the wife of the archer Yi, a subordinate of Emperor Jun of Heaven. The Yi couple was sent by Emperor Jun to assist Yao in the mortal world. Legend had it that there were ten suns living in the Donghai Valley, all of whom were the sons of the Heavenly Emperor. The Heavenly Emperor ordered them to take turns to illuminate the world for humanity in the sky. One day, ten suns ran together into the sky and refused to go back, making vegetation scorched and rivers dried up, causing unbearable suffering for people. Yi was ordered to persuade the suns to return, but no one paid attention to him. As a result, all remained in the sky. Yi couldn't bear it anymore and shot down nine of

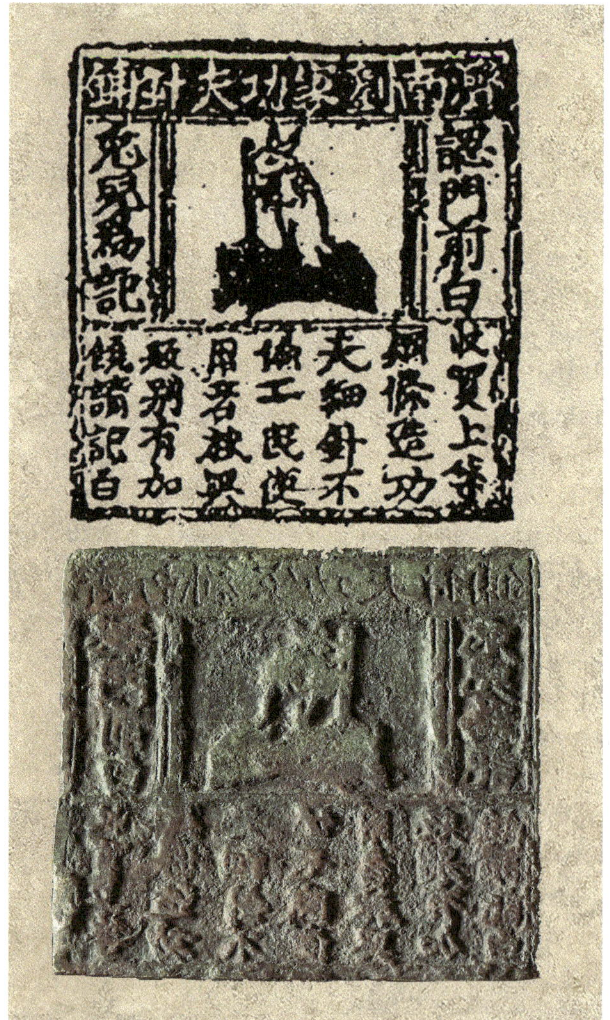

The copper printed plate of the advertisement for "Ji'nan Liu Family's Kung Fu Needle Shop," collected by the National Museum of China

the suns one by one. The earth then regained vitality with seedlings growing, vegetation reinvigorating, and rivers flowing smoothly. People have been able to live and work in peace and contentment. They were very grateful for Yi's kindness, and Yi was also respected by people. When Yi was shooting at the sun, Chang'e cut off her beautiful and tough long hair to make a string to tie it to Yi's bow, making Yi's shooting a success. She was also loved by people for this, but also implicated since she was punished as a mortal along with Yi. To seek immortality, Yi sought two elixirs from the Queen Mother of the West. Beautiful Chang'e was a curious woman. During Yi's deep sleep, she quietly took a vial of the elixir without feeling uncomfortable, and thus she took the other vial. She only felt herself suddenly floating towards the moon palace. After arriving at the Moon Palace, Chang'e was punished by becoming an ugly toad, constantly pounding the elixir of immortality. People had a strong affection for Chang'e, missing her dedication to helping Yi fight against drought. At the same time, they could not bear to see Chang'e's ugly appearance in the moon palace.

In the Jin Dynasty, Fu Xuan sent a white rabbit into the moon palace to replace the toad in making medicine in his work *Asking the Heaven*, thus changing the image of Chang'e. This gave rise to the beautiful image and legend of "White Rabbit Pounding Medicine." In the Tang Dynasty, under the pen of some literati, Chang'e was able to restore her personal image. Afterward, Duan Chengshi, in his *Youyang Zazu · Tianzhi*, also introduced an immortal cultivator, Wu Gang, to enter the moon palace to fell osmanthus trees, adding to the legendary color of Chang'e's journey to the moon.

The use of the Liu Family's Needle Shop of the white rabbit, which symbolizes "Chang'e" as its trademark, produced a profound meaning and was full of interest, naturally winning the love of the public and helpful to marketing. This "advertisement" has a certain level of proficiency in both product trademark selection and advertising language. To this day, it is still a good example of product promotion.

3.2 Printing Industry in the Liao Dynasty

Advocating Confucianism and Buddhism, the rulers of the Liao Dynasty worked hard to promote education nationwide, so the people's demand for books became increasingly high.

In the early period, the Liao Dynasty purchased a large number of books from the Song Dynasty through the border trade. The book trade between the Song and the Liao dynasties resulted in a significant influx of Song-edition books into the Liao Dynasty. As a result, Emperor Zhenzong of the Song Dynasty issued a decree in the third year of Jingde (1006), stating that "those who engage in book trade along the borders with the Liao are prohibited from selling any books other than *Jiu Jing*." Despite the prohibition, in practice, many books that were not confined to classics and histories also made their way into the Liao Dynasty. Su Zhe once remarked after visiting the Liao Dynasty, "Since the development of the printing industry in our country, I suspect the people in the Liao Dynasty have every copy of what we have printed." When envoys from the Liao Dynasty came to visit the Song government, they often asked for books. Most of their demands could be fulfilled. For example, once, a Liao envoy requested a copy of *The Poetry Collection of Wei Ye*, which was fulfilled by the Emperor of the Song Dynasty.

Under the influence of the Song Dynasty, the printing industry in such areas as Yanjing in the Liao Kingdom developed rapidly, eventually unleashing the widespread and prosperous development of the printing and publishing industry in the Liao Dynasty.

Historical records indicate that a wide variety of books were produced during the Liao Dynasty. Unfortunately, very few of them have survived to this day. For a long time, many scholars even have doubted the authenticity of these historical records. It was not until the discovery of the wooden pagoda in Ying County, Shanxi Province (formerly known as Yingzhou in the Liao Dynasty) that the mystery of Liao Dynasty printing was unveiled. The wooden pagoda in Ying County was built in the second year of the reign of Emperor Qingning of the Liao Dynasty (1056), which is a wooden structure Buddhist pagoda known as the Sakyamuni Pagoda of the Fogong Temple. In July 1974, during the renovation of the pagoda, a collection of richly varied Liao Dynasty printed materials was discovered inside the abdomen of the main statue of Sakyamuni on the fourth floor of the pagoda. These printed materials are precious cultural relics of the Liao Dynasty, reflecting the highly skilled engraving technique of that time.

During the Liao Dynasty, the printing of Buddhist scriptures flourished. From the royal family to the common people, most of them were devout Buddhists, which made pooling funds to engrave and print Buddhist scriptures a common practice. This was because, in the eyes of Buddhist believers, writing, engraving, reading, reciting, and spreading Buddhist scriptures were all considered supreme merits that could bring blessings to themselves and their families. The inscription at the end of the second volume of the *Well-Versed New Exegesis of the Lotus Sutra by Xuan Zan* stored in the wooden pagoda in Ying County reads, "Forty-seven sheets, carved

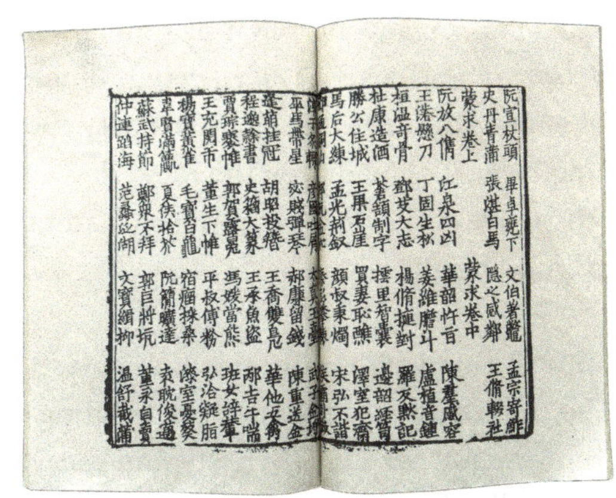

The engraved version of *Meng Qiu* from the Liao Dynasty, unearthed from the wooden pagoda in Yingxian County, Shanxi Province, is a kind of reading material for children. It mainly features historical allusions and dual rhyming sentences, each consisting of four Chinese characters containing a story of a historical or legendary figure. The book is butterfly-like binding.

together by forty-two persons, including twenty-two sheets by Nan Su, a military officer of three provincial offices, Sun Shoujie, and so on." The inscription at the end of the sixth volume of the same scripture reads, "Fifty-six sheets, carved together by forty-five persons, including two sheets by Zhang Su, the Deputy Commander of Yunzhou, three sheets by Li Shou, five sheets by Xu Yanyu, two sheets by Li Yin, the Deputy Commander of Yingzhou, and so on." The mention of "Yunzhou" in the inscription indicates the location of the engraving, which refers to present-day Datong City in Shanxi Province. The records in the inscription detailed the number of sheets, contributors, and carvers, indicating the prevalence of the engraved printing industry at that time.

During the reign of Emperor Shengzong of the Liao Dynasty, not only were Buddhist classics in Chinese printed, but also Confucian classics and historical books such as the *Five Classics and Commentaries*, *Records of the Grand Historian*, and *Book of Han* were printed in Chinese, which were then distributed to schools as textbooks. The Liao people also printed and published poems and essays by their favorite literati, Su Dongpo and Bai Juyi. Emperor Shengzong of the Liao Dynasty once translated such medical books as *The Political Program of Zhenguan Period*, *General History*, etc., into Khitan scripts for engraving. He also specifically translated Bai Juyi's *Collection of Satirical Admonitions* into Khitan, which was then engraved into larger characters and printed for the ministers who didn't know Chinese to recite.

In the first year of the Kaitai reign (1012), Emperor Shengzong of the Liao Dynasty once bestowed on the King Protector of the State each copy of the *Book of Changes*, *Book of Poetry*, *Book of Documents*, *Spring and Autumn Annals*, and *Book of the Rites*. In the first year of the Qingning reign of Emperor Daozong of the Liao Dynasty (1055), the *Commentary on the Five Classics* was officially published. In the tenth year of the Xianyong reign of Emperor Daozong (1074), the *Records of the Grand Historian* and *Book of Han* were promulgated. These books mentioned above were all engraved during the Liao Dynasty, and the boom of the printing industry of the Liao Dynasty had driven the rapid development of its culture. At the same time, the prosperity of the printing industry had taken the social culture of the Liao Dynasty to a new height.

3.3 Printing Industry in the Jin Dynasty

The Jin Dynasty developed its printing industry on the basis of the inheritance from the former Liao Dynasty and areas occupied by the Northern Song Dynasty. Especially after the Jin armies captured Kaifeng, the capital city of the Northern Song Dynasty, they transported all the books from the Imperial College, the Secretariat, the Three Offices, and the Secretariat of the Northern Song Dynasty, as well as the books from the Kaifeng Bookstore, the Imperial College printing editions, and the Honglu Temple sutra editions, to Yanjing and stored them in their Imperial College. The Jin government not only vigorously collected the existing books from the Song Dynasty, but also ordered the purchase and supplementation of the books that were missing from the *Chongwen Catalogue*. Besides, it extensively purchased private collections. If book collectors cherished their own books and were unwilling to sell them, the government also set regulations that the original books could be returned to the owners after borrowing and copying. In this way, the Jin government, on the one hand, collected and purchased books, and on the other hand, continuously translated and printed new books, rapidly increasing its collection of books and enriching the stock of books in society.

In the third year of the Tiande era (1151), the Jin government of the Liao Dynasty expanded and rebuilt the Yanjing City as its middle capital. In the first year of the Zhenyuan reign (1153), the capital was moved to Yanjing City, where the Imperial College was established. In the *History of Jin · Election History*, a list of books supervised by the Jin's Imperial College was provided, which were mostly printed with the Northern Song printing plate. These books include *Book of Changes, Book of Documents, Book of Poetry, Spring and Autumn Annals, Book of the Rites, Rites of the Zhou Dynasty, Analects of Confucius, Mencius, Classic of Filial Piety, Three Kingdoms Annals, History of the Jin Dynasty, History of the Song Dynasty, History of the Qi Dynasty, History of the Liang Dynasty, History of the Chen Dynasty, History of the Northern Zhou Dynasty, History of Sui Dynasty, History of the Tang Dynasty, History of the Five Dynasties*, and so on. These books basically belong to genres of classics, history, philosophy, and others. The Jin's Imperial College not only used the printing plate of its counterpart's version in the Northern Song Dynasty to print books, but also had a small number of books by engraving plate. It is regrettable that none of these engraved copies of books by the Jin's Imperial College have been passed down to this day.

The Jin government also established the Hongwen Academy, specifically responsible for translating and proofreading the Confucian classics. Emperor Shizu of the Jin Dynasty had repeatedly told his courtiers that the translation of the *Five Classics* was to help Jurchen understand the principles of benevolence, righteousness, and morality, in order to consolidate political power and cultivate useful talents to serve the government. Based on the experience of the Liao government, the rulers of Jin advocated the development of education by establishing schools. According to the historical records of the Jin Dynasty, most emperors studied classics and history, paying great attention to improving their cultural literacy and governance ability. Emperor Xizong of the Jin Dynasty once lamented that he had read very little, "When I was young, I idled away without any ambition to work hard. As time passed, I deeply regretted it." He realized that "although Confucius had no political power, his teachings were worthwhile to follow, which made him admired by all generations." Therefore, he personally worshiped the Confucian Temple and studied books day and night, such as *Book of Documents*, *Analects of Confucius*, and *History of the Five Dynasties*.

The Jin Palace Library was in charge of the preservation of classics. In addition to the Imperial College and the Hongwen Academy, the Bureau of Literary Creation, the Bureau of Calligraphy and Painting, and the Bureau of Astronomy also printed books. The Jin government had both a Bureau of Astronomy and an institute that complied calendars. At the beginning of the Jin Dynasty, the lack of calendars prevented Jurchen from knowing about their birth years. "Only when they see the grass gets green again do they know the fact that one year has passed." In the fifth year of the Tianhui era (1127), Yang Ji, an official in charge of the Bureau of Astronomy, created the "Daming Calendar," which was officially promulgated in the fifteenth year of the Tianhui era (1137). This marked a major progress in the development of the Jurchen society. The Jin Dynasty's "Daming Calendar" shared the same name as the Southern Dynasty's "Daming Calendar" created by Zu Chongzhi, but had different contents. Emperor Shizong of the Jin Dynasty ordered Zhao Zhiwei, an officer dealing with astronomical affairs, to revise the "Daming Calendar," which was continuously printed since the twentieth year of the Dading era (1180). The revised one was used until the early years of Mongolia.

Taoism was prevalent in the Jin Dynasty, so the engraving and printing of the Taoist scriptures were also very active then. Certainly, the development of Taoism benefited from the support of the rulers. Shizong of the Jin Dynasty, once invested in the printing of the Taoist scriptures, issued an edict in the 20th year of the Dading era (1180) to transfer the scripture edition of the *Taoist Canon* from Kaifeng Prefecture in Nanjing to the Shifang Da Tianchang Temple (today's Baiyun Temple) in the middle capital. The Taoist priests there, such as Sun Mingdao, Zhao Daozhen, and others, organized the repair and engraving of the *Taoist Canon* transported from Kaifeng Prefecture. After two years of efforts, a total of 1,074 volumes of the *Taoist Canon* were completed, and 21,800 engraved plates of the *Taoist Canon, Wanshou Edition,* were supplemented. In total, there were 602 volumes and 6,455 scrolls acquired, given the name *Taoist Canon, Jin Dynasty Edition* (hereinafter referred to as the *Jin-Edition Canon*).

THE STORY BEHIND CULTURAL RELICS
The legend of the *Jin-Edition Canon*

Jin-Edition Canon, also known as *Jurchen Jin-Edition Canon,* is one of the four treasures owned by the National Library of China. It was engraved based on the *Kaibao-Edition Tripitaka* of the Northern Song Dynasty. The existing copies of the *Kaibao-Edition Tripitaka* are extremely rare. In July 2018, at the Spring Auction of the Xiling Seal Engravers Society, only two remaining pages of the *Kaibao-Edition Tripitaka* were sold for a high price of 2.4 million yuan (excluding commission). Taking nearly 30 years, the block printing of the *Jin-Edition Canon* was completed in the 13th year of the Dading reign of the Jin Dynasty (1173). It consists of a total of 168,113 pieces of scriptures, a total of 6,980 volumes. It is scroll-bound, with simple cores made of thin wooden sticks.

There are two touching stories about the *Jin-Edition Canon.*

Story 1: In the Jin Dynasty, Cui Fazhen, the daughter of Cui Jin, was born in Zhangzi County in Luzhou (now part of Shanxi Province) and was devoted to Buddhism from a young age. At the age of 13, she vowed to engrave and print Buddhist scriptures, begging for alms with her broken arms. Many male and female believers were moved by her sincere asceticism, so they made generous donations. Not only did the wealthy donate, but even the poor also did their bit. Some donated donkeys, some donated cloth, some donated pear trees, some donated engraved scripture plates, and some donated carving knives. Names of the donors were all engraved on the back of many scrolls of the *Jin-*

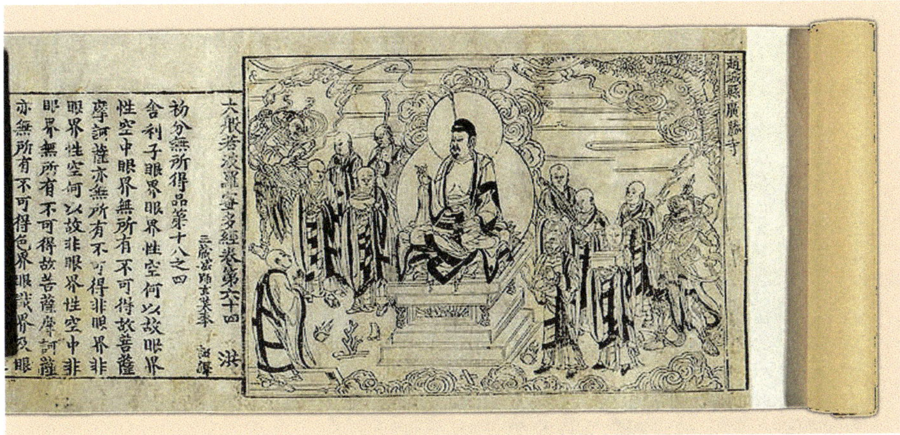

The picture in the front of the *Jin-Edition Canon*, with the inscription of Guangsheng Temple, Zhaocheng County

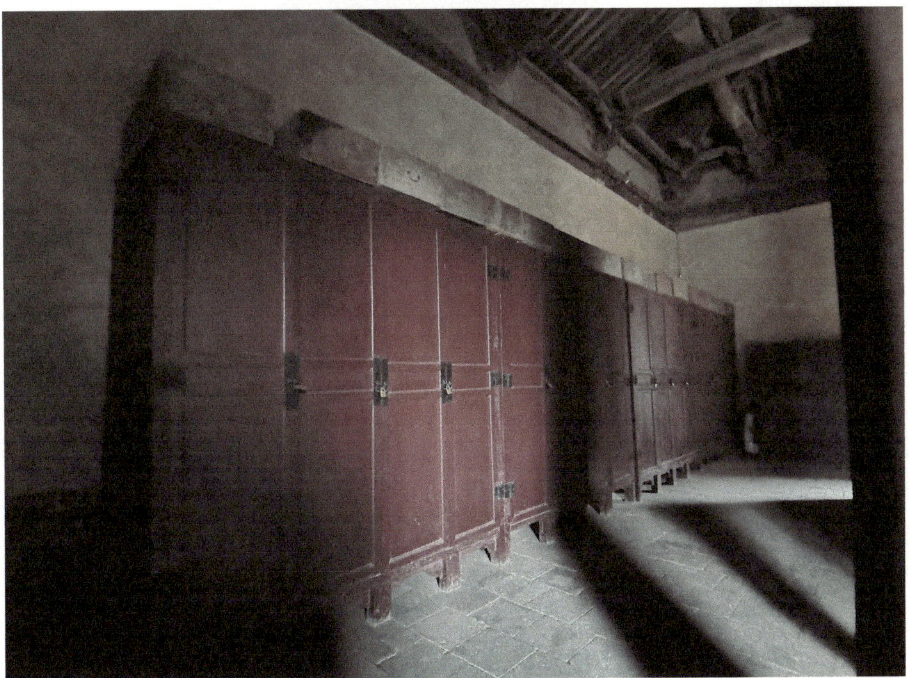

The red scripture cabinet in the Mituo Hall of the Guangsheng Temple, which houses the only copy extant of the *Zhaocheng Jin-Edition Canon*

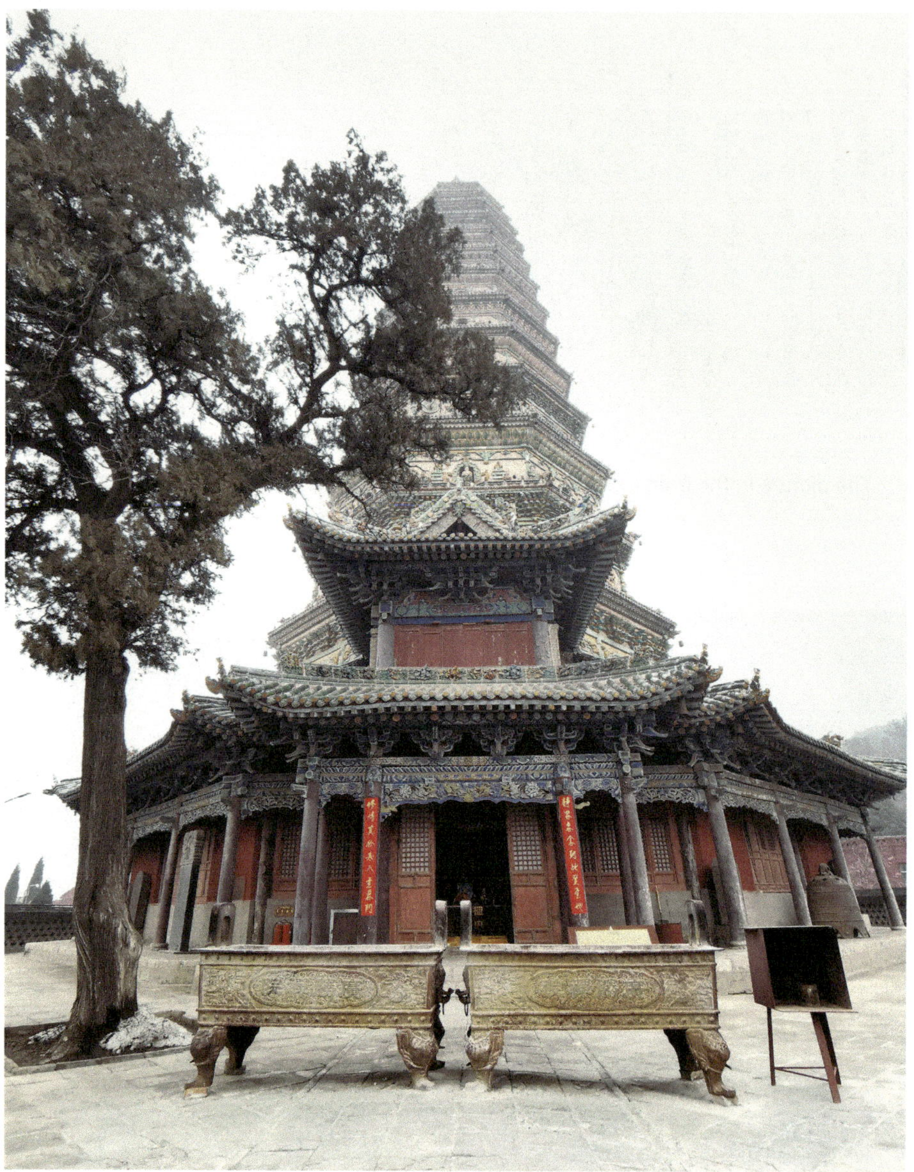

The Feihong Pagoda in the Guangsheng Temple

Edition Canon. From this, it can be seen that the donors were mostly believers from the southern part of present-day Shanxi Province, along with areas as far north as Taiyuan and as far west as Pucheng (now part of Shaanxi Province). In the 18th year of Dading of the Jin Dynasty (1178), Cui Fazhen presented a printed copy of *Tripitaka* to the imperial court and received great attention from Wanyan Yong, Emperor Shizong of the Jin Dynasty. At that time, the top ten monks in the middle capital held flagrant flowers to welcome the scriptures at the Dasheng'an Temple. A shrine was built for Cui Fazhen, who was granted a purple robe and conferred the title of Great Master of Hongjiao (spreading the teachings). Rewards were also given to 72 individuals who contributed to the engraving and printing of the scriptures, including Yang Huiwen. In the 21st year of the Dading reign (1181), Cui Fazhen transported all the scripture engraving plates to Yanjing City (now Beijing), storing them in the Dahaotian Temple of Yanjing. A scripture printing workshop was then established and began to print the works largely.

Story 2: There is a famous historical site named Guangsheng Temple in Hongdong County, Linfen City, Shanxi Province. It is an ancient temple originally named Julushe Temple, built in the first year of the reign of Emperor Huan of the Eastern Han Dynasty (AD 147). In the fourth year of the Dali era of the Tang Dynasty (AD 769), Guo Ziyi, the Prince of Fenyang, petitioned the imperial court to renovate and expand the temple. It was thus renamed Guangsheng Temple, meaning "vaster than the Heaven, famous beyond its time." In the 1930s, a collection of scriptures was discovered in 12 scripture cabinets in the Amitabha Hall of the Guangsheng Temple. After extensive research and verification, it was determined that these scriptures were engraved during the Jin Dynasty. As the Guangsheng Temple was located in Zhaocheng County then, the scriptures were named *Zhaocheng Jin-Edition Canon*. In February 1938, the Japanese invasion army occupied Zhaocheng County, whose nearest stronghold was only one kilometer away from the Guangsheng Temple. To prevent the Japanese from looting, Master Li Kong of the Guangsheng Temple hid the *Jin-Edition Canon* in the Feihong Pagoda in the temple. In April 1942, the Japanese government dispatched the "Eastern Cultural Survey Group" to Zhaocheng, threatening to visit the Feihong Pagoda on May 2. To ensure the safety of the *Jin-Edition Canon*, Master Li Kong immediately sought help from the Eighth Route Army. With the cooperation of the Eighth Route Army, the county's guerillas, and the monks, the *Jin-Edition Canon* was urgently transported out on the night of April 27. During the subsequent "mopping up" operations in May, comrades from the local committee fought against the Japanese enemies in rugged mountains with scriptures carried on their backs. Due to frequent battles and inconvenient moves, they hid these scriptures in caves and abandoned coal mines with assigned people guarding them for fear of losing. In 1949, the *Jin-Edition Canon* was transported to Beiping (now

Beijing) and handed over to the Beiping Library (now the National Library of China) for collection.

Jin-Edition Canon was the first large-scale ancient book restoration project funded by the Chinese government after the establishment of the People's Republic of China. On April 30, 1949, when over 4,300 volumes in 9 large packages of the *Jin-Edition Canon* arrived in Beiping, people were saddened to find that due to poor preservation over the years, most of the scriptures were damp, rotten, broken, and stuck together, with about five or six out of ten unable to open. The government specially invited four experienced bookbinding masters to assist in the restoration, which cost nearly 17 years and was finally completed in 1965. The original *Jin-Edition Canon* consisted of 6,980 volumes with over 60 million characters, but today, there are only over 4,000 volumes left. It is the only one of its kind in the world, and it is considered a rare treasure.

3.4 Printing Industry in the Xixia Dynasty

In 1038, the Khitan noble Li Yuanhao declared himself emperor and established a state named Daxia, also known as the Tangut Empire, referred to as Xixia by the Song Dynasty. At the beginning of the state's establishment, Li Yuanhao "intended to create characters at his own will, so he ordered his subordinate Yeli Renrong to take charge of it, with twelve volumes of books finished," which were immediately promoted nationwide for his people to record events as reference. The creation and spread of the Xixia characters laid the foundation for the rise of the Xixia printing industry. Before and after the establishment of the Xixia state, *Tripitaka* and other scriptures and wooden slips had been purchased from the Northern Song Dynasty six times, including books and calligraphy printed by the Song Imperial College. The Xixia government also set up departments for engraving and paper craftwork, which specialized in engraving and printing books. The earliest extant Xixia printed work is the dedication text of the Chinese Buddhist scripture *The Great Perfection of Wisdom Sutra*, engraved in 1073.

In 1908–1909, Russian archaeologist Pyotr Kozlov (1863–1935), commissioned by the Russian Geographical Society, conducted excavations twice in the Xixia ancient city named Blackwater City, located in the Ejina Banner, Alxa League, Inner Mongolia. They obtained about 24,000 volumes of documents from a tomb tower in the northwest corner of the city. Kozlov transported these documents, along with the ones he obtained in the city and other cultural relics, back to Russia with the help of 40 camels. The artifacts are now stored in the Winter Palace Museum in Saint

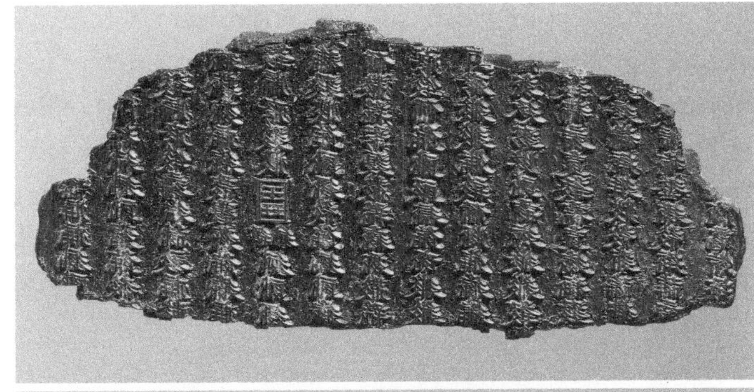

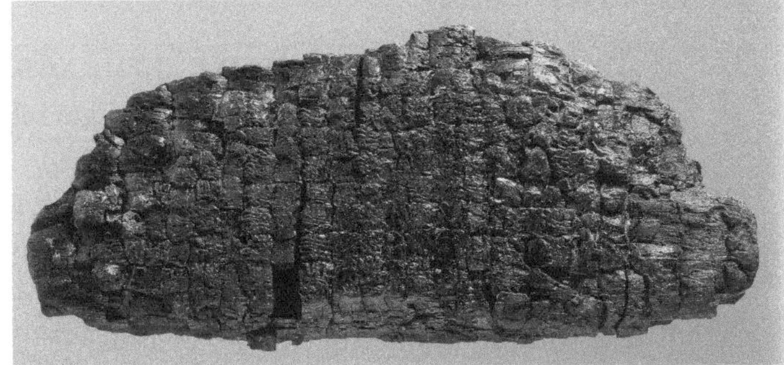

Xixia wooden engraved printing blocks unearthed from the Hongfo Pagoda

Petersburg (a palace within the Hermitage Museum), with the documents kept in the Institute of Oriental Studies of the Russian Academy of Sciences. Sorted out by several generations of Russian scholars over half a century, 8,090 registered Xixia documents were realized, with nearly 3,000 of them having been identified. Among them, there are about "60 secular works and about 370 Buddhist scriptures," which include 22 Xixia woodblock prints and engraved prints from the Song, Jin, and Yuan dynasties. In addition, there are six Xixia engraved stone blocks. These unprecedented and extremely rich cultural relics have opened a new era for Xixia studies, providing abundant materials for the research of Xixia printing.

In July 1990, a shocking discovery was made in the Hongfo Pagoda of the Xixia Dynasty in Helan County, Ningxia. Over 2,000 fragments of Xixia woodblock printing plates were unearthed, some of which had only half one character remaining, all charred through carbonization. There are single-sided plates, but most of them are double-sided. The plates are divided into three categories in terms of the size of characters: only seven large-sized plates, with the largest one measuring 13 centimeters in height, 23.5 centimeters in width, and 2.2 centimeters in thickness; most numerous medium-sized plates, accounting for over 50%, with the two largest medium-sized plates both in sutra-style binding, one fragment measuring 10 centimeters in height,

38.5 centimeters in width, and 1.2 centimeters in thickness, and the other fragment measuring 11 centimeters in height, 23.7 centimeters in width, with 14 lines and a maximum of 12 characters per line; the small-sized plates accounting for over 40%, with a thickness of 1.5 centimeters, mostly double-sided, and severely damaged. These precious fragments of woodblock plates are invaluable materials for studying the printing of the Xixia Dynasty and the medieval. The discovery also indicates that the Hongfo Pagoda Temple was once a place for engraving and printing in the Xixia Dynasty.

THE STORY BEHIND CULTURAL RELICS

***The Timely Pearl*, the earliest Chinese-Tangut bilingual dictionary**

There has always been a melancholy story circulating in the northwest region. Blackwater City was once a key city in the Xixia Dynasty, with its last general known as the Black General. He was mighty and invincible, but in a battle for dominance with the Han people in the Central Plains, he suffered a setback and had to retreat to the isolated city. The Central Plains armies besieged the city for a long time but couldn't conquer it. They noticed that the Ejina River flowed through the city, so they blocked the upstream with sandbags, cutting off the water supply to the city. After the water source dried up, the defenders dug wells inside the city, but even at the deepest point, they couldn't find a single drop of water. Under this circumstance, the Black General was forced to go all out in battle. Before the battle, he ordered more than 80 carts of white gold and other treasures to be dumped into the well and personally killed his wife and children to prevent them from falling into the hands of the enemies. He then led his troops into the battle, but ultimately succumbed to the overwhelming enemy forces and died. After the Central Plains armies captured the Blackwater City, they searched everywhere for treasures but found nothing.

In the early 20th century, Russian archaeologist Pyotr Kozlov (1863–1935) was attracted by the legend of the Black General's treasure. Before Kozlov, Russian traveler Grigory Potanin (1835–1920), geologist Vladimir Obruchev (1863–1956), and others had tried to search for the Blackwater City, but had no way to locate the site. It wasn't until 1908 that Kozlov and his expedition team were finally able to glimpse the true face of the Blackwater with the aid of some technologies. From April 1 to 13, 1908, Kozlov and his expedition team excavated various sites, including the government institutions, the residential houses, the temples, and the pagodas in Blackwater City. In a pagoda in the southwest of the city, they unearthed three Xixia documents and 30 Tangut brochures, Buddhist sculptures, Thangkas, coins, metal bowls, women's ornaments, daily utensils, articles for Buddhist ceremonies, as well as fragments of Persian scripts, Islamic scriptures, and Tangut manuscripts, and so on. These discoveries were fully packed with ten large boxes. Afterward, Kozlov returned to Blackwater City for "inspection" two times, taking away rich cultural relics. Kozlov excavated over 8,000 varieties of Tangut publications and hand-written copies from the Blackwater City, as well as a large number of books and scriptures in Chinese, Tibetan, Uighur, Mongolian, Persian, and so on. This is another disaster that Chinese literature has suffered since the Dunhuang Cataclysm.

Although a "Xixia Library" was unearthed in Blackwater City, literature research was impossible to carry out since Tangut was already a "dead language" that no one could read. In the first half of the 20th century, scholars from China and Russia were overjoyed by the discovery of an inconspicuous booklet among the treasures stolen by Kozlov in the Blackwater City. The booklet turned out to be *The Timely Pearl: A 12th Century Tangut-Chinese Glossary*, written in the 21st year of the Qianyou reign of the Xixia Dynasty (1190). It is a dictionary compiled by Gule Maocai of the Dangxiang people that combines the sounds and meanings of both Tangut and Chinese, equivalent to a dictionary of corresponding sounds in both Tangut and Chinese, commonly used for communication between the Xixia and the Chinese people at that time. Shi Jinbo, a member of the academic department of the Chinese Academy of Social Sciences, pointed out that the commonly used words in *The Timely Pearl: A 12th Century Tangut-Chinese Glossary* are divided into three parts: heaven, earth, and human, each of which is divided into three sections, namely one, two, and three. Each word has four explanations: Tangut, corresponding Chinese character, Chinese phonetic transcription of Tangut, and Tangut phonetic transcription of Chinese. It was a reference book for both the Xixia and the Han people to learn each other's language at that time.

The editor of the book clarifies this purpose in its preface: "If one does not learn Chinese, how can one socialize with them? If one cannot speak Chinese, how can one be respected by the Han people? Wise Chinese people are not respected by the Xixia people, and vice versa, which is due to the language

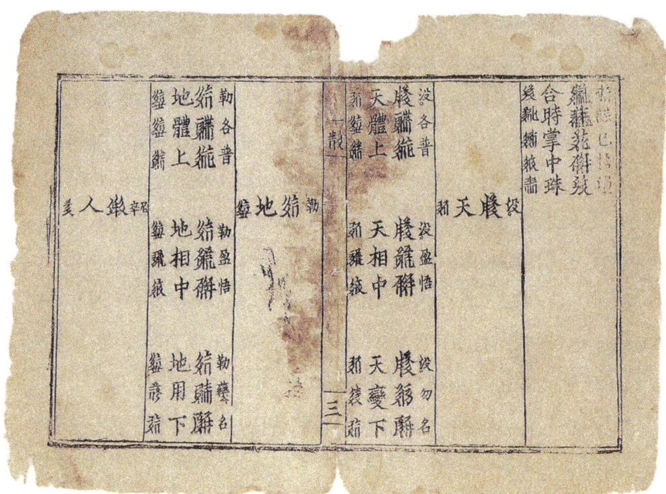

The Timely Pearl: A 12th Century Tangut-Chinese Glossary, currently housed in the Institute of Oriental Studies of the Russian Academy of Sciences

barrier between them." The four explanations of each word in the book are listed in order, with the middle two being the Tangut character and Chinese translation, the right side the phonetic transcription of Tangut noted with Chinese characters, and the left side the Chinese phonetic transcription noted with Tangut. The discovery of this precious literature is just like finding a key to open the door of Xixia studies. From then on, Tangut's secret was disclosed, and new disciplines studying Xixia literature and history emerged, gradually unveiling the mystery of the Xixia State.

This earliest Tangut-Chinese bilingual dictionary is not kept in its homeland—China, but in a foreign land, which is regrettable. In 1989, during the archaeological excavation of Cave B184 in the northern area of the Mogao Grottoes, a highly rare fragment of *The Timely Pearl: A 12th Century Tangut-Chinese Glossary* was unearthed, which is currently the only relatively complete surviving page of the book in China. Although it is only a fragment, it is extremely precious as it is the only copy extant in China.

4. Printing in the Yuan Dynasty

The establishment of the Yuan Dynasty united China as a whole, driving the further development of the printing industry. The main printing bases in the north were in Pingyang (now Linfen City, Shanxi Province) and Dadu (now Beijing), while in the south, Hangzhou and Jianyang (now Jianyang District, Nanping City, Fujian

Province) remained as the centers. There were also many printing workshops in Jiangsu, Jiangxi, Hubei, and Hunan provinces. Due to the country's unity, printing techniques began to spread to remote areas, represented by a certain scale of printing industries that had also developed in places like Tibet and Xinjiang today.

During the Yuan Dynasty, major headway was made in printing techniques, particularly in the following aspects. Firstly, in terms of bookbinding, in addition to butterfly-like binding, the back binding method emerged. The binding process involved folding the pages with the printed text facing outwards, and the binding adhesive was applied on the blank space on the left or right side of the folded pages. After arranging printed pages in order, the folded edges were aligned, with cotton paper twisted and inserted into the binding holes to secure the book as a whole. Then, the book was trimmed, and finally, a paste was applied to the book spine, completing the process of attaching the book cover. The back binding method not only overcame the inconvenience of reading with the butterfly-like binding, but also retained the advantage of the butterfly-like binding's adhesive spine. Additionally, the use of twisted cotton paper for binding increased the durability of the book. Therefore, this binding method became the most popular one during the Yuan Dynasty. Secondly, although editions printed in two colors originated from the Song Dynasty, there were only written records without physical evidence. The earliest known example of this kind is the *Annotated Diamond Sutra* printed in cinnabar and black ink by the Zifu Temple on Zhongxing Road (now in Jingzhou District, Jingzhou City, Hubei Province) in the first year of the Zhizheng era of the Yuan Dynasty (1341). Thirdly, books with illustrated covers also appeared during this period.

In the Yuan Dynasty, books were printed by such governmental institutions as the Xingwen Bureau, the Guangcheng Bureau, the Imperial College, and the Imperial Hospital. The books compiled by the government, such as *History of the Song Dynasty*, *History of the Jin Dynasty*, and *Essential Practice to Farming and Silkworm Rearing*, were all engraved in the areas of Zhejiang. Local governments also printed some books.

Schools also actively printed books during the Yuan Dynasty, with the West Lake Academy the most famous. Besides keeping the engraved plates of the Imperial College of the Southern Song Dynasty, the West Lake Academy also collected generous engraved plates, and printed a great number of books. The most notable block-printed edition by the West Lake Academy was the *Comprehensive Textual Research of Historical Documents*, compiled by Ma Duanlin, a historian at that time. This book featured beautiful lettering, clear and pleasing style, and elaborate engraving and printing, a truly representative of the Yuan Dynasty's block-printed edition. Another feature of school printing was the combination of several schools to print most books through teamwork. In this way, the whole book could be printed in a relatively short time. For example, during the Dade era, the *Seventeen History Records* were engraved by the joint efforts of the nine Confucian institutes in Jiangdong, so it only took over two years to complete this huge project.

THE STORY BEHIND CULTURAL RELICS
The "alchemy that could turn paper into gold" in Marco Polo's writings

In the 1270s, a young Western man followed his father across the oceans to China. In this mysterious country, he had traveled everywhere for 17 years, becoming the first Westerner in the Middle Ages to open his eyes to see the East. He was just Marco Polo, the son of a merchant in Venice, Italy.

The diverse Eastern civilization captivated Marco Polo, leaving him enthralled. He documented his legendary experiences in China in the book *The Travels of Marco Polo*. He witnessed the unimaginable use of paper money, which was printed on paper and had little intrinsic value but could be exchanged for all goods in the market. In Khanbaliq, also known as Dayidu (Beijing) of the Yuan Dynasty, he visited the Bureau of the Mint and experienced the process of producing paper money. Marco Polo saw that the paper money made from tree bark circulated nationwide, which could serve as military pay, just like gold and silver. "Paper money is made of tree barks of mulberry whose leaves are eaten by silkworms to spin silk. Mulberry trees are quite common to see here." In this connection, he regarded the paper money made in Dadu as a kind of "alchemy that could turn paper into gold."

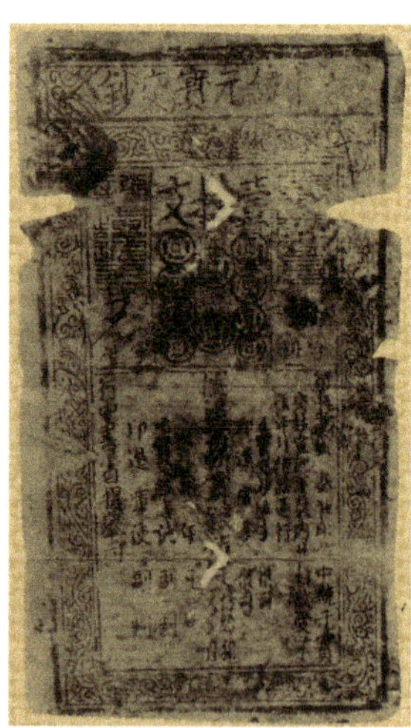

"Zhongtong Yuanbao Banknote" in the Yuan Dynasty

In fact, as early as the Song Dynasty, due to the need to develop the commodity economy and the rapid advancement of papermaking and printing techniques, as well as the severe shortage of raw materials for minting coins and the inconvenience of carrying heavy metal currency, paper money, known as "jiaozi," emerged. The Yuan Dynasty was the period when paper currency was most prevalent in China. In 1260, Emperor Kublai

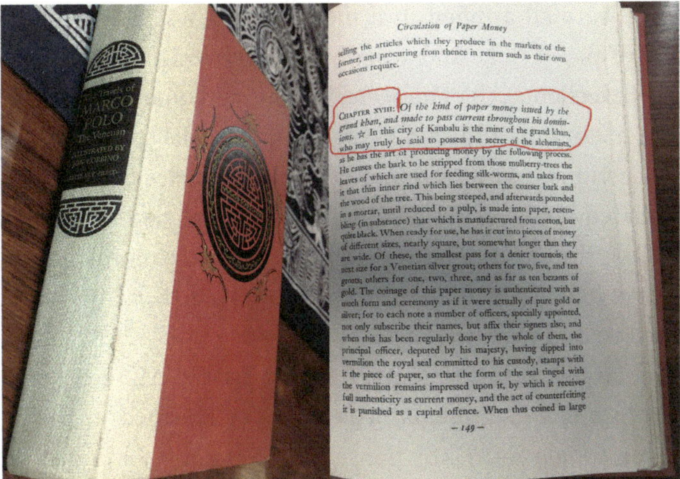

Circulation of Paper Money

selling the articles which they produce in the markets of the former, and procuring from thence in return such as their own occasions require.

CHAPTER XVIII: *Of the kind of paper money issued by the grand khan, and made to pass current throughout his dominions.* ☆ In this city of Kanbalu is the mint of the grand khan, who may truly be said to possess the secret of the alchemists, as he has the art of producing money by the following process. He causes the bark to be stripped from those mulberry-trees the leaves of which are used for feeding silk-worms, and takes from it that thin inner rind which lies between the coarser bark and the wood of the tree. This being steeped, and afterwards pounded in a mortar, until reduced to a pulp, is made into paper, resembling (in substance) that which is manufactured from cotton, but quite black. When ready for use, he has it cut into pieces of money of different sizes, nearly square, but somewhat longer than they are wide. Of these, the smallest pass for a denier tournois; the next size for a Venetian silver groat; others for two, five, and ten groats; others for one, two, three, and as far as ten bezants of gold. The coinage of this paper money is authenticated with as much form and ceremony as if it were actually of pure gold or silver; for to each note a number of officers, specially appointed, not only subscribe their names, but affix their signets also; and when this has been regularly done by the whole of them, the principal officer, deputed by his majesty, having dipped into vermilion the royal seal committed to his custody, stamps with it the piece of paper, so that the form of the seal tinged with the vermilion remains impressed upon it, by which it receives full authenticity as current money, and the act of counterfeiting it is punished as a capital offence. When thus coined in large

— 149 —

The Travels of Marco Polo, published in New York in 1948, in which "the alchemy that could turn paper into gold" was described.

Khan of the Yuan Dynasty, in order to achieve unified management, issued an official version of paper currency called "Zhongtong Yuanbao Banknote." To avert inflation and currency devaluation, the government then strictly controlled the total amount of paper money issued and commodity prices, with the department of Jiaochao Tiju established at all levels to manage currency issues. Zhongtong Yuanbao Banknote issued in the Yuan Dynasty not only circulated domestically, but also found usage in many Southeast Asian regions, with countries like India and Japan even imitating its style.

This seemingly insignificant piece of paper turning into gold-like magic shocked the West. In the third volume of his book, *Jami' al-Tawarikh*, published in 1310, Persian historian Rashid al-Din recorded the history of Persia, imitating China's printing and issuing of paper money in 1294. The Iranian banknotes then even had the Chinese character "钞" (banknote) printed on them. Subsequently, as the printing technique gradually spread to the West, it became a catalyst for motivating the European Renaissance. In 1660, Sweden issued the first paper currency in Europe.

5. Printing in the Ming Dynasty

During the Ming Dynasty, the handicraft industry and commodity economy flourished, marking the heyday of woodblock printing in China, which enjoyed the following main features. (1) The techniques of woodblock printing, wood movable type printing, metal movable type printing, integrated metal plate printing, and multicolor printing were all applied in a more refined way during the Ming Dynasty. (2) The quality of paper, ink, and woodblock engraving techniques reached unprecedented levels of excellence. (3) The scale, variety, and quantity of printing reached the highest level in history. In addition to traditional books such as classics, history, philosophy, and collections, a large number of local chronicles, scientific and technological books, skill-related books, popular literature, enlightenment literature, dramas, and novels were also printed. (4) The Song typeface became more mature and widely applied as a dedicated font for printing. (5) The innovative technique of woodblock overprint was introduced and widely adopted.

The largest printing factory set up by the Ming government was the Imperial Directorate of Ceremonials, which was established in the 19th year of the reign of Emperor Yongle (1421). By the reign of Emperor Jiajing, more than 1,000 craftsmen were engaged in engraving, printing, binding, ink making, and pen making in the factory, where many government publications were printed. The Imperial Celestial Supervisor also set up a printing workshop, which was mainly responsible for printing the samples of the annual calendar. Besides, the Imperial College was one of the main printing institutes in charge of the government.

The printing of books in the mansions of regional princes was a unique phenomenon in the Ming Dynasty. Due to their lack of actual duties and relatively abundant funds, they were engaged in writing and printing books in droves. According to incomplete statistics, over 500 different kinds of books were printed by the regional princes. Some of these books, such as chess-playing books, music books, and tea books, filled the gaps in the variety of books available. The printing of local chronicles just originated in the Song Dynasty, which had become a popular practice in the Ming Dynasty. Almost every region, state, and county then printed their own local chronicles. The publication of these books has left behind a large number of valuable historical records.

At the end of the Ming Dynasty, artists such as Wu Faxiang and Hu Zhengyan, together with the craftsmen from the Hui School, pioneered a technique dedicated to reproducing colored images, known as "woodblock overprint (dou ding)." This technique involves delineating and engraving in separate colors, then printing different colors layer by layer to produce colorful images that are quite similar to the original artwork. The reason why the technique is called "dou ban" lies in the fact that the plates with different colors for printing resemble "dou ding," also known as "ding dou," an ancient way of setting dishes in ancient China. In *The Food Classics* of the Tang Dynasty, people creatively stacked colorful small cakes in a box to form such shapes as peach, peach leaves, monkeys, and rocks as gifts for birthday celebrations.

Han Yu, a poet in the Tang Dynasty, wrote a poem titled *Joy about Hou Xi's Arrival, Presented to Zhang Ji and Zhang Che*: "Ask my wife to prepare cutlery and food, and 'ding dou,' fish, and vegetables are sufficient." Wu Faxiang of the Ming Dynasty used the woodblock overprint technique to print *Collection of Letter Paper Samples by Luoxuan*, while Hu Zhengyan used the same method to print *Shizhuzhai Studio's Painting Manual* and later *Shizhuzhai Studio's Stationery Manual*. In printing the *Shizhuzhai Studio's Stationery Manual*, Hu Zhengyan also introduced the Gong Hua technique, a colorless relief printing technique. The woodblock overprint technique later became known as woodblock watercolor printing during the mid-Qing Dynasty.

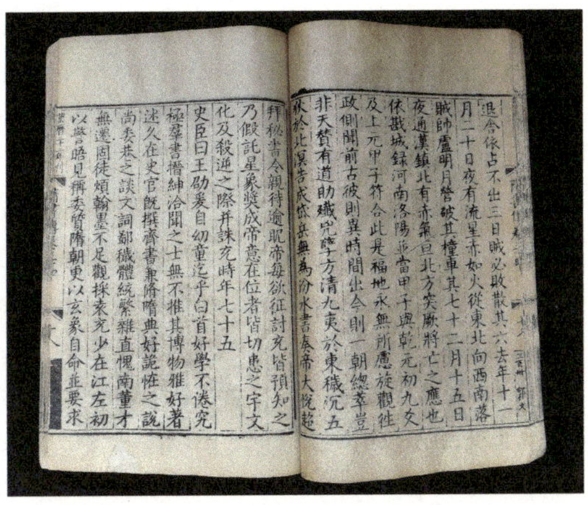

History of Sui Dynasty, printed by the Nanjing Imperial College in the 22nd year of the Wanli reign of the Ming Dynasty (1594)

THE STORY BEHIND CULTURAL RELICS

***Compendium of Materia Medica*, documentary heritage of the Memory of the World Register**

In the autumn of the 8th year of the reign of Wanli (1580), a long-traveling ship docked in the moat of Taicang Prefecture (now Taicang City, Jiangsu Province). An elderly man with a slim figure and white beard disembarked. He was Li Shizhen in his sixties, a native of Qi Prefecture (now Qichun County, Hubei Province). His coming to Taicang was to ask the literary leader Wang Shizhen to write him a preface.

Li Shizhen spent 27 years writing the monumental pharmacological work *Compendium of Materia Medica*, which has 52 volumes. He brought the manuscript to the publishing center in Nanjing, hoping to find a publisher to print it. However, since the voluminous book was costly to publish, and Li Shizhen had no reputation at the time, the publishers were concerned that the book would not sell well. Thus, no one was willing to print it. Li Shizhen thought that if he could invite Wang Shizhen to write a preface to introduce the book, the publishers would have confidence in publishing it. Wang Shizhen was known for his ability to write eloquently and effortlessly. However, being a serious man himself, he wanted to read Li Shizhen's manuscript before writing the preface, and it took him ten years to finally start writing the preface for the *Compendium of Materia Medica.*

In January of the 18th year in the era of Wanli (1590), Li Shizhen once again came to Taicang at the age of 73. Having read the manuscript carefully, Wang Shizhen let him stay at his home for a few days. Wang Shizhen wrote a passionate preface for the *Compendium of Materia Medica* on the Lantern Festival during Li's stay. Although it was only over 500 words, the preface was filled with deep emotions, singing high praise for the pharmacopoeia, providing detailed introductions, and describing Li Shizhen himself. In the preface, Wang Shizhen first depicted the image of Li Shizhen, then introduced the illnesses in Li's childhood and the purpose of compiling the book in his adulthood, as well as the hardships of revising the work three times in 30 years. The phrase "like entering the Palace of King Dragon, where all treasures are displayed" gave Li's work particularly high praise. This phrase, derived from the Buddhist scripture *Avatamsaka Sutra*, tells the story of the Bodhisattva Nagarjuna, who saw *Avatamsaka Sutra* in the Palace of King Dragon and brought it to the human world, benefiting humanity. Wang Shizhen used this allusion to compare the *Compendium of Materia Medica* to a pharmacy treasure that brings great benefits to humanity.

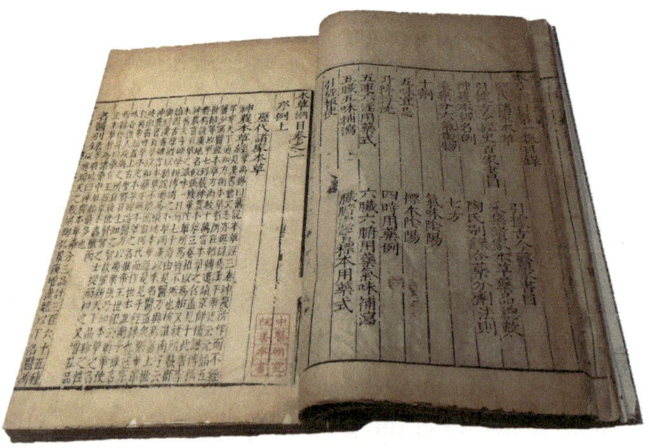

The Jinling edition of *Compendium of Materia Medica*, engraved by Hu Chenglong in the 21st year of the reign of Wanli of the Ming Dynasty (1593), housed in the Institute of Traditional Chinese Medicine, included in the UNESCO Memory of the World Register in 2011

Thanks to the preface by Wang Shizhen, Hu Chenglong, a book publisher in Nanjing, agreed to print the *Compendium of Materia Medica.* Six years later, in the 24th year of the reign of Wanli (1596), the book was finally printed and published in Nanjing. By this time, however, Wang Shizhen had been dead at home in Taicang in the winter of the 18th year of Wanli (1590). And in 1593, the third year since the beginning of the engraving of *Compendium of Materia Medica,* Li Shizhen also died of illness. Although Wang Shizhen and Li Shizhen had not seen the publication of the book at all, this scientific masterpiece eventually became an epoch-making milestone in the history of science in China and even in the world. Darwin, a British biologist, praised the book as "the encyclopedia of ancient China." From the 18th century to the 20th century, *Compendium of Materia Medica* was translated or abridged into more than 20 languages, including English, French, German, Russian, and Korean, and reprinted more than 100 times. It has been widely circulated in the world and become the research object of scholars in many Western fields.

Since 1997, the Memory of the World Project launched by UNESCO has established the Memory of the World Register, which is appraised and selected every two years. From May 23 to 26, 2011, at the UNESCO conference held in Manchester, England, *Huangdi Neijing* and *Compendium of Materia Medica* were successfully selected for the Memory of the World Register after being recommended by experts. *Huangdi Neijing* listed this time is just the earliest block printed version by Hu's Gulin Shutang, which is the most complete in the existing editions.

6. Printing in the Qing Dynasty

The Qing Dynasty witnessed the last glorious period of woodblock printing. Firstly, the scale of woodblock printing continued to expand. A printing and publishing network was gradually formed, covering both the central government and local areas, as well as workshops and private households. The variety and quantity of printed books far exceeded any previous era. Secondly, there was a scaled development of the printing industry and improvement in printing techniques. Various printing techniques invented and developed in ancient China were used during the Qing Dynasty, with some of the techniques further refined. In particular, movable type printing not only had a much larger scale of use at that time than any other era, but

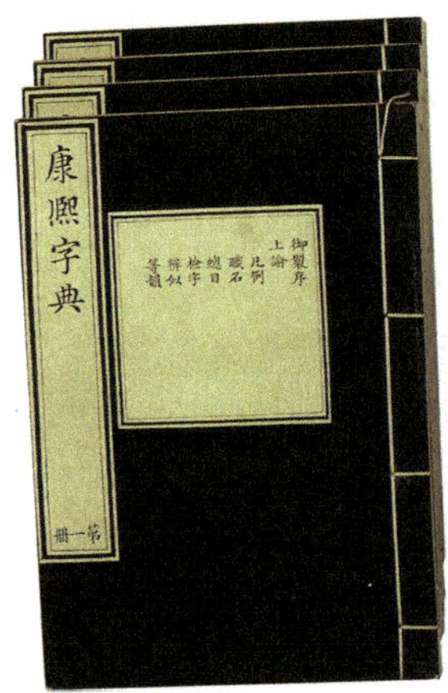

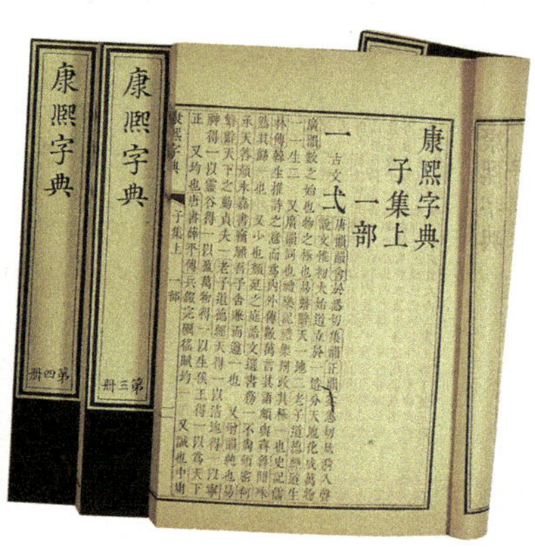

Kangxi Dictionary, the edition printed by imperial decree in the Qing Dynasty

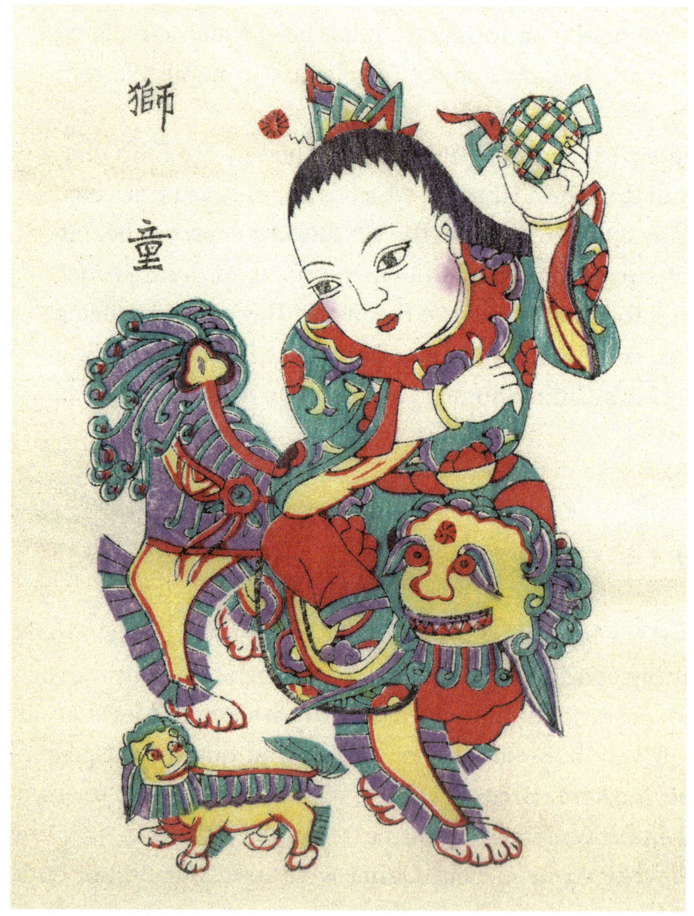

The New Year painting *Lion Boy Entering the Door* from Weixian County, Shandong (now Weifang, Shandong Province)

also achieved high levels of proficiency in wood, copper, and clay types. Woodblock color printing became more popular with more exquisite quality. The printing of New Year pictures had also developed into a large-scale industry. Printing institutes spread across the country, bringing printed products into thousands of households and reaching the highest popularity in history. Therefore, in terms of the application of traditional printing techniques, the Qing Dynasty became the last glorious period of woodblock printing.

During the reign of Emperor Shunzhi in the Qing Dynasty, the main printing technique used was woodblock printing, which had been inherited from the Ming Dynasty. In the 43rd year of the reign of Emperor Kangxi (1704), the Hall of Martial Valor began to proofread and print *Peiwen Yunfu*, which came to be a regular institution of the Inner Palatines to proofread and print books ever since. This hall also became the imperial publishing institution of the Qing emperors. Books printed by the Hall of Martial Valor, known as the "edition of classics printed by imperial decree," were the most influential official editions during the Qing Dynasty. However, after the reign of Emperor Jiaqing, printing activities in the Hall of Martial Valor gradually declined. In the 27th year of the reign of Emperor Guangxu (1901), books stored in the hall were burned into ashes in two separate fires.

During the Qing Dynasty, the printing units of local government and institutions were called "Shu Ju" (book bureau). The earliest known printing institution was the Yangzhou Poetry Bureau, established by Cao Yin, the Lianghuai Salt Supervisor during the reign of Emperor Kangxi. One famous book this bureau printed was the *Complete Collection of Tang Poetry*. In the reign of Emperor Yongzheng, provincial administrations also established printing institutions one after another.

The printing of New Year paintings achieved the most prominent development in the Qing's folk printing industry. The woodblock overprint technique, which emerged during the Ming Dynasty, was widely used in the mass production of New Year printings during the Qing Dynasty. Due to the widespread popularity of New Year printings among households, the printing industry experienced significant growth with larger sales. The most famous centers for printing New Year paintings included Yangliuqing in Tianjin, Yangjiabu in Weifang, and Taohuawu in Suzhou. There were also some workshops in places like Zhuxianzhen in Henan, Fengxiang in Shaanxi, Mianzhu in Sichuan, Linfen in Shanxi, and Foshan in Guangdong. New Year paintings often depicted folk stories, door gods, kitchen gods, court ladies, and auspicious symbols of abundance and prosperity. It was not until the mid-20th century, with the rise of modern printing technology, that the traditional handcrafted woodblock New Year paintings gradually gave way to mechanized printing methods.

THE STORY BEHIND CULTURAL RELICS
Rongbaozhai Studio and wood engraving water printing

Rongbaozhai Studio in Beijing has a history dating back over 300 years, starting from the establishment of South Songzhuzhai Studio Paper Shop in 1672. In 1894, the Songzhuzhai Studio was renamed Rongbaozhai Studio, and in 1896, the institution of "Tietaozuo" was established, laying the foundation for the later development of woodblock watercolor printing. In 1933, Lu Xun and Zheng Zhenduo collected the *Collection of Letter Paper in Beiping* and entrusted Rongbaozhai Studio to publish it. The following year, they also entrusted Rongbaozhai Studio to reprint the Ming Dynasty's *Shizhuzhai Studio's Stationery Manual.* The two books saved the endangered woodblock overprint technique to some extent. In 1945, Rongbaozhai Studio successfully printed Zhang Daqian's *Dunhuang Donors,* beginning the technique innovation based on the inheritance of ancient traditions. Over the next half-century, Rongbaozhai Studio developed traditional woodblock printing to a new stage, condensing this technique into an easily understandable term, "woodblock watercolor printing." "Watercolor printing" refers to water printing, as opposed to ink printing. By 1954, Rongbaozhai Studio's wood-

The process for creating the woodblock watercolor printing *Picture of Goldfish* at Rongbaozhai Studio

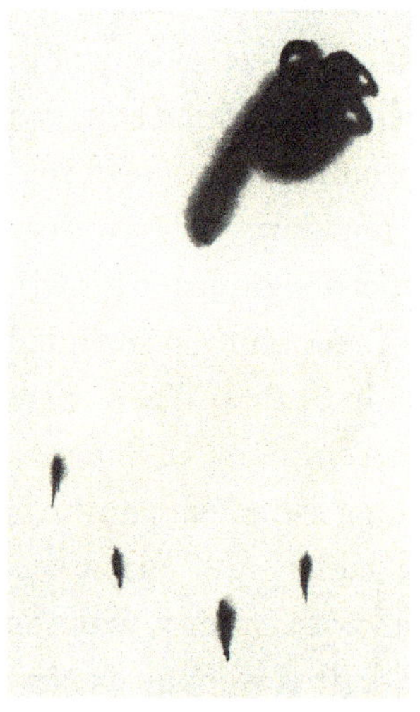

Step 1

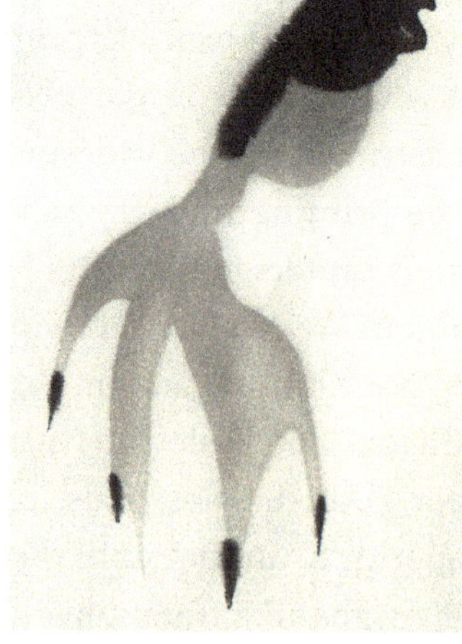

Step 2

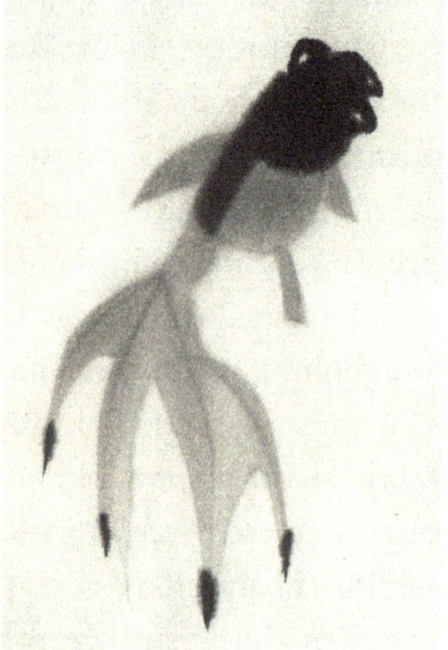

Step 3

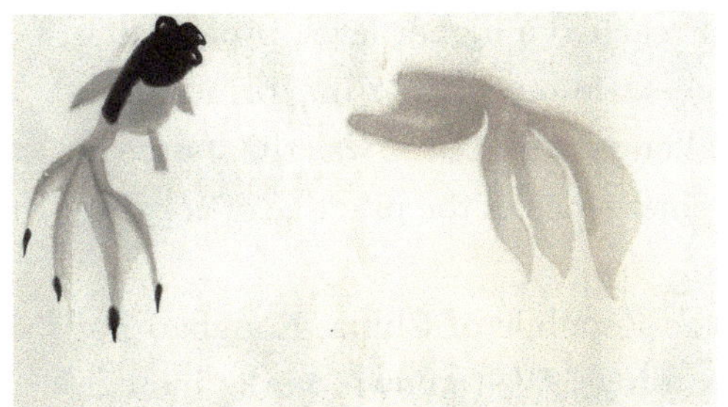

Step 4

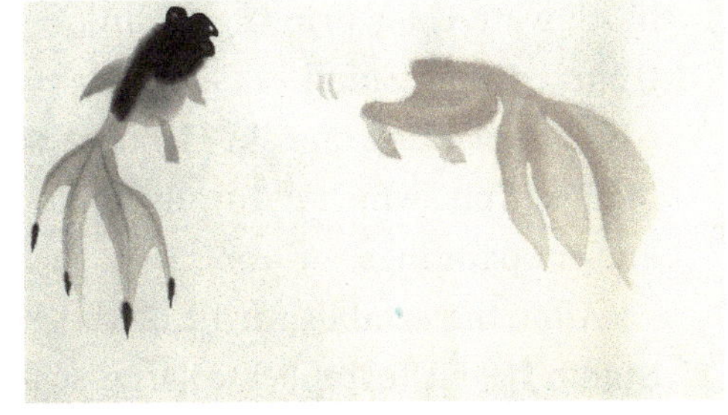

Step 5

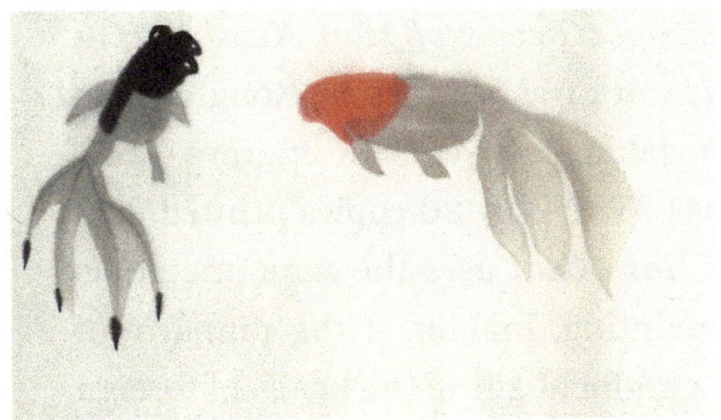

Step 6

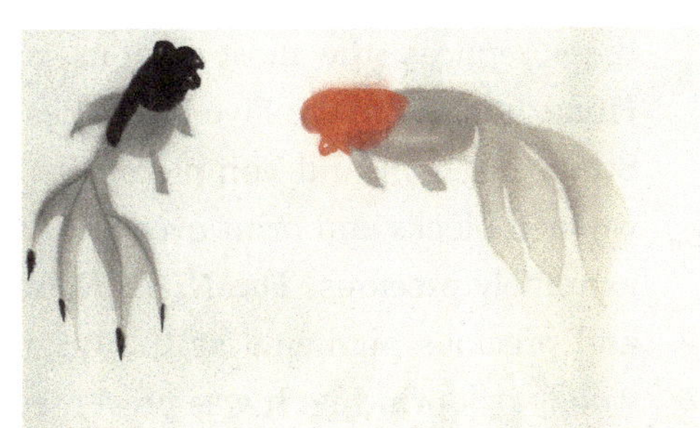

Step 7

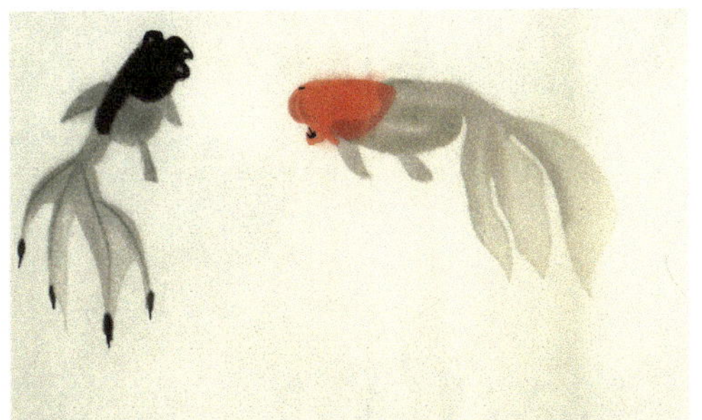

Step 8

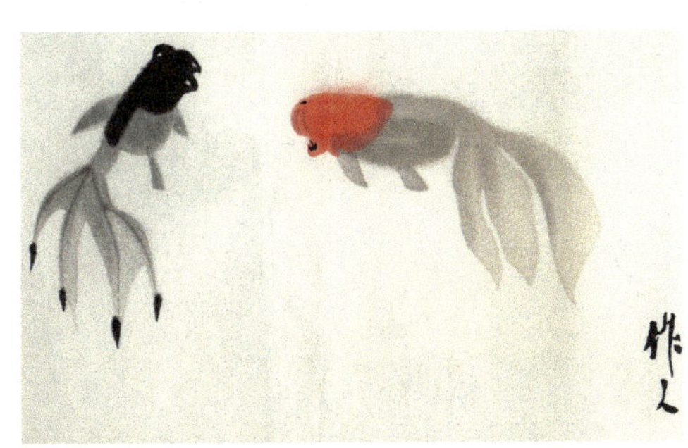

Step 9

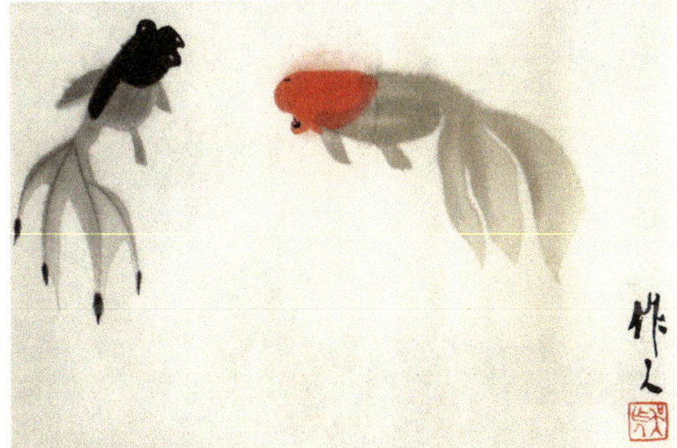

Step 10

block watercolor printing technique had reached a higher level, progressing from printing small-scale works to large-scale ones and from printing on paper to printing on silk. The biggest challenge at that time was the source of manuscripts, which naturally led to the emergence of the practice of copying ancient paintings.

After the establishment of the People's Republic of China, Rongbaozhai Studio began to replicate large-scale paintings. Well-known works include *Picture of Running Horse Painting*, *Picture of Maidens Wearing Flowers*, *Picture of Dancing and Singing*, and *Hundred Flowers in Full Bloom*. Among these replicas, the most famous is the *Night Revels of Han Xizai* by Gu Hongzhong from the Five Dynasties. This work was planned by Rongbaozhai Studio in 1959 and completed in 1979, taking 20 years to engrave 1,667 wooden blocks and print over 6,000 times. With only 30 copies printed, it is extremely precious. The *Night Revels of Han Xizai* uses the same materials and precious pigments as the original painting, making it the pinnacle of woodblock printing. It was presented as a national gift to the heads of foreign countries. Therefore, woodblock watercolor printing has a reputation of being "on par with genuine works" in the cultural and museum field.

CHAPTER III

The Invention and Development of Movable Type Printing

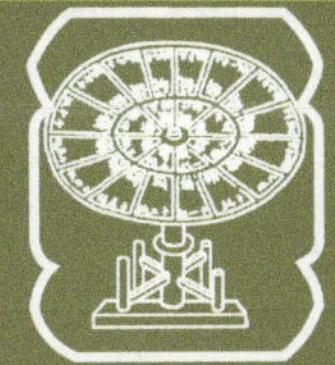

The invention of movable type printing is the second milestone in ancient Chinese printing history, coming after woodblock printing. Movable type printing involves engraving individual character blocks (movable type) made of materials such as wood, metal, or clay, which are then arranged and assembled into a printing plate. Ink is applied to the plate, and the characters are pressed onto the paper. In his *Dream Pool Essays*, Shen Kuo (1031–1095) not only recorded that Bi Sheng (972–1051), a commoner, invented movable type printing during the Qingli era of the Northern Song Dynasty (1041–1048) but also provided a detailed description of the technique. Over the following 900 years, various materials, such as wood, tin, copper, and lead, were used to create movable types for printing.

According to archaeological findings, there had been physical evidence of movable type dating back to the 13th–14th centuries along the Silk Road, including the paper products printed with the wooden movable type in Khwarazmian script and the clay and wooden movable type in Xixia script. In 1987, a Xixia Buddhist scripture titled *Vimalakirti Nirdesa Sutra* was discovered at the Haimudong Temple site in Gansu Province, which has been verified to be a movable type print in the 12th–13th

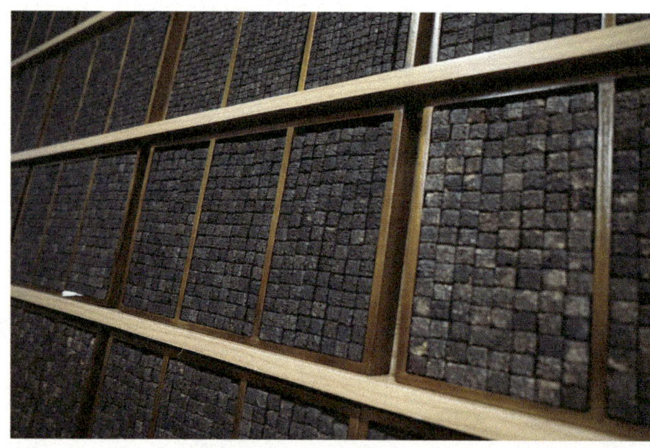

Wooden movable type in Jianyang, Fujian, during the late Qing Dynasty and early Republic of China

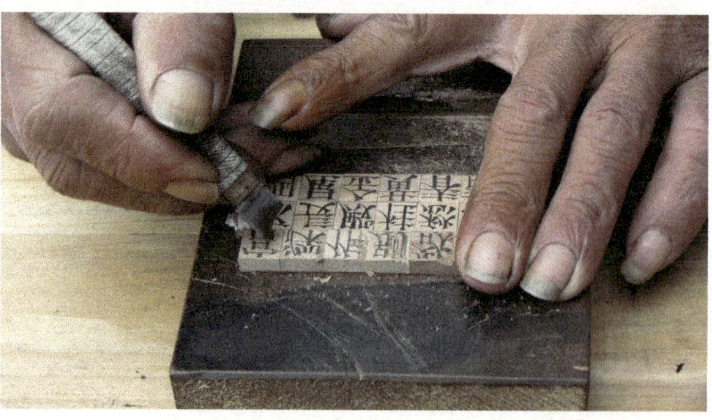

The movable woodblock engraving technique in Dongyuan Village along the Feiyun River, Rui'an

centuries, possibly made with clay movable type. In 1991, at the Fangta Pagoda in Baisigou, Helan County, Ningxia, nine volumes of *Auspicious Tantra of All-Reaching Union,* Buddhist scripture written in Xixia characters, were found, which are also printed with wooden movable type in the 12th–13th centuries. These two examples of movable type printing hold significant importance in the development of ancient Chinese printing history.

Both literature and physical evidence have proven that movable type printing has been continuously applied and innovated in China since the 11th century. After Bi Sheng, the development of movable type printing spanned the Song, Yuan, Ming, and Qing dynasties, continuing to spread eastward and westward and playing a significant role in the inheritance and dissemination of Chinese civilization as well as the progress of human civilization.

1. Bi Sheng and Clay Movable Type

During the Qianli period of the Northern Song Dynasty, the commoner Bi Sheng invented time-saving, material-efficient, convenient, and quick movable type printing, which opened a new era in the history of printing.

Shen Kuo, a politician and scientist of the Northern Song Dynasty, came from Qiantang (now Hangzhou, Zhejiang Province). He recorded the details of Bi Sheng's invention of movable type printing in his work *Dream Pool Essays*. In Volume 18, it is recorded:

> In the middle period of the reign of Emperor Qingli, there was a commoner named Bi Sheng who invented movable type. His method involved engraving characters with clay as thin as the edge of a coin, with each character serving as a separate stamp, which is made firm by heating. First, prepare an iron plate and coat it with a mixture of resin, wax, and paper ash. An iron frame is placed on the iron plate to print, and the stamps are densely arranged on the frame to form a complete plate. The plate is then heated until the mixture melts, and a flat board is pressed onto its surface, resulting in evenly printed characters. If only a few books are to be printed, this method is not particularly convenient. However, it is extremely efficient if hundreds or thousands of books are to be printed. Two iron plates are usually prepared, one for printing and the other for arranging the stamps. As soon as one plate is finished, the second plate has already been prepared and used interchangeably, allowing for rapid

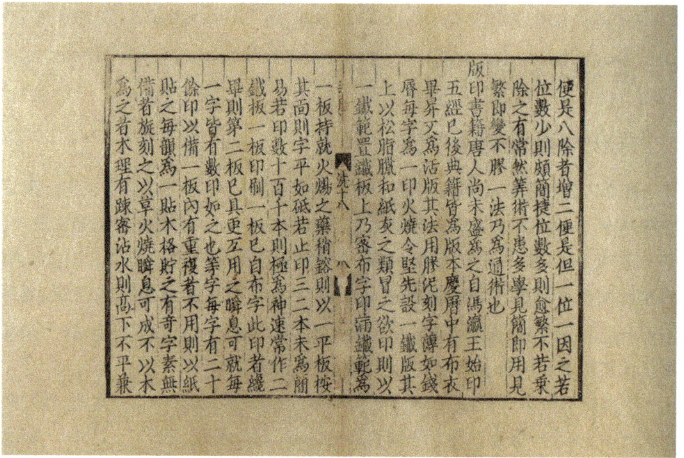

便昇八除者增二便是但一位一因之若
位數少則頗簡捷位數多則愈繁不若乘
除之有常然筭術不患多學見簡即用見
繁即變不膠一法乃爲通術也
版印書籍唐人尚未盛爲之自馮瀛王始印
五經已後典籍皆爲版本慶曆中有布衣
畢昇又爲活版其法用膠泥刻字薄如錢
脣每字爲一印火燒令堅先設一鐵版其
上以松脂臘和紙灰之類冒之欲印則以
一鐵範置鐵板上乃密布字印滿鐵範爲
一板持就火煬之藥稍鎔則以一平板按
其面則字平如砥若止印三二本未爲簡
易若印數十百千本則極爲神速常作二
鐵板一板印刷一板已自布字此印者纔
畢則第二板已具更互用之瞬息可就每
一字皆有數印如之也等字每字有二十
餘印以備一板內有重複者不用則以紙
貼之每韻爲一貼木格貯之有奇字素無
備者旋刻之以草火燒瞬息可成不以木
爲之者木理有疏密沾水則高下不平兼

Records of movable type in the block-printed version of *Dream Pool Essays* of the Yuan Dynasty

printing. Each character has multiple stamps, with more than twenty stamps for characters like "之" and "也," to account for the repetition of characters on the plate. When not in use, the stamps are covered with paper, with each rhyme having its own paper cover, stored in wooden compartments. If there are unusual characters that are not readily available, they can be quickly engraved and made by burning. Instead of using wood, which has uneven grain and becomes uneven and sticky to other ingredients when wet, it is better to use fired clay. After use, the stamps will fall off when brushed with the hand without any residue. After Bi Sheng's death, my cousins and nephews acquired his type, which is still kept as a treasure.

According to Shen Kuo's records, it can be proven that in the 11th century, movable type printing had already developed a complete process:

(1) Character engraving: Engrave characters with clay. Each character is a separate type, which is hardened by firing, actually ceramic-made movable type.
(2) Setting the frame: Prepare an iron plate and place an iron frame on top of it. Inside the frame, a mixture of rosin, wax, and paper ash is spread.
(3) Typesetting: Arrange the types closely on the plate, filling the iron frame.
(4) Setting the types: Heat the iron plate with fire to soften the mixture, then use a flat board to press the type surface, ensuring a smooth surface and firm typesetting.
(5) Printing: After fixing the type, ink can be applied, and paper can be printed. Usually, two plates are used simultaneously, one being typeset while the other being printed, improving efficiency.

(6) Disassembling the type: After printing, heat the iron plate again to soften the mixture and remove the movable types.
(7) Storing the type: Store the removed movable types in a wooden type case for future use.

In the poem *Jiejiao Yaozai Xiangzhi Er* (*Making Friends by Heart*) by Deng Su, a patriotic poet of the Song Dynasty, it is written, "My wrists are exhausted to copy books where are still in short supply, if only I have two Bi Sheng's printing iron plates." This means that his friend's poetry was so popular that people were eagerly copying it, almost dislocating their wrists, but demands still outstripped supply. It would have been much better if they had two Bi Sheng's two printing iron plates.

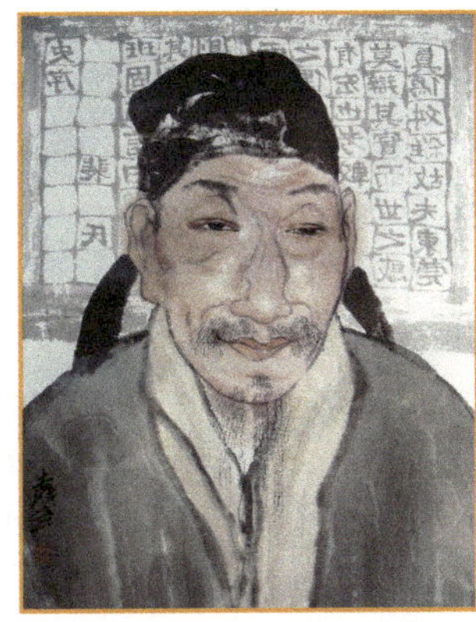

The portrait of Bi Sheng, painted by Yuan Wu

In 1193, Zhou Bida, a resident of Jiangxi in the Southern Song Dynasty, wrote in a letter to his friend, "Recently, I have been adopting Shen Cunzhong's method, using clay and copper plates to reproduce prints. Today, I have completed the printing of twenty-eight events of *Miscellaneous Records of Yutang*." Here, "Shen Cunzhong's method" refers to Bi Sheng's movable type printing technique recorded by Shen Kuo (courtesy name Cunzhong).

The invention of movable type printing has had revolutionary significance in the history of printing, promoting printing from engraved block type to movable type. The movable type printing technique developed by Bi Sheng was already quite mature. The subsequent emergence of the wooden type, tin type, copper type, lead type, etc., only involved changes in the material used to make the movable type without any substantial change in the printing principle.

2. *Wang Zhen and Wood Movable Type*

After Bi Sheng, another significant figure making great contributions to the development of movable type printing should be Wang Zhen of the Yuan Dynasty (1271–1368). Wang Zhen had craftsmen engraved over 30,000 wooden movable type characters, using them to print the *Jingde County Annals* in the second year of the Dade era (1298). Within less than a month, a hundred copies were completed, which was highly efficient. For the technique of movable type printing, Chinese character typesetting has always been a difficult technical challenge. With a large number of Chinese characters, it was always difficult to arrange, disassemble, and store the types. Wang Zhen creatively addressed the problem by inventing the wooden type rhyme wheel, where wooden movable type characters were arranged by rhyme and modeled in two large wooden rotating discs. Typesetters could sit and select characters simply by rotating the wheel to find the needed characters. Wang Zhen documented the techniques of wood movable type printing, character selection, and typesetting in his work "The Craft of Engraving Movable Type to Print," appended to the *Book of Agriculture*. This is the earliest known literature that systematically describes the technique of movable type printing. In 2015, Wang Zhen was inducted into the "Paper Industry International Hall of Fame."

Wooden movable type was widely used in ancient China. Emperor Qianlong of the Qing Dynasty considered the name "wooden movable type" indecent, so he named it "Juzhen." From the 38th year of the Qianlong reign (1773) to the 8th year of the Jiaqing reign (1803), the government produced over 250,000 pieces of jujube wood movable type and printed a total of 138 kinds of books with 2,416 volumes, making it the largest wood movable type printing project in Chinese history. Jin Jian was appointed as Vice President of the Office of *Complete Library in the Four Branches of Literature*, responsible for overseeing printing. Summarizing the technique of this large-scale wood movable type printing project, Jin Jian wrote the *Formulas for Prints with Moveable Types from the Hall of Martial Valor*. The book listed various items such as the production of wooden blocks, engraving characters, type cabinets, groove boards, clamps, top blocks, center blocks, classification plates, template grids, book arrangement, padding boards, proofreading, printing, classification, and daily rotation methods, accompanied by illustrations and brief explanations. This book is considered a milestone in the history of the Chinese movable type printing technique, which has been translated into German, English, Japanese, and other languages to achieve wide circulation.

In contemporary times, the ancient technique of wood movable type printing is still being inherited. Rui'an City in Zhejiang Province is a typical ancient immigrant city. Therefore, the revision of genealogical records is highly valued by every household in Rui'an, which has become the main reason for the continued inheritance of wood movable type printing in the city. The Dongyuan Village in Rui'an has established the Chinese Wood Movable Type Printing Exhibition Hall, with nearly a hundred masters who have mastered this technique. In 2010, "Chinese Wood Movable Type Printing" was inscribed on the Representative List of the Intangible Cultural Heritage of Humanity by UNESCO.

THE STORY BEHIND CULTURAL RELICS
Movable type printing rhyme wheel board invented by Wang Zhen

Wang Zhen, born in Dongping, Shandong Province, was an agricultural scientist and had served as a county official for several terms. He left behind a comprehensive agricultural book titled *Book of Agriculture.* This book also included the methods of engraving, repairing, selecting, arranging, and printing wooden types invented by Wang Zhen.

One of Wang Zhen's contributions to printing technology includes the invention of movable type printing rhyme wheel board, known as "ban yun lun" in Chinese. He used lightweight wood to create a large wheel

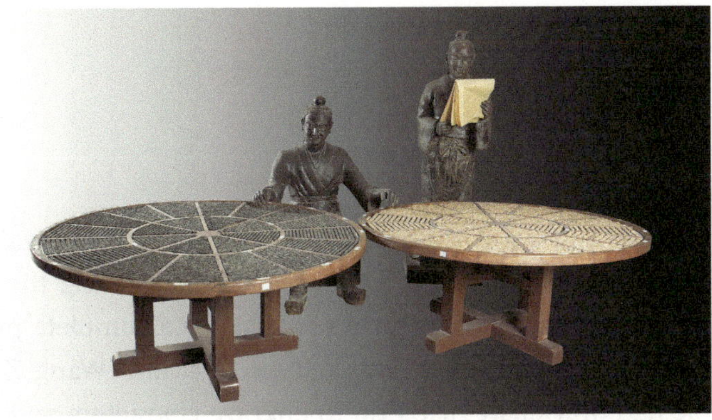

The model of movable type printing rhyme wheel board, invented by Wang Zhen in the Yuan Dynasty

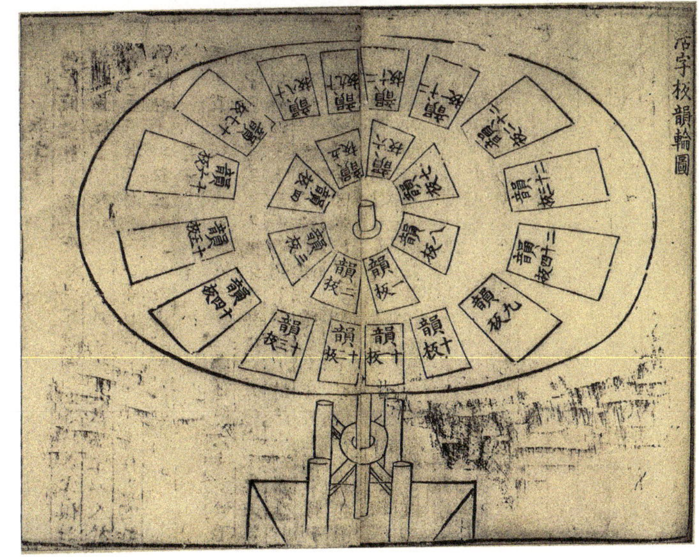

The diagram of the movable type printing rhyme wheel, published in "The Craft of Engraving Movable Type to Print"

with a diameter of about seven feet and a height of three feet. The wheel was mounted on an axle and could freely rotate. Categorized according to the ancient rhyme books, wooden movable type characters were placed in individual compartments within the wheel. Typesetters would sit between the two wheels made by Wang Zhen and rotate the wheels to find the desired characters. Wang Zhen described this method in his book as follows: "One person can sit in the middle, so can rotate to pick characters on both sides. It is difficult for a person to search for characters, but it is easy for characters to come to a person. This method of rotating the wheel allows for effortless sitting and getting a large number of characters. Characters can also be replaced to where they are after using, bringing huge convenience." This innovation not only improved typesetting efficiency but also reduced the physical labor of typesetters.

3. Copper Movable Type

Besides clay and wood, the materials used for making movable types in ancient China included metal, such as tin, copper, and lead. During the Northern Song Dynasty, people already used copper plates to engrave a complete printing plate. In his work "The Craft of Engraving Movable Type to Print," Wang Zhen also mentioned that people had previously "used tin to engrave characters and threaded them with iron bars."

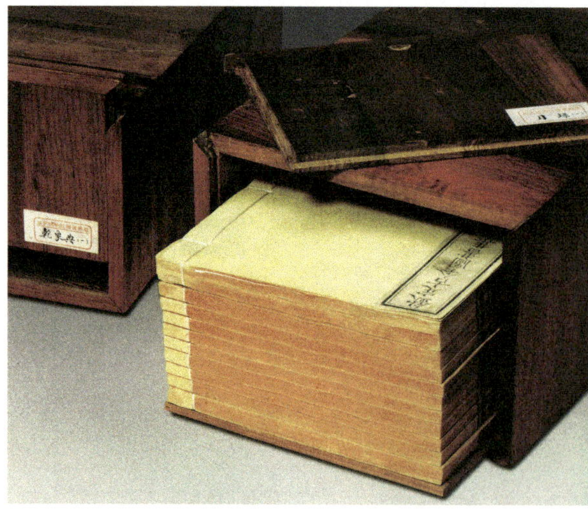

Compendium of Ancient and Modern Books, Copper movable type printing edition of the Qing Dynasty

In the late 15th century, there were many bookstores in Jiangsu that used metal movable type for printing. The most famous ones were the Hua and An families in Wuxi. In the Qing Dynasty, the metal movable type became more widely used. During the reigns of Emperors Kangxi and Yongzheng, the Hall of Martial Valor engraved a big and a small copper movable type, totaling about 250,000 pieces, and used them to print the large-scale series *Compendium of Ancient and Modern Books*. The printing and decoration of this edition were both exquisite. These copper movable types were in the Song typeface, making it the largest-scale copper movable type printing in history. During the reign of Emperor Qianlong, these copper movable types were melted and cast to construct the Trikalea Buddha statues in the Lamasery of Harmony and Peace.

South Korea learned the woodblock printing technique from China at an early stage, the clay movable type printing invented by Bi Sheng during the Northern Song Dynasty, and the following wooden movable type printing. Due to the abundance of copper in South Korea, copper movable type printing had been widely used, making significant contributions in the history of printing and holding an important position.

From the late 19th century to the second half of the 20th century, lead movable type printing became popular in China.

4. Uighur and Xixia Clay Movable Type

In February 1908, French sinologist Paul Pelliot led the French Central Asian Expedition to Dunhuang, where they conducted detailed and comprehensive surveys and investigations of the Mogao Caves. In the accumulated sands of Caves 181–182 in the northern area of the Mogao Caves (now numbered Caves 464–465 by the Dunhuang Research Institute), they discovered numerous documents written in Uighur, Tangut, and Tibetan scripts, as well as 968 pieces of Uighur wooden moveable type. In 1914, Russian explorer Sergei Oldenburg led an expedition to steal 130 pieces of Uighur wooden moveable type from the Mogao Caves. From 1988 to 1995, the Dunhuang Research Institute conducted further excavations and clearances of the caves in the northern area of Dunhuang, uncovering an additional 48 pieces of Uighur wooden moveable type. Together with the six pieces preserved in the Dunhuang Research Institute's warehouse (also unearthed from the northern area), the total number of surviving Uighur wooden moveable types reached 54. As of 2019, the total number of surviving Uighur wooden moveable types was 1,152.

The discovery of the Uighur wooden moveable type in Dunhuang is of great significance in the history of printing in both China and beyond. This indicates that the invention of movable type printing in China spread to the Xixia and Uighur regions soon after its invention. The discovery of Uighur wooden movable type serves as physical evidence for early movable type printing, further confirming the pioneering role of China in movable type printing and expanding the scope of its early use. More importantly, the Uighur wooden movable type contains a large number of movable type units based on the phonetic combination, which embodied the principles of formation used in the Western moveable type of letters. Its creation and use could date back to the 12th and 13th centuries, about 200 years earlier than the metal movable type used by Johannes Gutenberg in Germany. The Uighur people created the movable type that suited the features of their own language and characters,

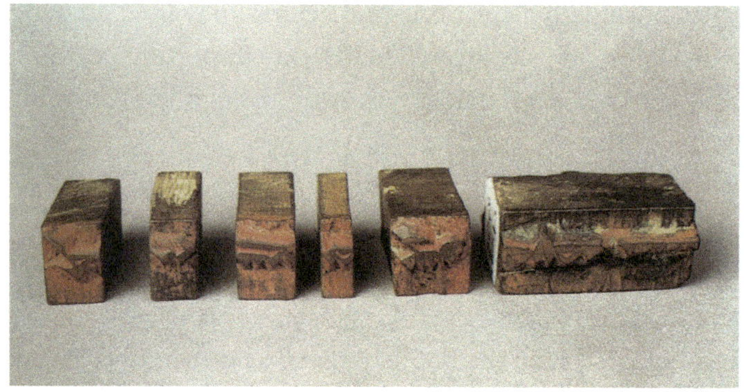

The 13th-century wooden movable type in Uighur (replica), unearthed in the region of Dunhuang

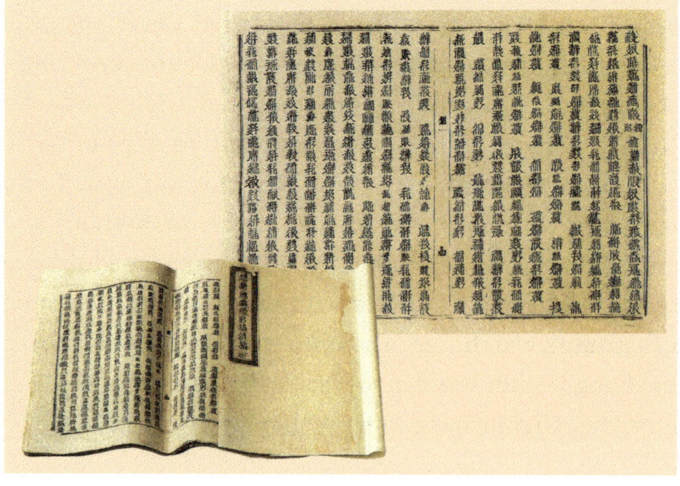

Auspicious Tantra of All-Reaching Union, woodblock-printed edition in the Xixia Dynasty

effectively pioneering alphabetic writing, which was an important innovation in the history of global movable type printing.

Since the 20th century, valuable Xixia printed materials have been discovered in various locations, including the Black City (also known as "the Blackwater City") site in Ejina Banner, Inner Mongolia; the Tiantishan Grottoes in Wuwei, Gansu; the Haimu Cave site; the Mogao Grottoes in Dunhuang; the 108 Pagodas in Qingtongxia, Ningxia; the Hongfo Pagoda in Helan; and the Fangta Temple in Baisigou, Helan. For example, among the stolen documents excavated by Kozlov in the Blackwater City in 1908–1909, which are now housed in the Oriental Studies Institute of the Russian Academy of Sciences, there are several Xixia movable type printing editions, including the *Collected Works of Three Generations Reflecting Each Other*, *Virtues*, and *Collection of the Hundred Dharmas of Mahayana* in Xixia script.

In 1987, the Xixia Buddhist scripture *Vimalakirti Nirdesa Sutra* was discovered in the Haimu Cave of Xinhua Township, Wuwei, Gansu. Scholars unanimously believe it is a clay movable printed edition. In 1991, nine volumes of the Xixia Buddhist scripture *Auspicious Tantra of All-Reaching Union*, consisting of over 240 pages and approximately 100,000 characters, were unearthed in the ruins of the Fangta Temple in Baisigou, Helan County, Ningxia. Scholars believe it is a late-period Xixia woodblock printed edition.

CHAPTER IV

The Invention and Development of Color Printing

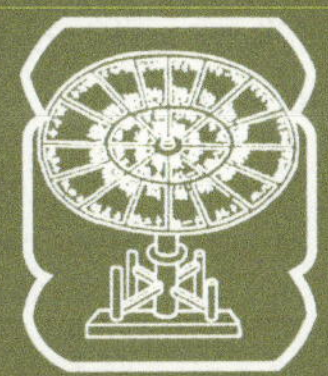

The technique of color printing emerged alongside monochrome printing. In the early stages, color printing involved applying different colors on a single plate to create a multi-colored print. Later, it developed into separate plates for each color, which were then printed layer by layer. The ability to reproduce gradation in color printing began in the late Ming Dynasty. The principle involved engraving separate plates for each color based on the original manuscript, resulting in color prints that closely resembled the original artwork. Color printing techniques are applied not only in book publishing but also in printing artworks and everyday decorative items.

Major Events of Color Printing Technique

Time	Event
Western Han Dynasty (202 BC–AD 8)	The fabric was printed by using block printing and three-color overprinting techniques.
Tang Dynasty (618–907)	Color resist dyeing technique became popular.
Song Dynasty (960–1279)	The printing of banknotes began to adopt two-color and multi-color overprinting techniques.
Song, Liao, Jin, and Xixia dynasties	Some objects with colored paintings were unearthed, such as the *Painting of the Mother of Silkworms*, the *Painting of Dongfang Shuo Stealing Peaches*, the *Painting of Prajvalosnisah Surrounded by Constellations*, and the *Painting of Bhaiṣajyaguru Preaching Buddhism*.
Yuan Dynasty (1271–1368)	Gold printing technology became popular.
The first year of the reign of Emperor Zhizheng in the Yuan Dynasty (1341)	The *Commentary on the Diamond Sutra*, the earliest book printed in black and cinnabar, was excavated at the Zifu Temple on Zhongxing Road.
Ming Dynasty (1368–1644)	Cinnabar or blue-colored printed books gained currency.
During the reigns of Emperor Wanli and Emperor Tianqi of the Ming Dynasty (1573–1627)	The overprinting technique of books was popular.
The sixth year of the reign of Emperor Tianqi in the Ming Dynasty (1626)	*Collection of Letter Paper Samples by Luoxuan*, engraved and printed by Wu Faxiang, was the pioneering work of woodblock watercolor printing.
Qing Dynasty (1644–1911)	There appeared editions printed in four, five, or six colors.
The reign of Emperor Qianlong in the Qing Dynasty (1736–1795)	The Hall of Martial Valor adopted the wood movable double-color printing technique.

From the 18th year of the reign of Emperor Kangxi to the 23rd year of the reign of Emperor Jiaqing in the Qing Dynasty (1679–1818)	*The Mustard Seed Garden Manual of Painting*, the edition printed in multiple colors, became one of the representative works of Chinese woodblock color printing.

1. Fabric Printing Technique

Fabric printing technique generally refers to the technique of printing patterns onto fabrics. Fabrics are the early substrates of printing, while block printing is mainly done on paper. In addition to the substrate, another main difference between fabric printing and engraved block printing is the different application areas. Fabric printing is mostly used for decoration purposes, while engraved block printing is mainly used for cultural dissemination. Early fabric printing techniques included skipping, clamp-resist dyeing, and relief printing.

The exact time when fabric printing was invented cannot be determined, but what we can be sure of is that humans have gone through thousands of years, from hand painting to fabric printing. Ancient fabric printing techniques can be divided into three types: direct printing, discharge dyeing, and resist dyeing. Since printed fabrics are mainly clothing, the application of fabric printing techniques allowed for quick, accurate, and uniform replication of silk patterns.

The earliest fabric printing technique was called clamp-resist dyeing. It involves using two engraved wood blocks, animal skins, or oil paper plates with the same pattern. The fabric to be printed is placed between the two blocks, tightly pressed, and then ink is applied to the engraved areas to print the pattern. The technique is characterized by symmetrical patterns and consistently polished colors on both sides, looking beautiful and natural.

Punched skipping is a technique where holes are punched on hard cardboard to create an image. Its disadvantages include that the pattern lines are not very fine; the patterns can be intermittently printed out. Hollow patterns must also retain several connecting points; otherwise, the pattern will not be complete. After the pattern plate is made, it can be drawn on or directly printed through the holes. Literature and artifacts prove that carved punched skipping had been widely used in China as early as the Spring and Autumn and Warring States periods. This method was the precursor to modern steel plate stencil sheet oil printing and the widely used screen printing.

After the Western Han Dynasty, fabric decoration widely adopted the relief printing technique. In relief printing, instead of hollowing printing plates out, patterns are engraved in relief. During fabric printing, ink or dye is applied to the raised lines on the printing plate and then pressed onto the silk fabric, resulting in patterns appearing on the fabric. This non-hollowed printing plate production technique not only allows for the printing of extremely fine pattern lines, but also enables the production of continuous patterns, avoiding the intermittent patterns between holes that occur in punched skipping and the broken joining points of patterns that occur in hollowed-out printing plates. The relief printing plate is stamped on the fabric like a seal during printing. In order to avoid leaving obvious marks at the joining points, it is best to design the patterns on the plate as continuous patterns in all four directions, so that the patterns on the upper edge of the plate match the lower edge of the neighboring plate above. The patterns on the left edge of the plate match the right edge of the neighboring plate on the left. This design concept is still widely adopted in the textile printing industry worldwide.

Later on, unlike the single block plate with four edges, the printing wooden roller was invented with only two edges, top and bottom, which can be continuously used by rolling left and right. This wooden roller is similar to the printing cylinder in modern printing technology. The length of this roller is designed to be the same width as or slightly smaller than the fabric, thus eliminating the need for joining plates, which greatly increases labor productivity.

Since modern times, there have been several major archaeological discoveries related to ancient printed fabrics. Here are some examples.

1.1 Changsha Mawangdui Western Han Fabric Printed Gauze

In 1972, the excavation of the Western Han Dynasty tomb in Mawangdui, located by the Liuyang River in the eastern suburb of Changsha City, caused a sensation. The female corpse unearthed from Tomb 1 of the Han Dynasty has a history of over 2,100 years, but has a complete body shape with a supple and moist body. Some joints can move, and the soft tissues still have elasticity, like fresh corpses. She is not only different from a mummy, but also from a tanned cadaver with adipocere and peat. She is a special type of corpse, a miracle in anti-corrosion studies, shocking the world and attracting many scholars and tourists for sightseeing.

More than 3,000 precious cultural relics have been unearthed from the three Han tombs in Mawangdui, with the vast majority well preserved. Among them, more than 500 pieces of various lacquerware are exquisitely crafted, with gorgeous patterns, shining as new. What is particularly precious is the large number of silk fabrics of a wide variety from Tomb 1, including spun silk, damask on tabby, leno, gauze, and brocade, all well preserved. There is a plain silk garment as light as smoke and as thin as cicada wings. With a length of 128 centimeters, the garment has long sleeves and weighs only 49 grams, which indicates its extraordinary weaving skills.

The various silk fabrics and clothing unearthed from the Han tombs in Mawangdui are of early age, large in quantity, diverse in variety, and well-preserved, greatly enriching the historical materials of ancient Chinese textile technology. Most of the fabrics unearthed from the boxes beside Tomb 1 were placed in several bamboo boxes. In addition to 15 relatively intact single and double-layered padded robes, skirts, socks, gloves, sachets, handkerchiefs, and cloth wrappers, there were also 46 rolls of single-sided silk, yarn, brocade, gauze, satin, and embroidered items, all neatly rolled with reed stems as the backbone, symbolizing bolts of silks. Most of the silk fabrics and clothing unearthed from Tomb 3 had already been damaged, with similar varieties to those in Tomb 1 but with more diverse patterns in the brocade. The most reflective of the development of textile technology during the Han Dynasty was the plain gauze and warp-faced compound tabby with piles. The light plain gauze robe, weighing less than 50 grams, was a symbol of the development level of spinning and weaving technology at that time. The warp-faced compound tabby with piles used as clothing trim has a three-dimensional effect in its patterns, requiring the complex jacquard mechanism of a double warp axis loom for weaving. Its discovery proves that pile fabrics were originally invented and created by China, refuting the previous belief that they only appeared after the Tang Dynasty or were introduced from foreign countries.

The several printed fabrics unearthed from Tomb 1 of the Han Dynasty in Mawangdui are the earliest physical specimens in the world related to pattern printing technology. These printed fabrics are divided into two types.

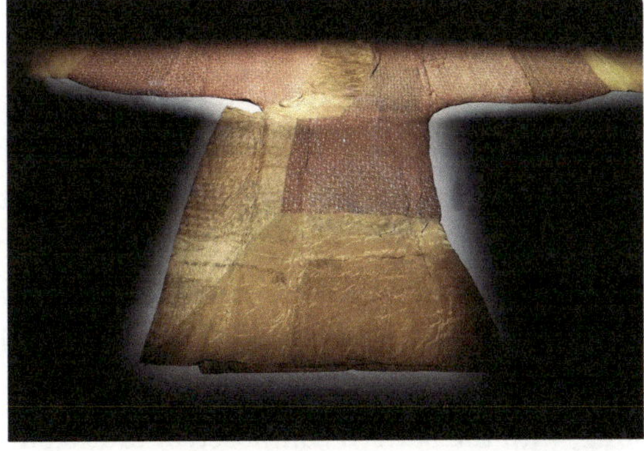

Printed and painted yellow floss silk padded gauze robe, with a length of 132 centimeters and sleeve length of 228 centimeters, unearthed from Tomb 1 of the Han Dynasty in Mawangdui, currently housed in the Hunan Provincial Museum

The first type is printed and painted floss silk padded gauze, which is the earliest discovered silk fabric in the world that combines fabric printing and color painting. It was processed by printing and dyeing on a lightweight plain weave

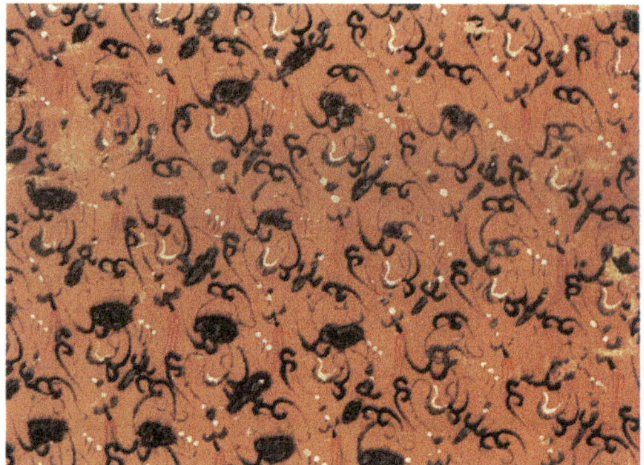

Printed and painted floss silk padded gauze of the Western Han Dynasty, unearthed at Mawangdui

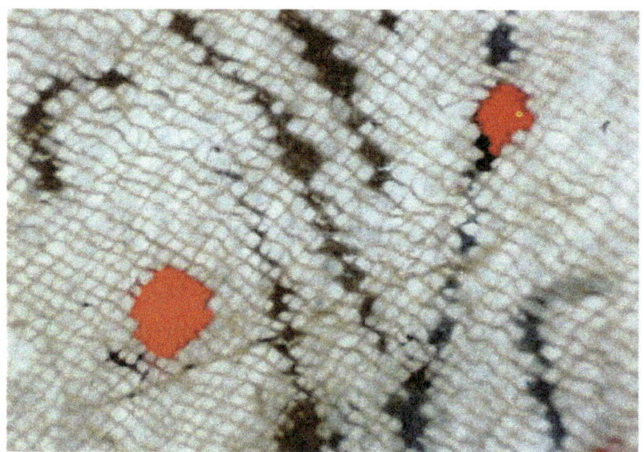

Part of the printed and painted floss silk padded gauze

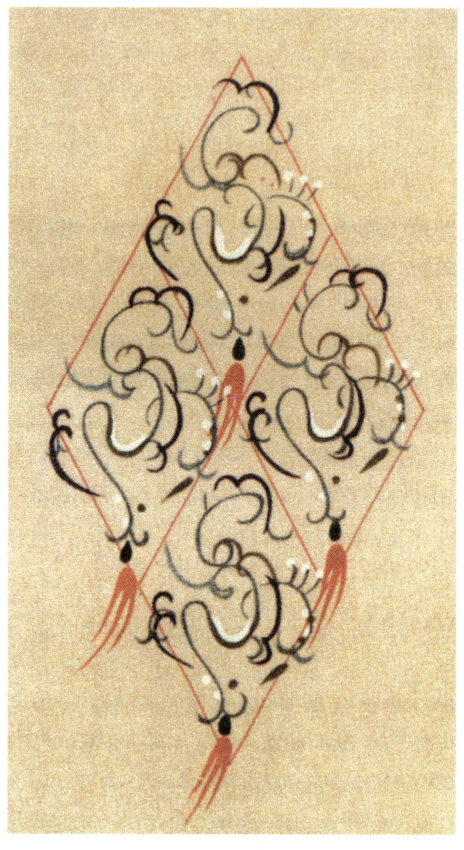

The pattern unit of printed and painted floss silk padded gauze

silk fabric with square-shaped holes. Among the silk robes unearthed from the Han tombs at Mawangdui, three were made of printed and dyed silk, indicating that this was a luxurious fabric used for fashionable attire by noble women at that time.

The second type is the gold and silver flame pattern printed gauze. Two complete "gold and silver flame pattern printed gauze" were unearthed from Tomb 1 of the Han Dynasty in Mawangdui. Both were exquisitely overprinted in three colors. The two fabric-printed gauzes are approximately 48 centimeters wide and 64 centimeters long, with the pattern composed of four changing cloud lines.

One such single pattern is 7.6 centimeters wide and 10.4 centimeters long, arranged in a staggered horizontal way. There are 13 patterns in one row and 12 in the other, with half a pattern on each side. The cloud lines are silver and decorated with small gold dots. The silver-white and silver-gray colors are overlaid to form delicate

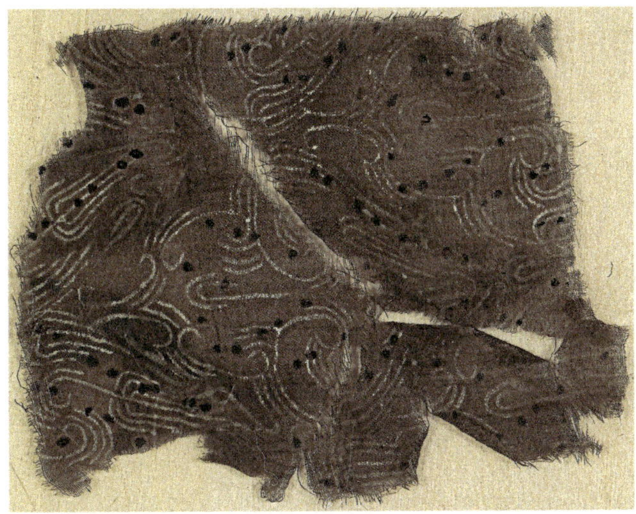

Fragments of a gold and silver flame pattern printed gauze, unearthed from the Han tombs in Mawangdui

and swirling cloud lines, while the gold color is overlaid to form stacked "山"-shaped small dots combined together like a flame.

1.2 Guangzhou Nanyue King's Tomb Silk Printing Plates

In 1983, a large number of precious cultural relics were discovered in the Nanyue King's Tomb in the Xianggangshan Mountain in northern Guangzhou City. During the sorting of the unearthed items from the tomb, several pieces of bronze fragments were found. After rust removing and repairing them, the cultural relic workers discovered that they were two bronze silk printing plates of different sizes. After studies, they were found to be the plates used for silk printing, which is a very important archaeological discovery.

The silk printing plates were unearthed in the western side room of the tomb, with a large amount of silk fabric on its west side room, all wrapped in silk when excavated. The larger one is mostly intact, with a flat and thin shape resembling a plate, with a pattern on the front resembling a small tree with swirling flame-like patterns. The pattern lines are in relief, most of which are very thin and sharp, with a thickness of about 0.15 millimeters. The patterns in relief are about 1 millimeter away from the copper plate vertically, forming grooves or concave surfaces between them. There is a small perforated button on the back of the printing plate. The total length of the artifact is 57 millimeters, with a width of 41 millimeters. The other one is flat and thin, resembling a plate, but smaller, which was already broken into four

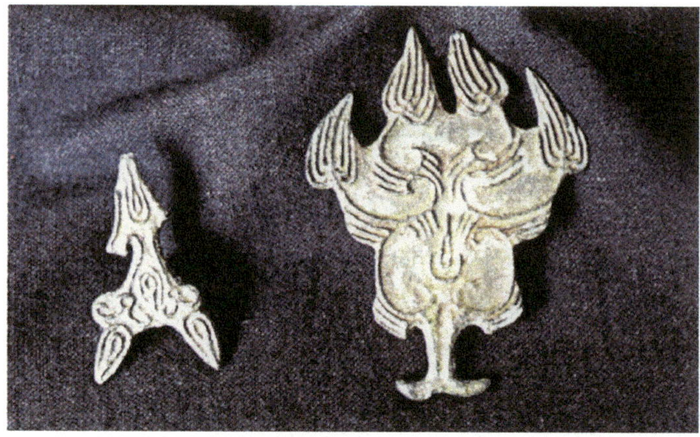

Bronze silk printing plates unearthed from Nanyue King's Tomb in Guangzhou

pieces when unearthed. Experts glued and reassembled them, with a pattern similar to the Chinese character "人." There are also raised cloud patterns on the front with a thickness of around 0.2 millimeters. The total length of the artifact is 34 millimeters, with the widest part being 18 millimeters. There is also a perforated button on the back. Patterns in relief at the back of the two bronze artifacts are on the same plane, with many worn signs, some of which have been rounded and dulled, indicating their previous usage. The buttons with small holes on the back are obviously convenient components for gripping and holding. Therefore, these two bronze artifacts are clearly printing plates used for dipping ink.

The combination of the two patterns is very similar to the gold and silver flame-patterned silk unearthed from Tomb 1 in Mawangdui, only the pattern unit is slightly larger than that in Mawangdui. Moreover, this patterned stamp was also found in charred fabrics from Nanyue King's Tomb. The fact that the fabric printing tools and the finished products came from the same tomb is extraordinary. The gold and silver flame pattern printed gauze unearthed from Mawangdui is considered to be the earliest color overprinted silk in the world, and the overprinting tools discovered in Nanyue King's Tomb provide strong evidence for this.

The production technique of these two printing plates, whether they are cast or engraved, has not been specifically identified by any department using modern technology. Based on the external characteristics of the printing plates and the bronze artifacts unearthed from the tomb, they are likely to be cast. Therefore, there may be several identical printing plates.

Over 2,000 years ago, craftsmen in the Kingdom of Nanyue were able to produce relief tools with clear and smooth patterns, which were used for printing on silk. It is truly a remarkable achievement. We can imagine that the craftsmen holding these standardized plates sequentially stamped them on the silk fabric in a horizontal and then vertical order, just like stamping seals. Each meter of fabric required over 600 stamps. This is not only a printing technique but also a multi-block overprinting technique. These two copper relief plates are the earliest preserved colored printing tools in the world, holding significant importance in the history of science and technology, dyeing and printing techniques, and engraved block printing.

1.3 Printed Dress Unearthed from Huang Sheng's Tomb in the Southern Song Dynasty

In October 1975, a tomb of the Southern Song Dynasty was discovered on Fucangshan Mountain in Fuzhou City. The tomb belonged to a young noblewoman named Huang Sheng. According to the *Fuzhou Huang Sheng's Tomb in the Southern Song Dynasty*, there were 201 burial garments found in Huang Sheng's tomb, including 153 whole pieces of silk fabric and remnants. Among them, there were a large number of silk garments with printed patterns on collars and cuffs. The garments had a total of 79

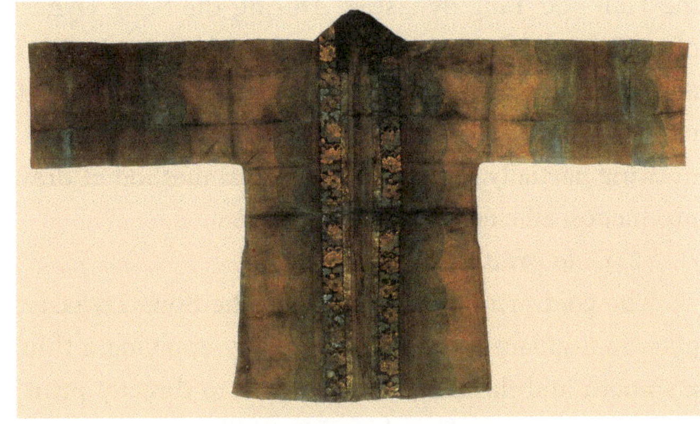

The unlined garment unearthed from Huang Sheng's tomb in the Southern Song Dynasty, featuring a pattern of smoke-colored plum blossom embroidered with floral borders and adorned with golden peach blossoms and tassels along the collar

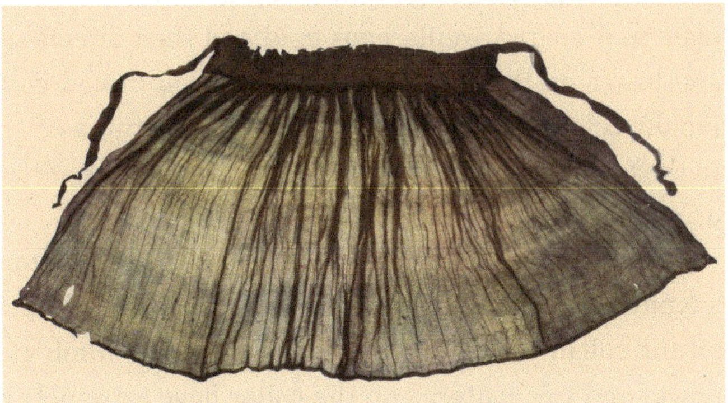

Printed and pleated brown gauze unearthed from Huang Sheng's tomb in the Southern Song Dynasty

pieces, with the front and edges of the clothing adorned with a combination of printed and painted or purely painted lace. Among them, there were eight robes, 39 tops, 15 skirts, nine single-piece laces, as well as three printed skirts, one swathe of printed fabric, three headscarves, and one printed sachet. This collection of printed fabrics is extensive in quantity and variety of patterns, representing almost all the popular printing techniques of the Song Dynasty. Therefore, it can be said that Huang Sheng's tomb is a treasure house of Chinese printed textiles of the Song Dynasty.

The printed fabrics unearthed in Huang Sheng's tomb can be divided into three categories according to the characteristics of the techniques.

(1) Relief printing added with colored drawing

Relief printing on fabric involves engraving the designed pattern on a smooth and flat hard wooden board, and then applying a suitable thickness of paint or adhesive on the board to create the outline of the pattern. This is the first step in the process of relief printing with colored drawings. Afterward, color is applied to the embossed pattern. Finally, petals and veins are outlined by using colors such as white, brown, and black or argillaceous gold. This technique has continued and developed since the Han and Tang dynasties. During the Song Dynasty, this type of relief printing often featured linear lace with grouped patterns. The ornamentation was patterned and decorated on robes, unlined garments, lined shirts, skirts, and linear lace, and various floral designs were adopted. The combination of relief printing and colored drawing partially replaced the manual method of drawing patterns, thus improving production efficiency to a certain extent.

(2) Gold printing technique

The gold printing technique in the Song Dynasty refers to dipping the pattern plate in argillaceous gold, followed by applying a thin paste and then fixing it onto a smooth and flat silk fabric surface to directly print the golden outline. The gold printing technique found in Huang Sheng's tomb mainly involves argillaceous gold printing. Argillaceous gold printing is done by dipping the relief-engraved pattern plate in prepared argillaceous gold and then directly printing the outline of flowers and leaves on the silk fabric that has been coated with a thin paste and smoothed. Finally, colors are filled inside the leaves, creating a colorful pattern with gold printing. In the tomb of Huang Sheng, the lace of 56 pieces of clothing and skirts were made by using this argillaceous gold printing technique.

Gold printing technology was also found in the tombs of the Liao Dynasty, with a typical example being a purple silk robe with gold-printed flower and tree patterns on the collar, which was unearthed from the tomb of Yelü Yuzhi. The gold-printed flower and tree patterns on the collar have extremely clear boundaries, and under a

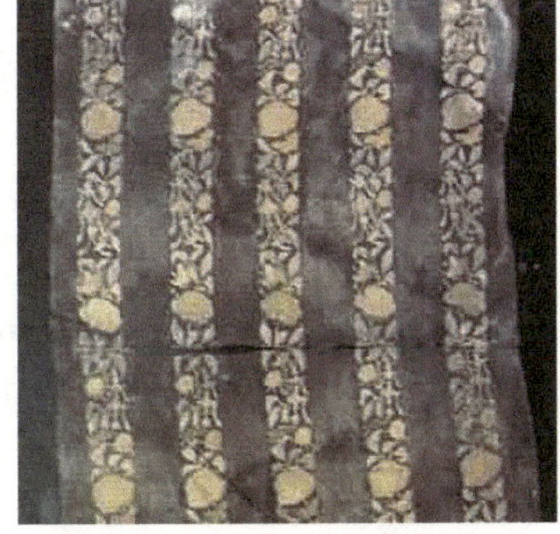

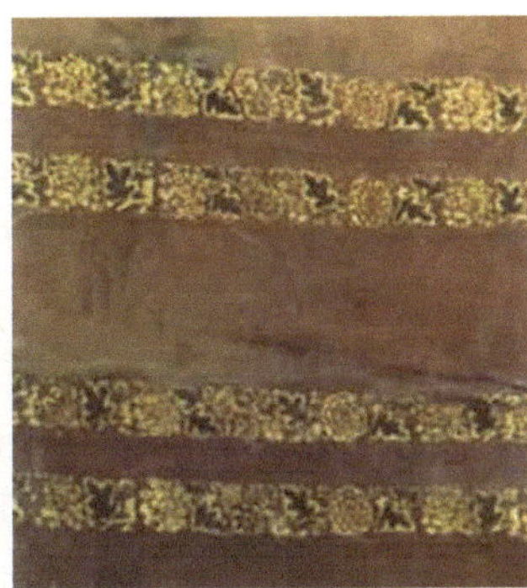

(RIGHT) The printed and painted peony tassel lace unearthed from Huang Sheng's tomb

(FAR RIGHT) The golden printed lotus and chrysanthemum lace unearthed from Huang Sheng's tomb

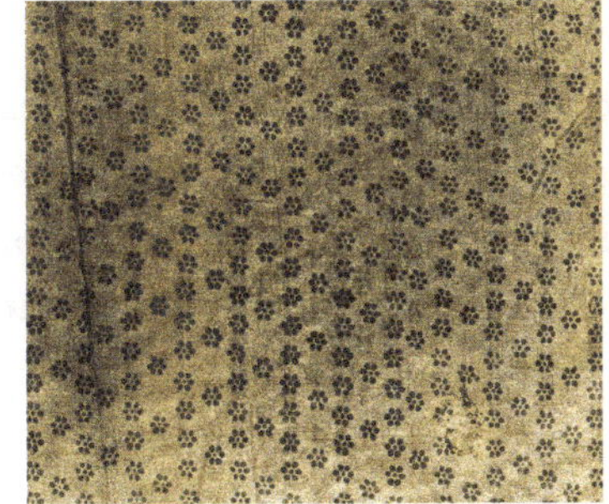

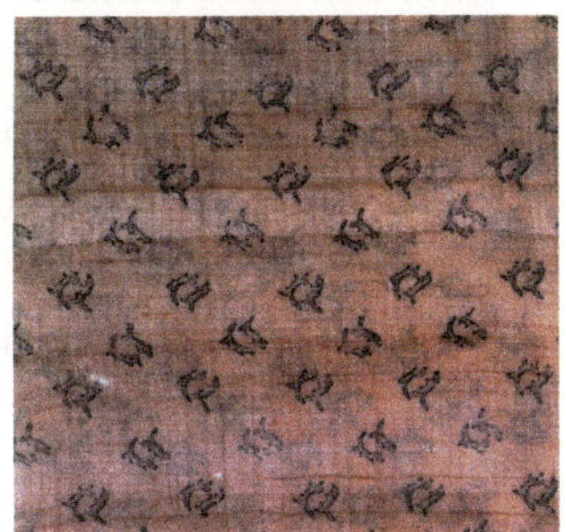

(RIGHT) The brown silk cloth unearthed from Huang Sheng's tomb, printed with indigo-blue dots on the skirt surface

(FAR RIGHT) Double-tiger pattern printed silk uncovered from Huang Sheng's tomb

microscope, no traces of adhesive can be seen. Still, it can be seen that the gold foil is warping, suggesting that a very weak adhesive was used to press the gold foil onto the collar.

(3) Stencil printing

From the excavated stenciled fabrics of Huang Sheng's tomb, it can be seen that the base pattern of the stenciled printed fabrics in the Southern Song Dynasty was created by hollowing out hard cardboard to form a pattern. The pattern was then placed flat on a smooth silk fabric and directly brushed for printing. The pigments used for printing were mixed with adhesive. Due to the repeated application of color paste, the paste covered the yarn holes of the fabric, resulting in raised lines and a certain thickness. In some areas, there were even instances of color bleeding. However, overall, the pattern lines were still relatively smooth and flowing. Generally speaking, the main parts, such as flowers and buds, were processed and depicted after the base pattern was printed.

1.4 *Sakyamuni Preaching the Dharma* in the Liao Dynasty

In July 1974, during the renovation of the wooden pagoda in Ying County, Shanxi Province, a total of 61 engraved prints were discovered, including 12 volumes of

Khitan-Edition Tripitaka, 35 other Buddhist scriptures, two block-printed books, six miscellaneous stone engravings, and six block-printed Buddha statues in colors. It can be said that this is another groundbreaking discovery in the history of printing, following the discovery of the Dunhuang Caves and the documents in the Xixia Blackwater City.

The three paintings of *Sakyamuni Preaching the Dharma* unearthed from the wooden pagoda are extremely precious. These paintings have a relatively large size, with the dimensions of all three being almost the same (with slight variations), approximately 66 centimeters in length and 61.5 centimeters in width. All painted on silk, the three paintings were originally folded and stored in a six-curved silver tray inside the pagoda. The paintings depict Shakyamuni Buddha sitting on a lotus blossom, wearing a red robe, with the inner cycle of a halo around red and outer blue. The top of the painting is adorned with a canopy decorated with a composite flower design and a silk curtain hanging down. Both sides of the canopy are decorated with heavenly grass. Outside the canopy, there are characters "Namo Shakyamuni Buddha" printed, with both sides of the characters mirrored on the silk. In front of the Buddha, there are four groups of monks, nuns, male and female lay Buddhists, all standing respectfully with their hands clasped together. There are also donors wearing

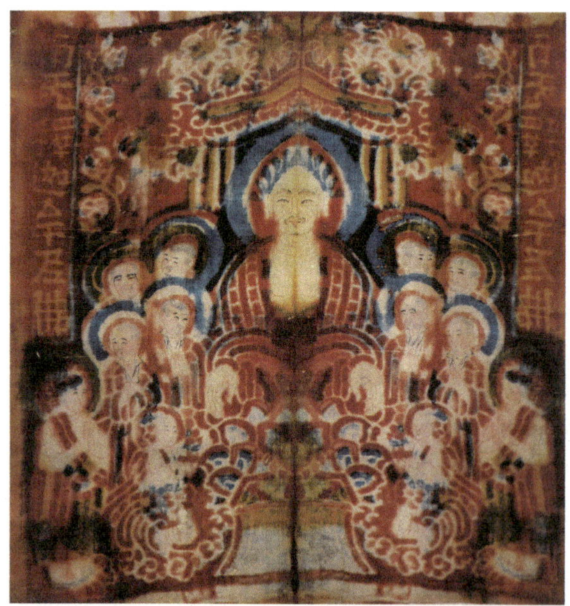

Sakyamuni Preaching the Dharma, unearthed from the wooden pagoda in Yingxian County, Shanxi Province

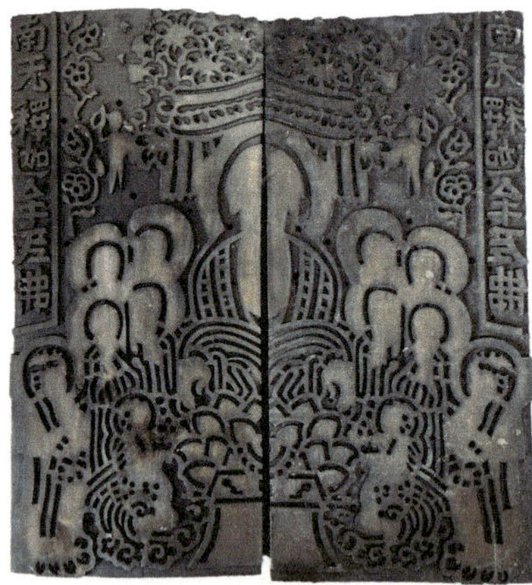

Sakyamuni Preaching the Dharma, the copy of the clamp-fabric dyeing plate

decorative hairpins, standing with their hands clasped together. Two children born in lotus flowers are surrounded by auspicious clouds. The overall composition of the painting is intricate and compact.

These three paintings may have been produced by skipping and overprinting in three colors. It is possible that, in order to allow both the front and back worshippers to see the Buddha's picture and read the inscriptions of the standard script in a line, the three precious Buddha paintings were made of almost transparent thin silk with front and back folding. They were most likely used for hanging in religious ceremonies or temples without obstructing the light. Even when there is wind, the figures in the paintings can still be seen vividly despite the swaying silk banners. The three-color printed Buddha paintings on silk of the Liao Dynasty boast larger size and three-color printing, holding significant importance in the history of printing.

2. *Color Printing of Books*

The history of the practice of color printing in the field of books is less than 1,000 years. However, the technique of color printing has had a long history since ancient times, as detailed in my book *Chinese Color Printing for Two Thousand Years*. Generally speaking, color printing has gone through a path from decorative painting to color printing on paper. When books and pictures are printed in monochrome, black is often used. Whether it is talking about brushes, ink, paper, inkstones, or scholars, whenever the word "ink" appears alone, it seems to refer to the color black. If referring to other colors of ink, a color-relating adjective must be added before it. Each woodblock will be printed hundreds of thousands of times, but it will gradually wear out due to the constant expansion that happens after the absorption of ink, drying, and brushing. As a result, the characters will become more distorted over time. Therefore, the earliest printed versions of books have the clearest characters, thus being the most precious one. The first printed copies are called the "first edition," and the later copies with blurred characters are called the "painted-face edition." Since the rise of "handkerchief books" in the Ming Dynasty, in order to indicate the preciousness of the first edition and also to indicate that it could be presented for improvement, the first edition would be printed with cinnabar or blue ink, known as "cinnabar edition" or "blue edition." The term "blueprint" in dictionaries just refers to the original work or picture based on which other works are created. This is how it originated. With the development of culture, the demand for printed books has increased, leading to the creation of books with multiple colors printed on a single sheet, known as multi-color printing.

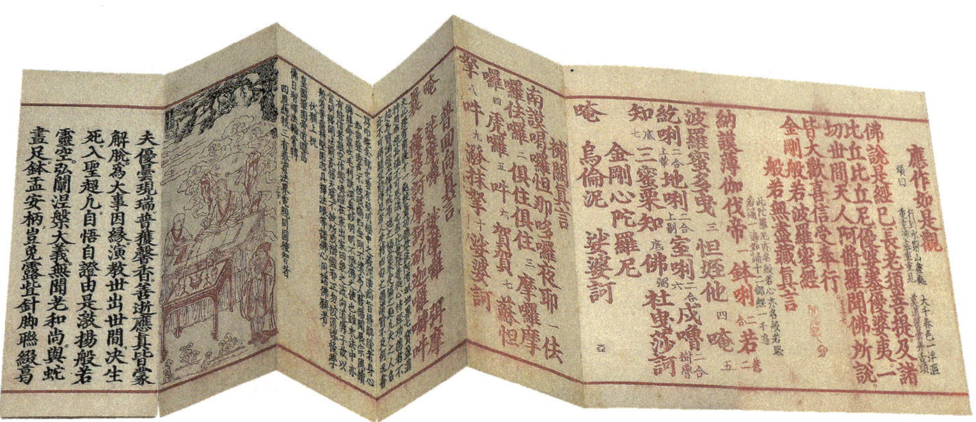

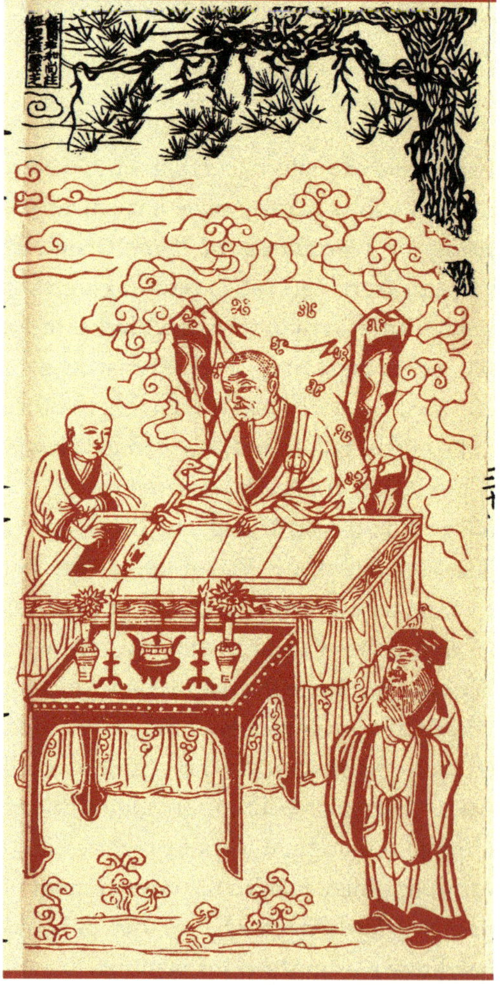

(ABOVE) The black and cinnabar dual-color edition of *Commentary on the Diamond Sutra*, published in the Zifu Temple on the Zhongxing Road

(LEFT) *Picture of the Lingzhi Mushroom Growing during the Sutra Annotation by Wise Monk Wuwen*

There are two methods for multi-color printing: one is to brush different colors on one plate at a time, and the other is to engrave separate plates for each color and then print them layer by layer. Originating in the Song Dynasty, the method of multi-color printing was used to print banknotes. In the Yuan Dynasty, books printed in cinnabar and black appeared. The earliest surviving printed book in multiple colors is the *Commentary on the Diamond Sutra* in the collection of Taiwan Province. It was annotated by monk Wuwen of the Zifu Temple on Zhongxing Road in the Yuan Dynasty, printed in the first year of the reign of Emperor Zhizheng (1341). There is a postscript written by Liu Jueguang in the book, which says, "When the master was annotating the sutra in a small room in the Zifu Temple, in the fourth month of the Gengchen year, a Lingzhi mushroom suddenly grew, with a yellow stem and a purple cloud covering it. On the first day of the first month of the following year, Liu Jueguang dreamed of a gathering of dragons and heavenly beings at the printing place of the sutra." The *Picture of the Lingzhi Mushroom Growing during the Sutra Annotation by Wise Monk Wuwen* in the book vividly tells the story. In the Qing Dynasty, Zhou Kefu wrote *The Diamond Sutra: A Record of Examination and Practice*, which detailed this legend: "Monk Wuwen of the Zifu Temple, a native of Xiangshan in Ruyi, was invited by Elder Wu'ai of the Zifu Temple in the first year of the Zhiyuan era. He was asked to annotate the *Diamond Sutra*. It took thirty-two parts. At that time, there was a purple cloud covering the temple. After the annotation was completed, there were five Lingzhi mushrooms of different colors growing in front of the Dharma seat. The annotated sutras have been circulating to this day. Besides the annotations by Master Wuwen, there are also praises attached to each part, which can open the heavenly eye of humans to see through the Diamond Mountain. It is expected that there will be auspicious signs of purple clouds and miraculous Lingzhi mushrooms. There are also carved sutras, from which relics flow out. Those who receive the relics are all wise people who have achieved wisdom."

The book has been a subject of debate since the era of the Republic of China (1912–1949) regarding how it was printed. In fact, most of the debates stemmed from not having seen its true appearance. The book was printed with two engraved plates in red and black, first printing the red color, then overprinting the black color. Two overprints were made on one sheet, and then the pages were glued, folded, and bound to form the book. It is indeed the earliest and most unique edition, with exquisite illustrations and brilliant black and cinnabar ink, and it is indescribably marvelous.

If the Song Dynasty was the golden age of engraved block printing, then the Ming Dynasty was the golden age of color printing. Since books in the Ming Dynasty became souvenirs for the upper class, there was a wider demand for pleasant-looking books, thus making color printing of books a trend. However, if color-printed books were delivered to the tasteful literati of the Song Dynasty, such as Su Dongpo and Wang Anshi, they would most likely be heavily criticized. Even in modern times, it is rare to see adult books printed in color. However, color overprinting represents a new peak in the development of printing technology, which is both a law of historical development and the basis for further innovation. Overprinted editions can be divided into categories such as red and black dual-color, cinnabar, black, and blue tricolor, cinnabar, black, blue, and green four-color, and cinnabar, black, blue, green, and yellow five-color. Generally, black ink is used for the main text, which is printed first, while cinnabar ink is used for the annotations and comments in the margins, printed afterward. The texts represented by the two colors, cinnabar and black, have a distinction between the main and subordinate.

There are many color-printed books of the Ming Dynasty that are surviving. Among them, the books printed by the Min and Ling families during the Wanli and Tianqi periods were particularly well-known for their extensive circulation. In the Min

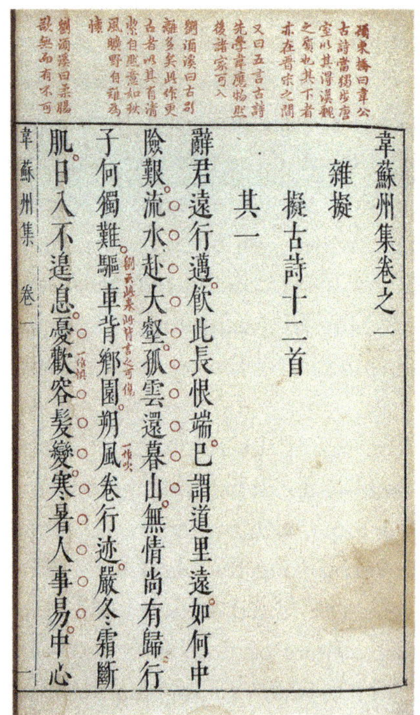

韋蘇州集卷之一

雜擬

擬古詩十二首

其一

辭君遠行邁飲此長恨端已謂道里遠如何中險艱流水赴大壑孤雲還暮山無情尚有歸行子何獨難驅車背鄉園朔風卷行迹嚴冬霜斷肌日入不遑息憂歡容髮變寒暑人事易中心

韋蘇州集 卷一

The Collected Works of Wei Yinwu, written by Wei Yingwu, overprinted in black and cinnabar by Ling Mengchu

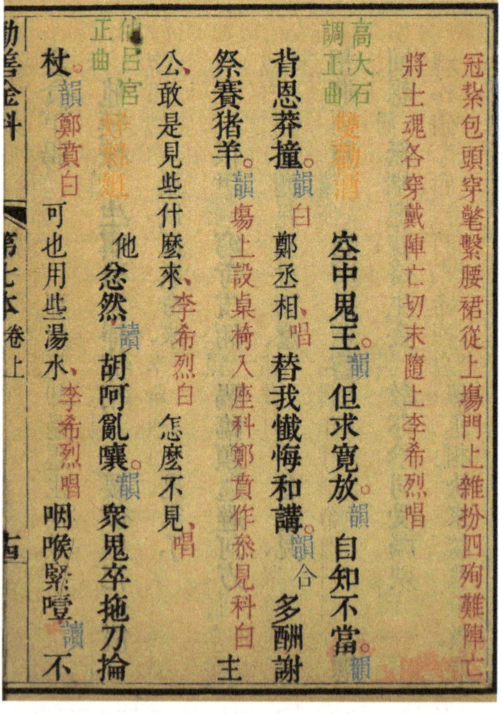

冠紫包頭穿氅繫腰裙從上場門上雜扮四殉難陣亡將士魂各穿戴陣亡切末隨上李希烈唱

高大石調正曲 雙勸酒 空中鬼王。韻 但求寬放。韻 自知不當。韻 背恩莽撞。韻白 鄭丞相、唱 替我懺悔和講。韻合 多酬謝祭賽豬羊。韻場上設桌椅入座科鄭賁作祭見科白 主公敢是見些什麼來、李希烈白 怎麼不見、唱

仙呂宮正曲 好姐姐 他忿然、讀 胡阿亂嚷。韻 衆鬼卒拖刀掄杖。韻鄭賁白 可也用些湯水、李希烈唱 咽喉緊噎讀 不

勸善金科 第七本 卷上

Quan Shan Jin Ke, the overprinted edition in five colors during the reign of Emperor Qianlong of the Qing Dynasty family, the editions in black and cinnabar of *Dongpo Yizhuan, Dongpo Shuzhuan, The Collection of Rites, Among the Flowers: The Hua-Chien Chi,* and other works printed by Min Qiji during the Wanli period were very famous. The overprinted books in black and cinnabar engraved by other families with the Min family name included *Sunzi Cantong,* printed by Min Yuchen; *Deeds of the Qin and Han Dynasty,* printed by Min Risi during the Wanli period; *Jiuhui Yuanyao,* printed by Min Qihua During the Tianqi period, and so on. Ling Mengchu was the mainstay of the Ling family in terms of block-printed editions in multiple colors. The block-printed editions in black and cinnabar by him were mainly on literature, and the most printed books during the Wanli period included *The Book of Songs, The Collection of Tao Yuanming, The Collection of Wang Wei,* and *The Collection of Rites of Zhou.* Both the main bodies of editions, overprinted in multiple colors by the Min and Ling families, adopted the popular square characters during the Wanli period and the rectangular characters used during the Tianqi period, which looked very neat.

Quan Shan Jin Ke, engraved by the Hall of Martial Valor, is a masterpiece of interlaced printing from the reign of Emperor Qianlong of the Qing Dynasty. The book was printed in five different colors: titles and melodic models in the margins were printed in yellow, the names of plays inside the book were printed in green, the lines and spoken parts performed by the actors were printed in black, characters and descriptions of their actions were printed in red, and rhymes, repetition, and sentences between the actors' lines were indicated with blue ink. The different colors also had variations in font size. With its five colors, the book looks truly vibrant and visually appealing.

3. Woodblock Overprint

The breakthrough in printing technology in the Ming Dynasty was the creation of woodblock overprint and the "Gong Hua" technique.

The so-called woodblock overprint ("dou ban" in Chinese) refers to the process of engraving separate blocks for each color based on the colors of the original painting. After sketching and dividing, each color is printed in a sequence from light to dark, following the principle of "from shallow to deep, from light to dark." Finally, a colored print resembling a hand-painted artwork is completed. Why is it called "dou ban"? "Dou" means stacking or piling up, and it is often used in the word "dou ding," which was a popular pastry in the Jiangnan region during the Ming and Qing dynasties. In the *Food Classics* section of *The Complete Works of Sheng'an,* it is described as "small cakes of five colors, shaped like flowers and treasures, stacked in a box, called 'dou ding.'" Tang Yin, born in Suzhou, wrote in his poem *Tao Hua Wu Fu Xi*, "During the Grain Rain when flowers blossom, beautiful women gather together, and at the banquet, dou ding is something new." Woodblock overprint divides the same page into several different-sized blocks, each representing a part of the page. Different colors are brushed onto each block, then printed onto the same sheet of paper and pieced together to form a complete image. It resembles dou ban in appearance, hence the name. The process and division of modern woodblock watercolor printing techniques have developed based on the woodblock overprint technique.

The reign of Emperor Wanli of the Ming Dynasty (1573–1620) was a watershed in the history of ancient Chinese woodblock overprint. In the history of Chinese printmaking, works of woodblock overprint from the Ming Dynasty are the most numerous, recording the highest achievements. Since the Song and Yuan dynasties, the woodblock overprint technique that people had been exploring made a qualitative leap into full application in the Ming Dynasty. In the late Ming Dynasty, Hu Zhengyan in Jinling (today's Nanjing) was the first to use woodblock overprint to print the *Shizhuzhai Studio's Painting Manual*. He divided a large engraved block into smaller blocks according to the different colors needed for the pictures and then stacked the engraved blocks with color ink on top of each other. This method is similar to the process of movable overprint, presenting multiple colors on one printed work, solving the problem of unclear color layers, which brings woodblock prints closer to the original paintings. This is representative and innovative in the history of ancient printmaking. Hu Zhengyan put a lot of effort into publishing this collection of paintings. According to Cheng Jiajue's *Mengwai Oulu*, Hu Zhengyan did not consider the engravers as mere craftsmen but discussed with them day and night for ten years. Due to the complexity of woodblock overprint and the high requirements for craftsmanship, there could be no carelessness in the process of block dividing, block engraving, block matching, coloring, and printing. Therefore, before printing, he personally inspected and checked to ensure the quality of the engraving, resulting in the finished products reaching an unprecedented level. Yang Wengeng said in the preface of this collection, "With light and heavy ink, each piece has its own charm; with sparse and dense typesetting, each scroll is lifelike."

Collection of Letter Paper Samples by Luoxuan is currently the earliest book to be discovered using the woodblock overprint technique. The book was compiled by Yan Jizu, engraved by Wu Faxiang, and was published in the sixth year of the Tianqi period of the Ming Dynasty (1626). The name of the book highlights the concept of "Biangu" ("changing the old practice"). In the postscript written by Yan Jizu at the

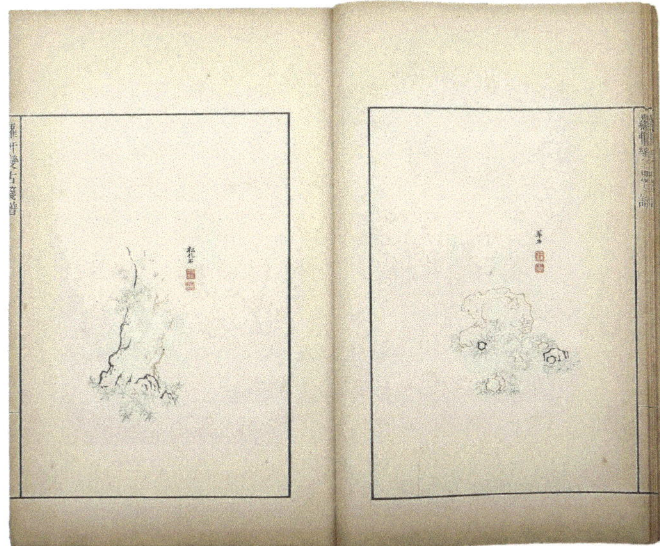

Collection of Letter Paper Samples by Luoxuan, the earliest surviving edition of the book using the woodblock overprint technique

end of the book, it is explicitly stated, "We do not blindly pursue the present while abandoning the past, nor do we have to reject the present in favor of the past. What I hope today is to return to simplicity through engaging in engraved block printing." In addition to the innovative use of woodblock overprint to change the old practice, the *Collection of Letter Paper Samples by Luoxuan* also pioneered the technique of "Gong Hua," which is commonly known as intaglio printing, is a craft that carves patterns and lines into the wooden block, creating a concave effect, and when printed, the paper surface becomes arched, creating a three-dimensional effect.

Shizhuzhai Studio's Stationery Manual, the representative work of woodblock overprint, was published in the 17th year of the reign of Emperor Chongzhen of the Ming Dynasty (1644), edited and printed by Hu Zhengyan. Hu Zhengyan was a publisher and a master in seal carving of calligraphy and paintings during the late Ming Dynasty, with the courtesy name Yuecong. He named his residence "Shizhuzhai" (Ten-Bamboo Studio) because he had more than ten bamboo plants in his courtyard. Hu Zhengyan, with his reputation and financial resources, often hired skilled craftsmen to work in his studio, and they would "discuss and study together day and night, like this for ten years," thus continuously improving their craftsmanship. *Shizhuzhai Studio's Stationery Manual* used the popular woodblock overprint and Gong Hua technique of that time, pushing the art of woodblock process printing to a new peak. Lu Xun praised *Shizhuzhai Studio's Stationery Manual* as the "highest achievement of literati's refined cultural pursuits in the late Ming and

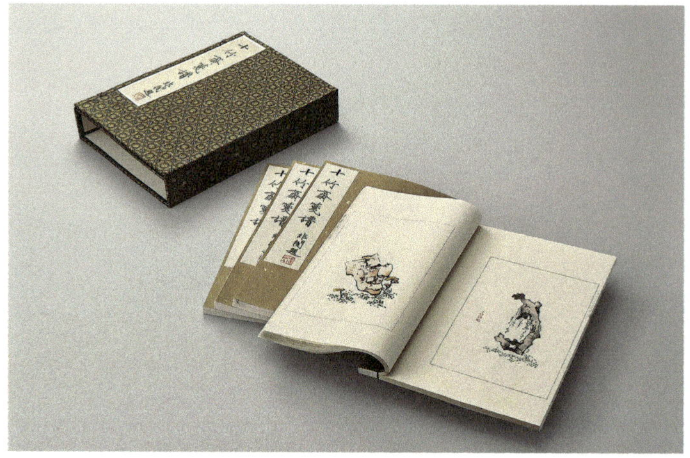

Shizhuzhai Studio's Stationery Manual, the representative work using the technique of woodblock overprint in the late Ming Dynasty

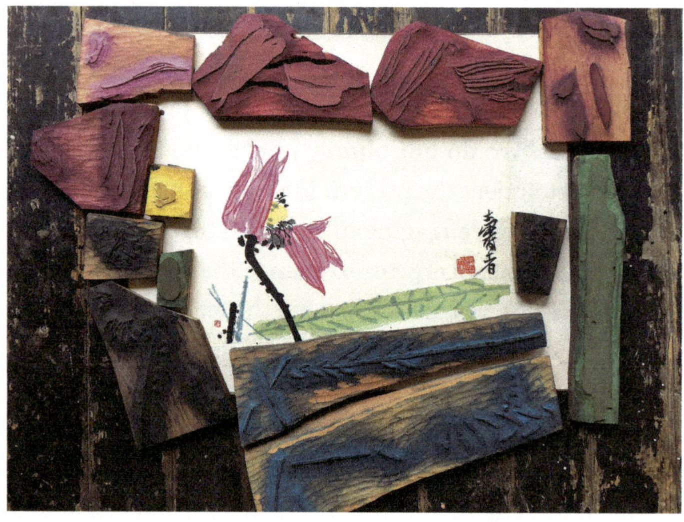

"Five-colored small cakes"—woodblock overprint and letter paper

early Qing dynasties." The whole work consists of four volumes, with a total of 283 illustrations featuring various themes such as precious stones, auspicious artifacts, scenic views, elegant crafts, gifts, symbols of longevity, auspicious signs, accessories, and miscellaneous drafts.

4. The Art of New Year Paintings Printing

New Year paintings, a traditional Chinese art form, originated from the ancient "Door God paintings." As early as the Han Dynasty, there had already been rudimentary images of "Door God." The development of Buddhist sutra block-prints, the maturation of woodblock printing techniques during the Tang Dynasty, and the flourishing of urban culture during the Song Dynasty greatly promoted the prosperity of woodblock New Year paintings. The woodblock New Year paintings gradually evolved from their initial monochrome form to colored prints, with the technique of hand coloring developed into process printing.

The traditional Chinese New Year paintings have a history of over 1,000 years. However, the term "New Year paintings" itself is relatively new, undergoing a process of evolution. During the Song Dynasty, New Year paintings were referred to as "zhi hua" (paper painting), while in the Ming Dynasty, they were commonly called "hua tie" (picture paste). In the early and middle Qing Dynasty, they were often referred to as "hua pian" (picture slice), "hua zhang" (picture piece), or "wei hua" (guarding painting), and so on. It wasn't until the 29th year of the reign of Emperor Daoguang of the Qing Dynasty (1849) that the term "New Year paintings" appeared in Li Guangting's book *Xiangyan Jieyi*. These folk art pieces are mostly posted during the Chinese New Year for decoration, conveying blessings for a prosperous and joyful new year. Therefore, the name "New Year paintings" fits well, and it has continued to be used until today.

The wide influence of New Year paintings has made them a specialized category in the history of printing. They are characterized by a sense of joy, celebration, and auspiciousness, with vibrant and lively scenes, simple lines, and vivid colors. The forms of New Year paintings include door paintings, wall paintings, and bedhead paintings. The content of these paintings is very diverse, including themes such as court ladies, flowers and birds, landscapes, babies, social customs, history, and literary stories, which mainly reflect people's aspirations for a happy life, abundant offspring, and bountiful harvests. New Year Paintings are also designed to promote traditional moral values such as respecting the elderly, loving the young, harmonious family relationships, and frugality. They often depict auspicious

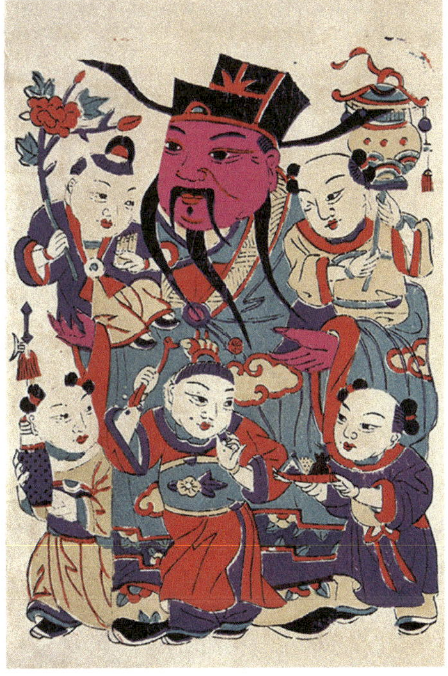

The famous New Year painting of the Qing Dynasty

patterns, which are loved by the public. Due to different regional preferences, several regional production bases of woodblock New Year paintings have gradually formed. Famous production areas include Yangliuqing in Tianjin, Yangjiabu in Shandong, Taohuawu in Suzhou, and Mianzhu in Sichuan.

4.1 Yangliuqing in Tianjin

The New Year paintings produced in Yangliuqing, located southwest of Tianjin, are one of the most widely spread and influential folk woodblock prints in northern China. The Yangliuqing New Year paintings originated in the reign of Emperor Chongzhen of the Ming Dynasty and gradually prospered during the Qing Dynasty, particularly during the reigns of Emperor Yongzheng and Qianlong. Every year, from October to the end of the year, merchants from various places would gather here to purchase New Year paintings and then sell them elsewhere. Within a hundred miles of Yangliuqing, many villagers engage in printing New Year paintings as a secondary occupation for their families.

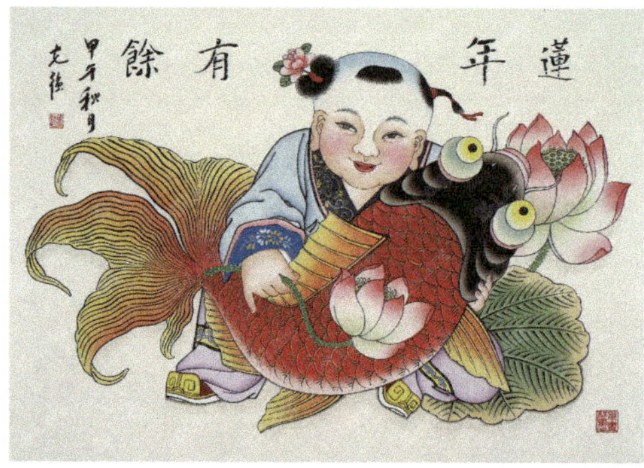

Surplus Year after Year, the Yangliuqing New Year painting

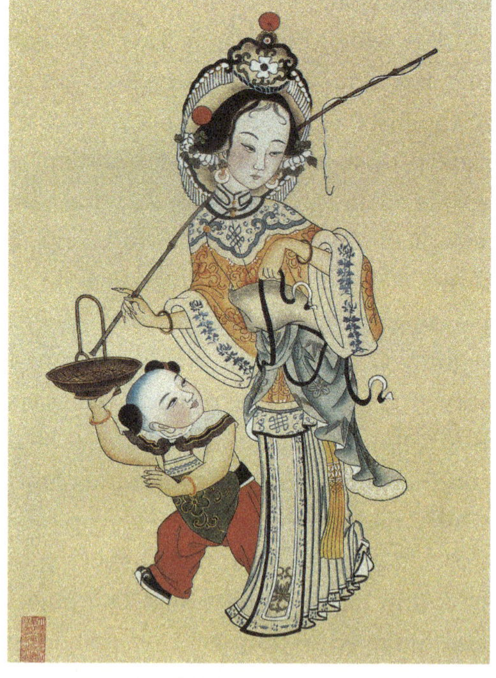

Fishermen's Return, the Yangliuqing New Year painting of Tianjin produced in the reign of Emperor Qianlong of the Qing Dynasty

The characteristics of Yangliuqing New Year paintings lie in their production method, which is a combination of printing and painting. First, the image lines are carved on a wooden block; then, ink is applied and printed onto paper. After several layers of single-color prints, the painting is filled in with colored brushes. This method ingeniously combines the techniques of woodblock printing and painting, creating a unique artistic style that distinguishes it from other paintings and New Year pictures. Due to different techniques used by painters, the same unfinished edition (ink lines without color or a semi-finished product printed in multiple colors) can be painted in either a meticulous and detailed style called "fine work" or a bold and rough style called "coarse work," thus creating distinct artistic styles, each with its own artistic value.

4.2 Yangjiabu in Shandong

The history of woodblock New Year Paintings in Yangjiabu, Weifang City, Shandong Province, could date back to the late Ming Dynasty. It flourished during the Qing Dynasty, with a history of over 400 years. Yangjiabu Woodblock New Year Paintings are renowned both domestically and internationally for their rich rural features and distinctive artistic style. During the Qing Dynasty, there were "hundreds of painting shops and thousands of types of New Year paintings, with tens of thousands of printing blocks" in Yangjiabu, making it one of the three major painting markets in the country at that time. The themes of the New Year paintings were very diverse, with a wide range of deity paintings for blessings, auspiciousness, and warding off disasters. During the Xianfeng period of the Qing Dynasty, Yangjiabu woodblock New Year Paintings reached their peak, with numerous painting shops scattered throughout the area. In just the western part of Yangjiabu, there were 82 shops owned by the Yang family alone.

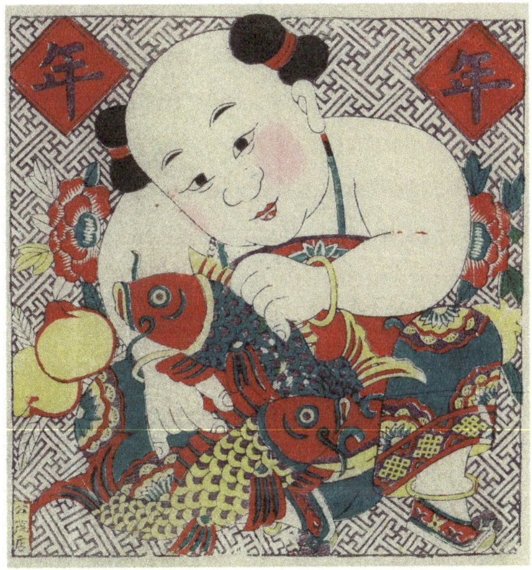

Surplus Every Year, Yangjiabu New Year painting of Shandong Province

The printing method of Yangjiabu New Year paintings is simple, with exquisite craftsmanship and unique characteristics. The process involves three steps: sketching, engraving, and printing. The artists first use willow charcoal sticks and incense ash to create a preliminary draft called "xiugao." Based on the preliminary draft, they then complete the final draft, outlining the lines, and then paste it in reverse on a pear woodblock for engraving, creating separate blocks for lines and colors. After color adjusting, paper mounting, plate alignment, and color correction, the paintings are finally hand-printed. The craftsmen of Yangjiabu continuously innovated the printing process of New Year paintings, initially using small consoles to print with craftsmen sitting and later switching to large consoles with craftsmen standing. After paintings are printed, various colors are hand-painted to make them more natural and vivid.

4.3 Taohuawu in Suzhou

Taohuawu New Year paintings are named after the area of Taohuawu in Suzhou, where they were originally produced. Taohuawu woodblock prints flourished during the reigns of Emperor Yongzheng and Emperor Qianlong in the Qing Dynasty, and it is one of the largest production centers for New Year paintings in southern China. Taohuawu New Year paintings are mainly printed in multiple colors, with red, yellow, blue, green, and black as the basic color tones. Influenced by Hu Zhengyan's woodblock printing technique and the early Qing Dynasty's *The Mustard Seed Garden Manual of Painting*, Taohuawu New Year paintings have achieved a high level of craftsmanship in composition, engraving, and printing. Taohuawu New Year paintings mainly depict southern landscapes, famous scenic spots, and folk customs, with representative works like *Gusu Longevity Bridge* and *Xuanmiao Temple Fair*.

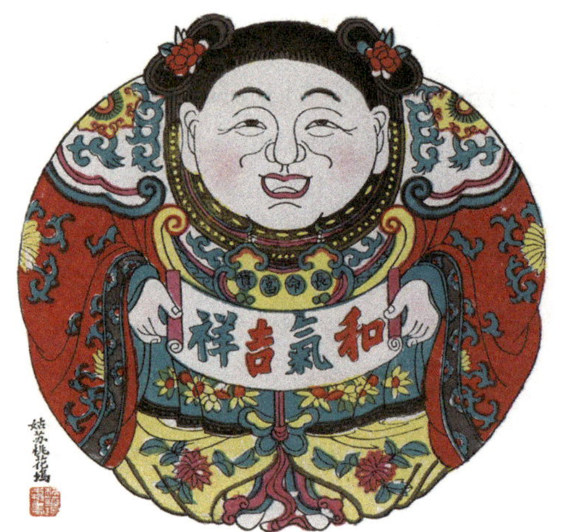

Taohuawu New Year painting made in Suzhou

The production process of Taohuawu woodblock print generally involves five steps: sketching, engraving, printing, mounting, and polishing by hand. The engraving process can be further divided into four parts: creating a sample, engraving the blocks, smoothing out the remaining blank areas with a chisel, and making modifications. The main tools used include a punching knife, as well as tools such as curved chisels, flat chisels, Jiucaibian (one celadon pigment), needle chisels, root chisels, skew chisels, water bowls, iron rulers, and small brooms. The process of multi-color printing also follows a set of procedures, including plate inspection, color mixing and adhesive

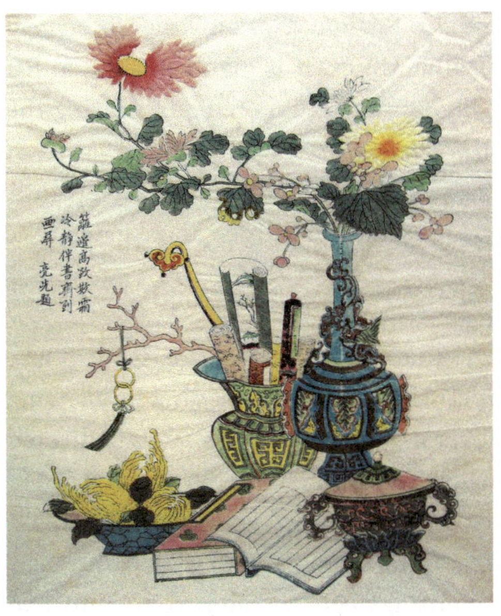

The woodblock color print of flowers and birds produced by Ding Liangxian, collected by Mr. Christer Vonder Burg

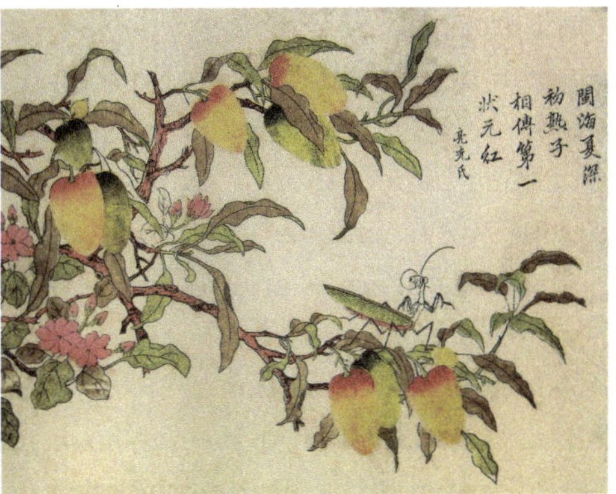

The woodblock color print of flowers and birds produced by Ding Liangxian, collected by Mr. Christer Vonder Burg

preparation, paper selection (clipping paper), plate rubbing, paper cutting, printing, and drying.

Taohuawu woodblock New Year paintings mainly adopt the forms as door paintings, central scrolls, and hanging scrolls, usually depicting auspicious and festive scenes, folk customs, opera stories, flowers, birds, and fruits, which are traditional aesthetic contents in folk culture. In the folk painting community, Taohuawu woodblock New Year paintings are known as the "Gusu version." The *Painting of the God of Longevity* is the earliest discovered Taohuawu woodblock New Year painting, included in the Japanese book *Illustrated Catalog of Ancient Chinese Woodblock Prints*, with the inscription "25th year of the reign of Emperor Wanli (1597)" carved on the picture.

During the reign of Emperor Qianlong, Ding Liangxian from Suzhou used the woodblock overprint and the Gong Hua technique to print many flower and bird paintings on white paper, displaying exquisite engraving and vibrant colors, which are rare gems in the field of process printing. They are collected by institutions such as the National Library of France, the British Museum, and Mr. Christer Vonder Burg from Sweden. According to the archival documents in France, Ding Liangxian was a Catholic living in the mid-Qianlong period. He had frequent interactions with the European missionaries who were preaching in Suzhou. Not only did he engage in printing himself, but he also traded Western paintings. It is highly likely that his works were sold to Europe through missionaries and foreign merchants. During the Qianlong period, there were also people in the Suzhou area who imitated Western perspective techniques to create New Year paintings and other literary-themed prints. Some of these prints are still preserved in some museums in Europe and Japan.

4.4 Mianzhu in Sichuan

Mianzhu, Sichuan Province, is also one of the main production areas for Chinese New Year paintings. During the reigns of Emperor Qianlong and Jiaqing in the Qing Dynasty, over 300 workshops were staffed by over a thousand professionals dedicated to producing New Year paintings in Mianzhu. The annual production exceeded 12 million paintings, which were also exported to countries such as India, Japan, Vietnam, and Myanmar, as well as Hong Kong and Macau in China. Mianzhu New Year paintings can be categorized into two types based on their themes: "red product" and "black product." "Red product" refers to colored paintings, including door paintings, square paintings, and decorative strips. Door paintings come in different sizes, such as "bigger size," "big size," and "small size," and are used for posting on main doors, hall doors, room doors, and kitchen doors. Decorative strips include central scrolls, hanging scrolls, horizontal scrolls, and single strips, which are used for posting in halls, rooms, corridors, and livestock pens. "Black product" refers to woodblock rubbings printed with soot or cinnabar ink, mostly depicting landscapes, flowers and birds, deities, and calligraphy by famous individuals, which are mainly in the forms of central and hanging scrolls.

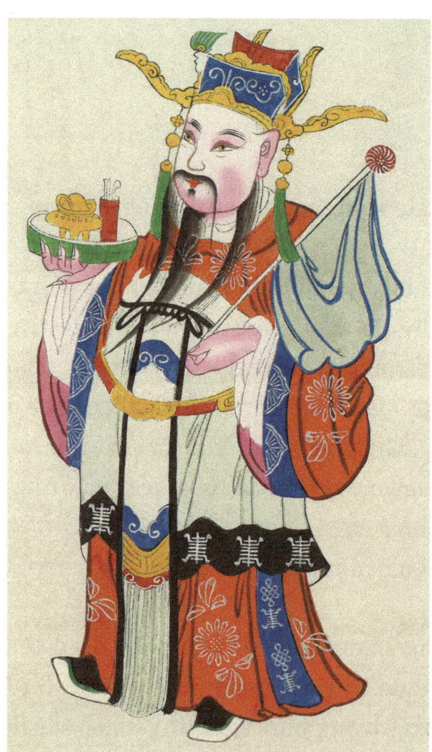

The God of Wealth, a New Year painting created in Mianzhu, Sichuan, in the Qing Dynasty

Mianzhu New Year pictures, like other Chinese New Year pictures, should first be engraved into a version with lines. However, the line version only plays the role of outline in Mianzhu New Year pictures, and the remaining works rely on manual color painting instead of process printing. The production procedures and features are all embodied by manual color application and line drawing. The specific processes are as follows: (1) Clearly painting, whose skill is exquisite and beautiful. (2) Outline patterns with gold powder. Dip the pen in gold or silver powder to draw the pattern. (3) Patterned golden stamp, which belongs to the reprocessing after color painting. It uses wooden flower stamps with gold or silver patterns. There are about 30 kinds of flower stamps, including clothing flowers, hat flowers, corner flowers, and cuff flowers. (4) Printing gold. After printing the ink line and color painting, use the original printing plate to copy the glue (except face and hand), and then sprinkle the gold powder or silver powder. After cleaning the remaining powder, the gold or silver lines will appear. (5) Painting with watercolor. Work to create an elegant tone through lines. (6) Simple pattern, that is, strive to make the color simple. (7) "Tianshuijiao," a few freehand brushwork, which is the characteristic painting method of Mianzhu New Year pictures.

In addition, New Year paintings in Mianzhu are unique in terms of paper, brush, and color. Traditional Mianzhu New Year paintings are usually made with locally produced tribute paper and Mandarin Duck-kind brushes (specially-made flat brushes that are dipped in water and color at the same time). The colors are mostly made from mineral pigments and folk dyes mixed with alum, which are resistant to wind and sun, resulting in vibrant and harmonious artistic effects. The main colors include Buddha blue, peach red, scarlet, grass green, followed by gold, sky blue, etc.

4.5 New Year Paintings in Other Areas

Till the middle and late Qing Dynasty, woodcut New Year paintings had almost developed across the country. In addition to the above four regions, there are many well-known places of origin, such as Zhuxian Town in Henan Province, whose woodcut New Year pictures mainly adopt overprinted editions. The edition is characterized by a transparent color used for printing, showing slight wood grain in the New Year pictures. Zhuxian Town woodcut New Year paintings have distinctive features such as bold lines, simple and vivid images, and strong colors, which are unique among many New Year painting schools in the country.

The woodcut New Year paintings in Wuqiang of Hebei have a strong local flavor and local characteristics. Wuqiang New Year paintings are mainly engraved in relief, coupled with intaglio designs. They use the technique of black-and-white contrast to give full play to the effect of woodcut engraving. In terms of coloring, it mainly uses red and green, which are rather distinct and unique.

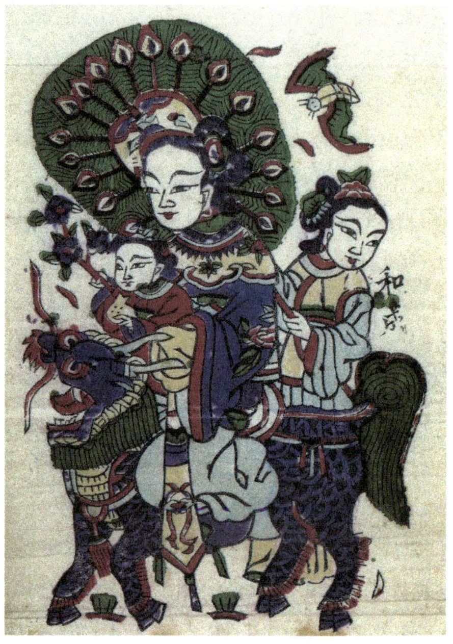

Guanyin Sending Children, a woodcut New Year painting made in Zhuxian Town of Henan in the Qing Dynasty

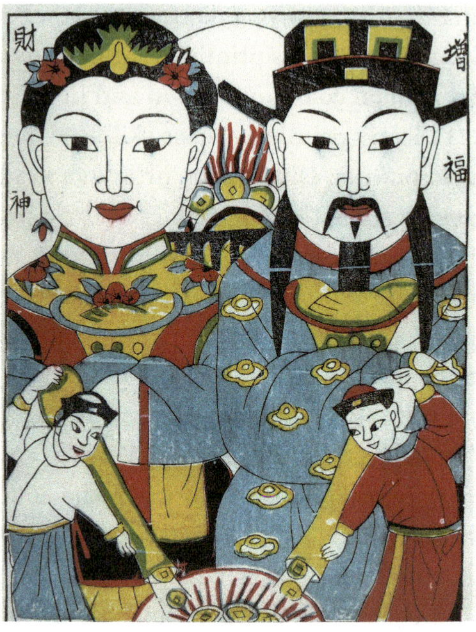

The New Year painting made in Wuqiang, Hebei, in the Qing Dynasty

In addition, the New Year paintings printed in Jinnan, Shanxi Province, inherit the unique style of block printing tradition in the Pingyang area formed in the Jin Dynasty. Most of the Jinnan New Year paintings are colored after full pages printing with ink. The New Year paintings printed in Guanzhong and Hanzhong, Shaanxi Province, are of primitive simplicity, with various content and strong colors. There are also New Year pictures with local characteristics in Foshan, Guangdong; Quanzhou, Fujian; Shaoyang, Hunan; Hanyang, Hubei; Baotou, Inner Mongolia; Dali and Lijiang, Yunnan; Tainan, Taiwan, and some ethnic minority areas.

CHAPTER V

The Spread and Influence of Printing

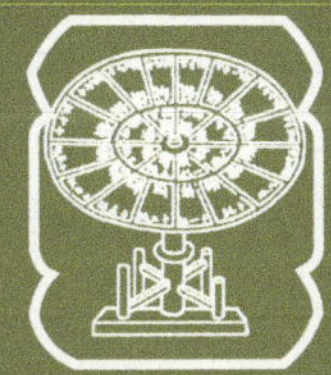

China is the birthplace of printing, which was invented in China and spread to the world, achieving great glory.

Over 2,000 years ago, Zhang Qian's mission to the Western Regions officially opened the "Silk Road on Land" that connected Chang'an with Rome. During the Sui and Tang dynasties, the "Maritime Silk Road" emerged. For over 2,000 years, through the Silk Road, China's silk, tea, ceramics, and other goods continuously flowed into the West, while the West introduced spices, Persian brocade, fruits, and vegetables to the East. The Silk Road is not only a route for material exchange, but also a major path for economic, political, and cultural exchanges between the East and the West. Through this route, China's papermaking, compass, gunpowder, and printing techniques spread to Europe through the Arab region, while Arab astronomy, calendars, and medicine are introduced to China, leaving an important chapter in the history of civilization exchange and mutual learning.

The invention of Chinese printing inspired and led the development of printing in other parts of the world, playing a huge role in promoting a community with a shared future for mankind with merits recorded in the annals of history, shining brightly for thousands of years. It was pointed out in the speech at the 12th Conference of academicians of the Chinese Academy of Engineering: "Through the course of over 5,000 years development of civilization, the Chinese nation has created a highly developed civilization as our ancestors had invented papermaking, gunpowder, and printing... They have contributed countless achievements in scientific and technological innovation to the world and made far-reaching and huge contributions to the progress of world civilization, putting China among the world leaders for a long time."

1. The Spread and Influence of Printing in Asia

After it was invented by China, printing gradually spread to other parts of the world. Many countries either adopted printing techniques from China or developed their own printing techniques influenced by China. It first spread eastward to the Korean Peninsula and Japan and southward to Vietnam and the Philippines in Southeast Asia. Later, it spread westward through Central and West Asia, reaching various European countries. Here, we take the examples of the Korean Peninsula, Japan, the Philippines, Vietnam, and Iran to illustrate the early transmission of printing techniques in Asia.

1.1 The Korean Peninsula

Throughout history, China has had close ties with various regimes on the Korean Peninsula. In 2015, a burial site was discovered in Beijing's Daxing District, where a tomb brick inscription recorded the death of the tomb owner in AD 539, stating that he was from "Nakrang commandery, Joseon County." Nakrang commandery was one of the four Han commanderies established by the Han Dynasty on the Korean Peninsula. Therefore, it is natural that the printing industry developed earlier on the Korean Peninsula.

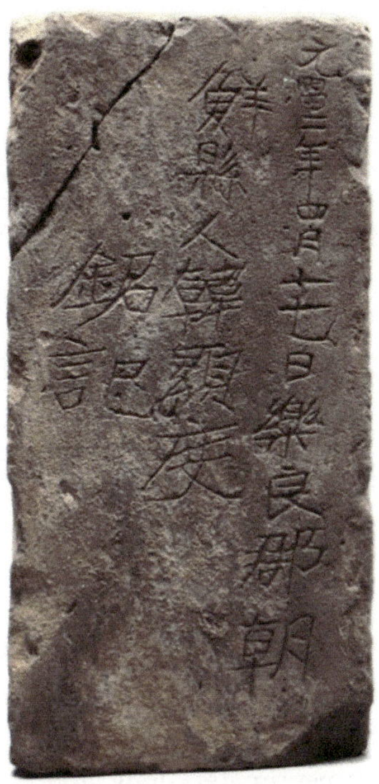

The tomb bricks unearthed from the tombs in Daxing District, Beijing, in 2015

In the late 7th century, the Silla Kingdom unified the Korean Peninsula. Afterwards, Silla absorbed Tang Dynasty culture, sending many students to China to study Confucianism and Chinese culture. China's high-quality handmade paper, especially leather paper, also took root during the Goryeo Dynasty on the Korean Peninsula with its own local characteristics. Goryeo paper produced on the Korean Peninsula was thick and sturdy, suitable for writing various scripts. The ink-making technique was also introduced from China to the Korean Peninsula during the Tang Dynasty. The ink produced on the Peninsula boasted a glossy appearance with excellent texture. The development of paper and ink laid the foundation for the emergence of printing technique.

- *Block printing*

At first, the Korean Peninsula brought back printed materials from China through cultural exchanges. Gradually, the peninsula residents began to use the printed works brought back by China as a blueprint to start their printing industry. In 1966, an ancient pagoda in the Buddhist temple in Gyeongju, South Korea, was found in Chang'an, a printed version of the Tang Dynasty, *Great Dhāraṇī Scripture of Immaculate Radiance*, which was brought back by monks from the Korean Peninsula. In recent years, according to research, silk, iron, and other ancient cultural relics have been found in the Korean Peninsula, many of which come from mainland China.

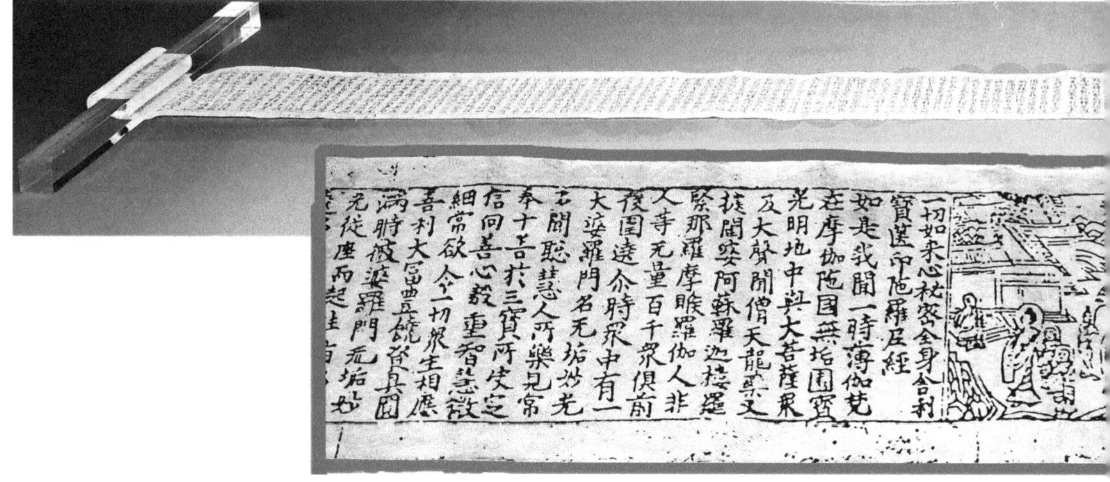

一切如来心秘密全身舍利
寶篋印陀羅尼經
如是我聞一時薄伽梵
在摩伽陀國無垢園寶
光明池中與大菩薩衆
及大聲聞僧天龍藥叉
揵闥婆阿蘇羅迦樓羅
緊那羅摩睺羅伽人非
人等无量百千衆俱前
後圍遶尒時衆中有一
大婆羅門名无垢妙光
多聞聡慧人所樂見常
奉十善於三寶所深之
信向善心殷重智慧微
細常欲令一切衆生相應
善利大富豐饒資具圓
滿時彼婆羅門无垢

The earliest extant print on the Korean Peninsula is the *Sutra of the Whole-Body Relic Treasure Chest Seal Dharani* (hereinafter referred to as *Dharani Sutra*), which was block printed at the Zongchi Temple in Kaesong in 1007. The printed work is 240 centimeters long and 7.8 centimeters wide; its contents and layout are the same as the one unearthed in Zhejiang Province but with different engraving levels. The title painting at the beginning of the volume is slightly different, with the only obvious difference being the inscription. In 1917, the inscription on the *Dharani Sutra* unearthed from the Tianning Temple in Huzhou was: "Eighty-four thousand volumes of the *Dharani Sutra* were printed for placement and worship in the pagoda by the Commander-in-Chief, King Qian (Hong) Chu of Wuyue in 956, the third year of Xiande." The inscription of the *Dharani Sutra* of Goryeo was: "The master of the Zongchisi Temple in Goryeo, Zhennian Guangji master Shi Hongzhe, respectfully made the *Dharani Sutra* for placement in the pagoda in the 25th year of the Tonghe reign." The Koryo edition is obviously based on the Scriptures printed by Qian Chu, which was printed 51 years later.

From the time of King Seonjong (1010–1031), the official organization of the large-scale printing industry began in the Korean Peninsula. Taking the Song Dynasty's *Kaibao-Edition Tripitaka* and the Liao Dynasty's *Khitan-Edition Tripitaka* as references, the first complete collection of Buddhist scriptures in the Korean Peninsula, called the *Tripitaka*, was engraved. It consisted of 5,924 volumes, known as the *Goryeo Great Treasure*, which was later destroyed in wars and re-carved during the 24th year of King Gojong of Goryeo (1237). The project was completed in the 38th year of King Gojong (1251), totaling 6,791 volumes. Undergoing multiple repairs and

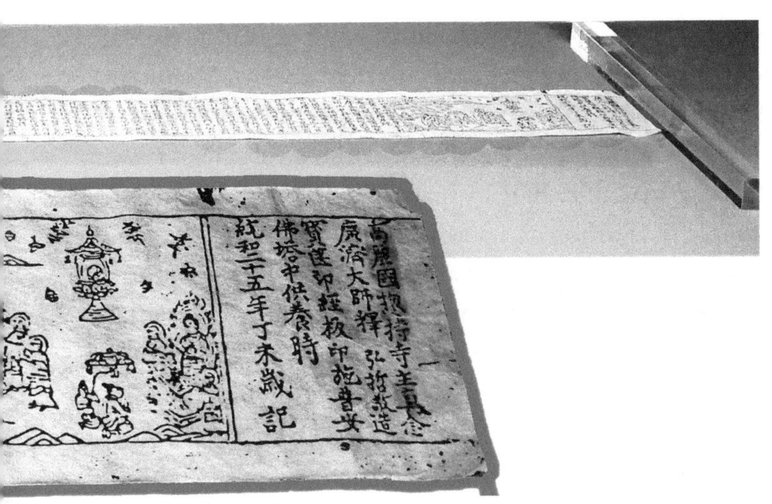

Sutra of the Whole-Body Relic Treasure Chest Seal Dharani, the earliest extant print on the Korean Peninsula

printings, this edition has been preserved to this day, and it is known as the famous *Koryo-Edition Tripitaka*.

There were no written characters on the Korean Peninsula in ancient times, so Chinese characters were used all along. It was not until 1446 that the Korean language known as "Hangul" (now commonly known as the Korean Peninsula language) was created. From then on, printed Hangul books and bilingual Chinese-Hangul books appeared. The earlier Hangul publication on the Korean Peninsula was *The Lotus Sutra*, printed in 1463. The Taoist *Interpretation of the Book of Rites and Trustworthiness in Hangul* was an early Chinese and Hangul bilingual version.

Due to the importance of the Koryo royal family in the printing industry, printed works on the Korean Peninsula were not limited to Buddhist scriptures and Taoist books. The government also printed a large number of Chinese scriptures, histories, books, collections, and medical works, most of which were reproduced exactly as they were in China. It can be seen that the Korean Peninsula was deeply affected by Chinese printing.

- *Movable type printing*

In the second half of the 11th century, when monk Yitian lived in Hangzhou, he probably learned about the invention of clay movable type printing, which was recorded in *Dream Pool Essays* by Shen Kuo, who was contemporary with Yitian. In 1102, the method of coin-casting in ancient China was also introduced into Korea. Both favorable timing and geographical conditions promoted the adoption of movable type printing in Korea.

In the 14th century, the Korean Peninsula was in the late period of Wang's Korea. In 1351, Baiyun, a 54-year-old monk, went through hardships to the Xiawu Mountain in Huzhou, China, to ask Master Shiwu of the 18th generation of Sect Linji for Dharma. Monk Baiyun paid a visit to Master Shiwu, who gave him a volume of *Buljo Jikji Simche Yojeol.* After returning to China, Baiyun served as Abbot in the Anguk Temple and the Shingwang Temple in Haizhou and devoted himself to cultivating the younger generation. At the same time, he tried to print and disseminate the scriptures imparted by Master Shiwu. With the efforts of Baiyun's followers, three years after his death, the movable type version of *Buljo Jikji Simche Yojeol* was published in the Xingde Temple in Cheongju. It was divided into two volumes, but only one volume was passed down to the present, which is now kept in the French National Library. The scripture's name is abbreviated as *Jikji,* which is widely spread. Although the extant copy of *Jikji* is not in South Korea, it is still listed as No. 1132 of South Korea's national cultural heritage. In 2001, UNESCO listed it in the Memory of the World Register. In order to promote the printing culture of South Korea, since 2003, the Cheongju municipal government of South Korea has held the Jikji Festival every other year, and its Department of Education, Science, and Culture will also confer the Jikji Award.

In 1403, a type foundry was established on the Korean Peninsula, initiating large-scale casting of copper movable type. Over the next 460 years, nearly 30 sets of metal movable type were cast, totaling millions of characters. All others were made

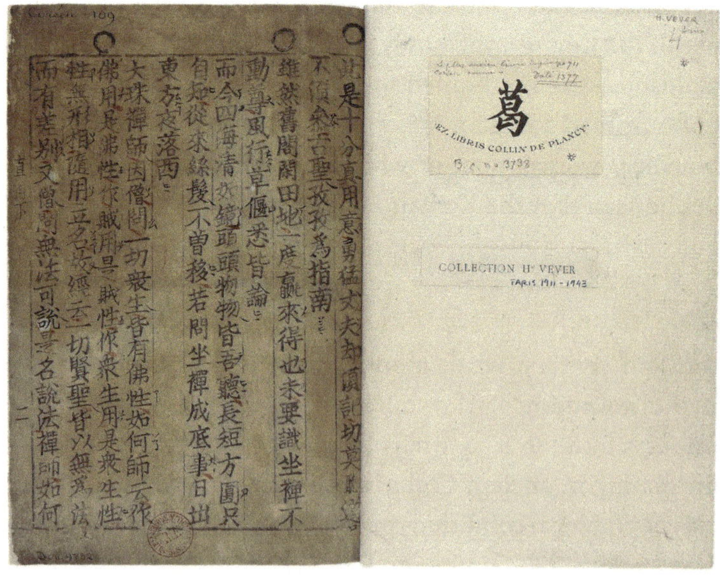
此是十分真用意勇猛丈夫都須記切莫
不復參吾聖教我為指南
雖然舊閣閑田地一度贏來得也未要識坐禪不
動尊風行草偃悉皆論
而今四海清如鏡頭頭物物皆吾聽長短方圓只
自知從來絲髮不曾移若問坐禪成底事日出
東方夜落西
大珠禪師因僧問一切衆生皆有佛性如何師云作
佛用是佛性作賊用是賊性作衆生用是衆生性
性無形相隨用立名故經云一切賢聖皆以無為法
而有差別又僧問無法可說是名說法禪師如何

直指下 二

Buljo Jikji Simche Yojeol, copper movable type printing edition of copper except for one set of lead type and two sets of iron movable type. From then on, printing books with copper movable type became the main printing method in the Korean Peninsula. Among the various sets of copper movable type, the typeface created in 1434 (said to be modeled after the calligraphy by the famous calligrapher Madame Wei from the Eastern Jin Dynasty) was the most exquisite and beloved. Since it was invented in the "Jia Yin Year," the typeface became known as the "Jia Yin Character," which is treated as the "Eternal Treasure of the Democratic People's Republic of Korea."

The method of casting type on the Korean Peninsula, according to the 15th-century Korean scholar Seong Jeon, involved carving characters with boxwood, pressing them into soft clay to create a mold, pouring molten metal into the mold for solidification and then processing it into usable metal type. This method is almost identical to the casting of bronze seals in China.

1.2 Japan

From the Three Kingdoms period in China to the Tang Dynasty, the Silla and Baekje kingdoms on the Korean Peninsula served as a bridge for the spread of Chinese culture to Japan. It was through the Korean Peninsula that papermaking techniques were introduced to Japan. In AD 645, Japan underwent the "Taika Era Reforms" and began sending envoys and students to the Tang Dynasty to learn about Confucian culture and advanced technologies. These individuals brought back many writing brushes, ink, paper, inkstones, manuscripts, and printed books. Among them, the Japanese monk Genbō brought back over 5,000 Buddhist scriptures when he returned to Japan in AD 734. The Japanese envoy to the Tang Dynasty, Kibi no Makibi, arrived in China in AD 750 and later became the teacher of Emperor Shōtoku. Additionally, the renowned monk Jianzhen traveled to Japan from Yangzhou in AD 754 to propagate Buddhism. These three individuals not only provided scriptures for printing, but also brought woodblock printing technique and pushed for the printing of *Hyakumanto Darani* (The one million pagodas and Dharani prayers) in AD 764, ordered by Emperor Shōtoku, also known as Empress Kōken.

The earliest surviving woodblock print in Japan is just the *Hyakumanto Darani*, which is currently housed in the Tokyo National Museum. Printed in AD 770, its content excerpted from the Chinese Buddhist scripture *Great Dhāraṇī Scripture of Immaculate Radiance* of the Tang Dynasty, including the fundamental, the compassionate, sōrin, and six paramitas. According to the historical records such as the thirty volumes of *Continuation of Japanese Chronicles*, *Records of Tōdaiji Temple*, and *Origin of Yakushiji Temple*, in the eighth year of the Tenpyō-hōji era (AD 764)

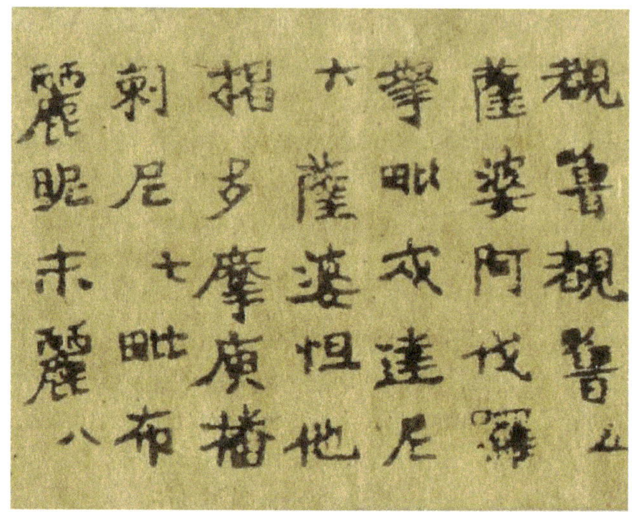

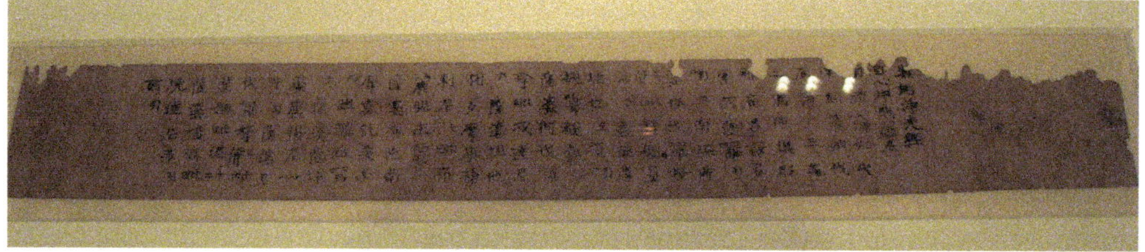

Hyakumanto Darani in Chinese, collected by the Tokyo National Museum, Japan

during the reign of Emperor Kōken, after suppressing the Fujiwara no Nakamarō Rebellion, the emperor made a vow to build one million small pagodas and place the printed content of the four Darani (the fundamental, the compassionate, sōrin, and six paramitas) inside the pagoda bases. Later, it became known as *Hyakumanto Darani*. After six years of construction, these pagodas were divided into ten major temples, collectively known as "One Million Pagodas." As an early example of printing, *Hyakumanto Darani* is not only an important cultural artifact in the history of Japanese printing, but also holds significant importance in studying the origin of printing technology in East Asia. However, there are no records or physical remains of woodblock printing in Japan for the next 200 years after *Hyakumanto Darani*.

In AD 983, Emperor Taizong of the Song Dynasty gifted a Japanese monk with the *Kaibao-Edition Tripitaka*, which was brought to Japan by the monk, promoting the development of Japan's printing industry and inspiring Japanese interest in block-printed books. In addition, as Buddhism was prevalent in Japan at that time, there was a high demand for Buddhist scriptures, which could only be satisfied through printing, rendering printing Buddhist scriptures a trend. According to records, 1,000 copies of *The Lotus Sutra* were printed in Japan in 1009, with another 1,000 editions printed in 1014, using the same binding method as *Kaibao-Edition Tripitaka*. This is probably the beginning of the official printed books in Japan. The earliest woodblock printing work in Japan that can be traced back to an exact date is the *Vijnapti-matrata-siddhi* (*Establishment of the Thesis of Cognitions-Only*), printed in 1088, which was the result produced after the introduction of the Song Dynasty block-printed books into Japan.

The early development of Japan's printing industry was inseparable from the help of Chinese craftsmen. During the late Yuan and early Ming dynasties, about forty to fifty Chinese craftsmen fled to Japan to avoid the chaos and participated in the engraving work of the Five Mountain edition (referring to the engraved edition centered around Kamakura five mountains and Kyoto five mountains from the mid to late 13th century to the late 16th century Muromachi), with the most famous figures Chen Mengrong from the late Yuan Dynasty and Yu Liangfu from the early Ming Dynasty. The former boasted exquisite craftsmanship, claiming to be the "Meng Rong Skilled Engraving." The latter had been living in Japan for a long time, engraving over ten types of books known as the "Yu Liangfu Edition." They not only engraved Buddhist scriptures, but also literacy textbooks such as *Mengqiu*, the dictionary of Chinese characters *Yupian*, and works of famous scholars in the Tang and Song dynasties such as *Du Gongbu's Poems* and *Mr. Changli's Collection of Coupled Sentences*, which had enabled many Chinese works to be circulated in Japan. At the same time, they also trained a group of excellent engravers for Japan, greatly improving Japan's printing quality. Chinese craftsmen made significant contributions to the development of Japan's printing industry, whose achievements cannot be forgotten by Japanese people even today.

In Japan, the introduction and use of movable type printing were relatively late, and it did not begin to spread until the late 16th century. In early Japanese movable type prints, sometimes the sentence "this method originated from Korea" appeared. For example, the book *Encouraging Learning*, printed with Japanese movable type in 1597, clearly records that "The method from North Korea is very convenient." Why? This is because Japan's movable type printing technique was introduced from the Korean Peninsula. In 1592, Toyotomi Hideyoshi invaded Seoul, the capital of Korea. In the school library of Seoul, copper movable type and movable type printing tools were found and then shipped back to Japan along with other treasures and books from Korea, which were all presented to Emperor Go-Yōzei. In the second year of the Bunroku era of Japan (1593), Emperor Go-Yōzei ordered the use of movable type to print the *Classic of Filial Piety in Ancient Chinese*, which was Japan's first movable type printed edition, opening a new chapter in the history of Japanese movable type printing. However, there are only written records without any physical objects. From then on, movable type printing gradually spread among the Japanese governments, private individuals, and temples.

Afterwards, the Japanese Emperor ordered the production of wooden movable type based on Korean bronze movable type. From the second to the eighth year of the Keicho era (1597–1603), a series of books including *Jinxiu Duan*, *Encouraging Learning*, *Chang Hen Ge Pipa Xing*, *Nihon Shoki Shindai Kan*, *Zhiyuan Chao*, *The Great Learning*, *The Doctrine of the Mean*, etc. were continuously printed, collectively known as the "Keicho edict edition." Later, Emperor Go-Mizunoo ascended the throne and continued to print books such as *New Engraved Imperial Categorized Garden of Historical Facts* with wooden movable type in the seventh year of the Genwa era (1621), which were called the "Yuanhe edict edition." At the same time, Tokugawa Ieyasu, who rose to power in the Japanese political arena after Toyotomi Hideyoshi, appointed a monk named Kanshitsu to engrave over 100,000 wooden movable types in Fushimi. Starting from 1599, books such as *Kongzi Jiayu*, *San Lue*, *Liu Tao*, and *The Political Program of Zhenguan Period* were successively printed. This batch of books with wooden movable type was called the "Fushimi edition." Afterward, Tokugawa Ieyasu moved to Suruga and appointed a Chinese man named Lin Wuguan as his technical advisor. Using the batch of bronze movable type introduced from the Korean Peninsula, 10,368 pieces of type were recast, with books such as *Dazang Yilanji* and *Qunshu Zhiyao* printed. The printed books with bronze movable type at this period were called the "Suruga edition."

In ancient Japan, there were no written characters of its own. Instead, it used Chinese characters to record events. Later, referring to the side of cursive and regular script of Chinese characters, it created the Japanese character "kana," but Chinese characters were still popular. However, until the 17th century, there were not many printed books in Japanese, compared with the most printed books in Chinese, which only had different ways of reading.

In the late Ming Dynasty, woodblock overprinted works represented by the *Shizhuzhai Studio's Painting Manual* were popular both at home and abroad, becoming a bridge for scholars to study the art of calligraphy and painting, which exerted a direct and profound impact on the Japanese ukiyo-e prints at that time.

There is also a beautiful story in the history of the printing exchange between China and Japan, which is about the printing, distribution, and inheritance of *Qunshu Zhiyao*. The *Qunshu Zhiyao* consists of 50 volumes, which were compiled by Wei Zheng, Yu Shinan, Chu Suiliang, and others under the order of Emperor

Taizong of the Tang Dynasty. Although this book has no longer existed in China, there are still ancient written versions circulating in Japan. The "Suruga edition" *Qunshu Zhiyao* was based on the Kanazawa library edition transcribed by Kamakura monks. Tokugawa Ieyasu had passed away before the book was completed, so it was not widely published around the world. At that time, only 51 copies were printed, barely spreading. In the first year of the Tenmei era in Japan (1781), impressed by the rarity of this book, Dainagon Muneyoshi compared it with the "Kanazawa edition" and "Suruga edition" to proofread and reprinted the *Qunshu Zhiyao*. He also entrusted Japanese merchants to send three copies of the book to China. After nearly 500 years of loss in China, the book *Qunshu Zhiyao* by Wei Zheng and others returned to their homeland in such a wonderful way. It can be seen that the introduction of the Chinese printing technique to Japan not only promoted the development of Japanese culture, but also enhanced cultural exchanges between China and Japan.

1.3 Vietnam

As Vietnam borders China, Vietnamese people have used Chinese characters for a long historical period, so most of Vietnam's ancient books are also in Chinese. The introduction of the Chinese printing technique to Vietnam was later than the Korean Peninsula and Japan. Still, the way of transmission was the same, that is, both introducing books from China through exchanges, gifts, and other forms and then learning China's engraving and printing techniques, gradually developing their own printing industry.

In the 11th century, Chinese books were introduced into Vietnam. At the request of Vietnam, the government of the Northern Song Dynasty presented it with three *Tripitaka* and one *Tao Tripitaka*. Vietnamese envoys often bought books in Bianjing, the capital of the Northern Song Dynasty, or exchanged local products and spices for books. Numerous Chinese books spread to Vietnam, which undoubtedly enlightened block printing in Vietnam.

The earliest printing records in Vietnam date back to the printing of household registers from 1251 to 1258. When the Mongolian army attacked Vietnam during the Yuan Dynasty, the three copies of the *Tripitaka* and one copy of the *Dao De Jing* that Vietnam had obtained from China during the Northern Song Dynasty were destroyed in the war. The *Full History of Great Vietnam* recorded that in 1295, Vietnamese Emperor Trần Anh Tông sent envoys to the Yuan Dynasty and obtained a copy of the *Tripitaka*, which was kept in Thiên Trường Phủ (now Imo Commune, My Loc District, Nam Dinh Province, Vietnam) with replica published. In the seventh year of Hưng Long (1299), new texts and official document formats for Buddhist rituals and ceremonies were printed and distributed throughout the country. However, these books are no longer extant. Although Vietnam did not engrave the entire *Tripitaka*, many scattered Buddhist scriptures were privately printed. The Vietnam Institute of Archaeology preserves more than 400 different types of these scriptures. These scriptures were mostly published by donors or monks, whose engraving plates are stored in the 70 temples in Hanoi, Vietnam, Bac Ninh, Hà Nam, Hải Dương, Thái Bình, Bắc Giang, and Thua Thien-Hue, among other places, for printing and circulation, among which the Trúc Lâm Chánh Giác Temple in Hanoi alone has 20 sets of printing blocks.

To learn Chinese woodblock printing techniques, Vietnamese people made a special trip to China. In 1443 and 1458, Lương Như Học, a native of Hồng Liễu Village in Trường Tân County, Vietnam, visited China twice to learn Chinese engraved block printing technique. After rcturning to his home country, he taught this skill to local people, thereby promoting the development of Vietnam's folk printing industry. During the Later Le Dynasty in Vietnam (1428–1789), Confucian classics were first published in Vietnam. In 1467, the *Complete Collection of Four Books* was published, and in the same year, a version of "The Five Classics" was engraved. The Vietnamese government attempted several times to control the printing and circulation of books. In 1743, the government prohibited the purchase of Chinese versions of the classics, only allowing the Vietnamese versions. In 1796, the Nguyen Dynasty ordered the nationwide publication of the official editions "Four Books" and "Five Classics" printed in Hanoi. In 1806, Vietnam obtained an almanac from China and compiled the Vietnamese almanac based on it. Since then, the government had issued almanacs every year, with the format and content completely following the Chinese almanacs.

The categories of privately printed books in Vietnam are similar to those of printed official books, including Confucian classics, official history, and textbooks, which were mainly used by scholars taking the imperial examination. In addition, poetry collections, genealogies, novels, and medical books were also published from time to time.

The three types of early printed books in Vietnam are those entirely printed in Chinese, those printed in Vietnamese using the Chu Nom, and those with the main text in Chinese but with Chu Nom annotations for pronunciation and meaning. Most of the Chinese books printed and published in Vietnam were works related to Buddhism and Taoism, with a smaller number of Confucian classics, literature, history, medicine, and so on.

Most of the ancient books in Vietnam were block-printed editions, but there were also movable-printed ones. The earliest known adoption of movable type printing

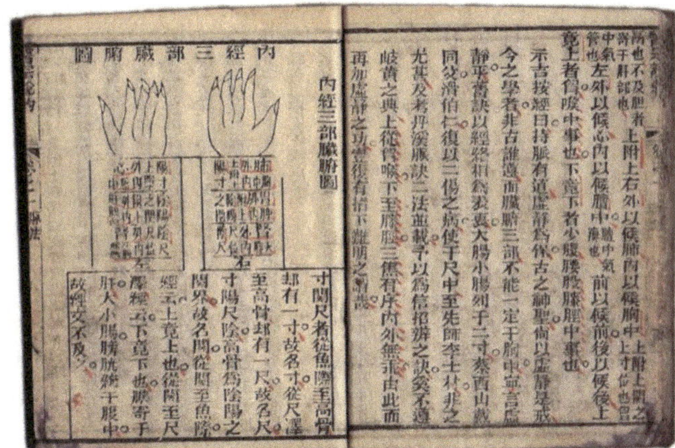
內經三部臟腑圖

Yi Zong Shuo Yue in Chinese, Vietnamese block-printed edition in the first year of the reign of Emperor Kangxi (1662)

technique was in 1712, with the printing of *Wandering Records of Legends* using wooden movable type. Later, Vietnam also purchased a set of wooden movable types from China and used it to print books such as *Qin Ding Da Nan Hui Dian Shi Li* and *Si De Yu Zhi Wen Ji Shi Ji.*

The block-printed New Year paintings industry in Vietnam also thrived, with themes and printing methods similar to Chinese New Year paintings. Many of the paintings were actually copied from Chinese originals. For example, the widely circulated Chinese painting *The Rat's Wedding* also has a Vietnamese version, depicting a lively scene of a group of rats playing the roles of the groom, gift bearers, sedan carriers, and trumpet players. There is also a color-printed New Year painting, *Guan Yu Riding a Horse*, which depicts Guan Yu riding a horse with one hand holding the reins and the other hand holding the Green Dragon Crescent Blade, looking ahead and walking slowly, just like the Chinese New Year painting *Guan Yu Riding a Horse*. This shows the deep influence of Chinese printing in Vietnam. In addition to religious statues, Buddhist paintings, and animal paintings, there are also paintings depicting agricultural labor, satirizing society, beautiful women, and humorous subjects. For example, in a painting depicting farming activities, the phrase "Agriculture is the foundation of the world" is written in Chu Nom, illustrating agricultural production processes such as "plowing the field," "harrowing the field," "sowing seeds," "transplanting seedlings," and "harvesting rice."

1.4 The Philippines

The spread of Chinese printing techniques to the Philippines also began with the introduction of printed materials through mutual envoys. Additionally, many Chinese immigrants settled in the Philippines, especially in the Chinese community centered around the Binondo market in Manila, which was formed in the late 16th century. Among these Chinese immigrants were skilled craftsmen in engraving and printing, who naturally brought Chinese printing techniques to the Philippines. These craftsmen not only engaged in engraving work but also trained local engravers, so generally, it can be said that the Philippines' printing technique and industry were directly taught or operated by Chinese engravers.

The earliest extant printed book in the Philippines is *Doctrina Christiana*, a bilingual edition in Spanish and Tagalog. It was published in 1593 by the Dominican Order in Manila, the capital of the Philippines. This block-printed edition book consists of 38 pages, currently housed in the Library of Congress in the United States. There is also a Chinese block-printed edition of *Doctrina Christiana* that was printed with Chinese stencil tissue paper. The title and front page of the book are printed in Spanish, but the content is written in Chinese, with a vertical layout and Chinese-style binding. According to a letter written by Governor-General Gomez Perez Dasmariñas to King Philip II of Spain on June 20, 1593, "Your Majesty: Considering the urgent need, permission was granted to print Christian doctrine in the Philippines. It has been printed and completed, with two books

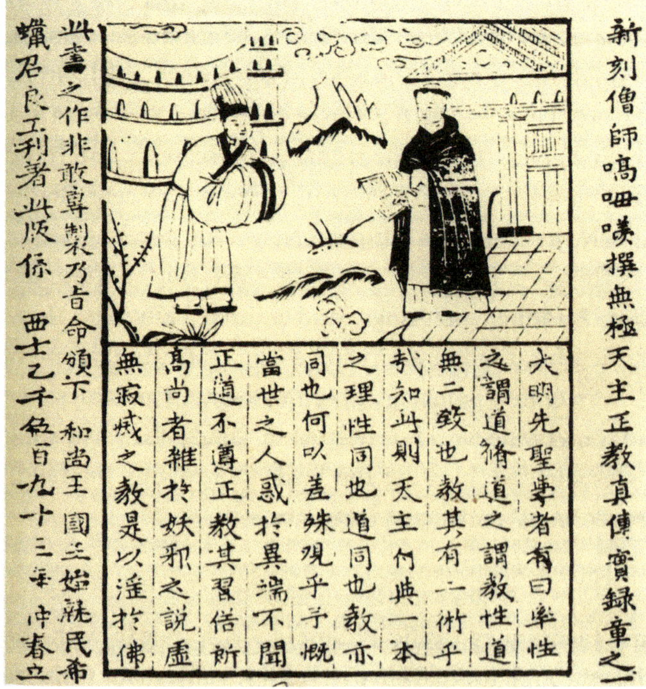
新刻僧師嗃呣嘆撰無極天主正教真傳實錄章之一

大明先聖學者有曰率性之謂道脩道之謂教性道無二致也教其有二術乎哉知此則天主何典一本之理性同也道同也教亦同也何以差殊覩乎予慨當世之人惑於異端不聞正道不遵正教其習俗所高尚者雜於妖邪之說虛無寂滅之教是以淫於佛

此書之作非敢尊製乃旨命頒下和尚王國主始就民希蠟召良工刊著此版係

西士乙千伍百九十三年仲春立

Doctrina Christiana, the earliest surviving printed book in the Philippines enclosed: one in the best Tagalog language among these islands and the other in Chinese. Henceforth, it will be more convenient to spread the gospel in these two countries," it can be inferred that this Chinese edition was also published in the first half of 1593. Importantly, the front page of the Chinese edition states that the book was printed by a Chinese craftsman named Keng Yong in the market of Binondo with permission. In 1556, the Spanish royal family issued a decree, stating that any publication or printing related to the residents in the colonies must obtain a permit from the authorities. The two Spanish lines on the front page of this book explicitly state, "Printed with special permission by Keng Yong, a Chinese person in the Binondo market in Manila."

The introduction of printing techniques played a significant role in the cultural heritage and dissemination in the Philippines, marking an important chapter in the history of cultural exchanges between China and the Philippines.

1.5 Iran

In the 9th century, Uighur people, the ancestors of the Uygurs, lived in the Hexi Corridor and Xinjiang region. Served as a hub for East-West trade, this area was an important route for the western spread of printing technique, known as the "Silk Road." In the early 20th century, an expedition team composed of German, Japanese, and Chinese discovered documents written in 17 different scripts and woodblock prints in 6 different scripts at the ancient temple sites in Turpan. The most common scripts found were Chinese, Uighur, and Sanskrit. In 1907, the wooden movable type of Uighur script, created by the Uighur around the 13th or 14th century, was discovered in Dunhuang. Analysis of these printing artifacts indicates that the printing industry in this region was quite advanced during the 13th and 14th centuries when it served as a meeting point for Eastern and Western civilizations.

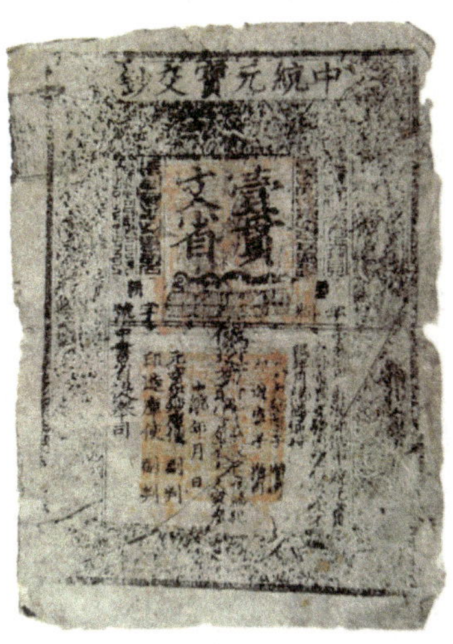

The "Zhongtong Banknote" in the Yuan Dynasty

After the consolidation of political power in the Yuan Dynasty, there was a strong push for large-scale printing of paper money. In 1260, Emperor Kublai Khan printed the "Zhongtong Banknote" to establish a unified currency system. From then on, paper money replaced gold, silver, and other general equivalents, becoming a "necessity" in people's lives.

Paper money also became the earliest Chinese printed material accessed by travelers from Central Asia, West Asia, and Europe. The production of paper money combined advanced papermaking and printing technologies of the time. After foreigners returned to their countries from the Yuan Dynasty, they accurately described the material, size, text, denomination, and circulation of the Yuan Dynasty paper money in their writings. Its excellent craftsmanship and circulation capabilities amazed people from other countries and regions around the world, who marveled at the magic of "turning paper into gold."

The Ilkhanate was the first to copy the printing form of the Yuan Dynasty banknotes and attempted to issue banknotes throughout the country. The Ilkhanate was located in the southern part of present-day Central Asia to West Asia, with its capital in Tabriz (northwest of Iran). In 1283, the envoy of the Yuan Dynasty, Bolad, submitted a detailed report to the rulers of the Ilkhanate on how to print and issue the "Zhiyuan Banknote," bringing knowledge of paper currency printing to the Ilkhanate. In May 1294, the Ilkhanate began printing paper currency in its capital. At that time, the Ilkhanate was proficient in Chinese papermaking techniques, with a large number of papermaking workshops producing flat, beautiful, high-quality paper. The layout design and content of the banknotes were basically modeled after those of the Yuan Dynasty, printed with woodcut blocks on both sides of a single sheet, stamped with a seal, filled in official information, and finally cut into banknotes. This was also the first time that the Ilkhanate used woodblock printing. Tiberius was located in the political center of Central and West Asia, where many merchants and monks from various countries gathered to engage in commercial, religious, cultural, and other activities. As a result, the circulation of paper currency had expanded, with printing knowledge spreading to many countries in Central and West Asia and Europe that had not been exposed to paper currency. *Jami' al-Tawarikh*, written by Prime Minister Rashid of the Ilkhanate, was first published in the form of a manuscript in 1311, recording the process of the Ilkhanate issuing paper currency.

Although the issue of paper money in the Ilkhanid failed due to the subsequent shock, this printing practice had epoch-making significance in the history of external transmission of Chinese printing. This was the first time that China's block printing had been used in central and Western Asia to pilot the Chinese paper currency system. Hence, the Arabs had gained printing knowledge and realized the value of Chinese printing. Since then, printing greatly contributed to the protection of Arab heritage, Arab civilization, and scientific knowledge.

2. *The Spread and Influence of Printing in Europe*

The papermaking technique invented by China was introduced to Europe in the 12th century, but it was not until the 14th century that the papermaking industry flourished in Europe. The development of the papermaking industry had laid a material foundation for printing to take root in Europe. When and by whom printing spread to Europe cannot be confirmed, but what is certain is that during the long process of exchanges between China and the West, European businessmen, travelers, and missionaries who came to China through the routes of Persia, Egypt, and Russia, introduced Chinese printed cards, paper money and books to Europe, which not only broadened the horizons of Europeans, but also enhanced their printing needs and developed the European printing industry. Printing spread to Europe not only through the Silk Road, but also through the northern route. In the Yuan Dynasty, Mongolia's wars against central Asia, Persia, Russia, and Europe led to the emergence of new trade and cultural centers, which facilitated China's contacts with Persia, Arabia, and Europe. During this period, religious and cultural exchanges between the East and the West reached an unprecedented level, creating a favorable environment for the westward spread of printing.

During the Yuan Dynasty, Europeans came to the Dayidu of the Yuan Dynasty to spread teachings. At that time, woodblock printing had already been very common in China, with the invention and adoption of movable type printing in the Central Plains and Western Xia having a history of more than 100 years. Therefore, it was natural for Western missionaries to use woodblock or movable type to print scriptures. The earliest surviving printed material in Europe is the *St. Christopher and Christ Crossing the Water*, engraved in 1423, whose layout can be seen as impacted by China. In Qian Cunxun's *Paper and Printing*, he quoted the viewpoint of British traveler Robert Curzon: the woodblock printing techniques in Europe and China are almost so similar in every aspect, "We speculate that the printing of these books may have been copied from samples from ancient China, which were brought by some early travelers from China whose names have

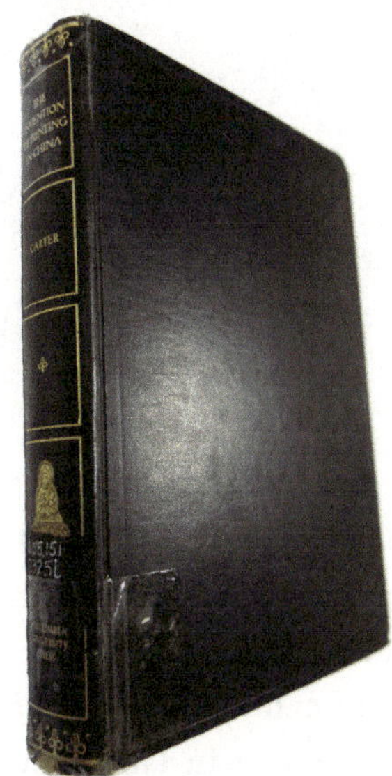

The Invention of Printing in China and Its Spread Westward, published by Columbia University Press in 1925

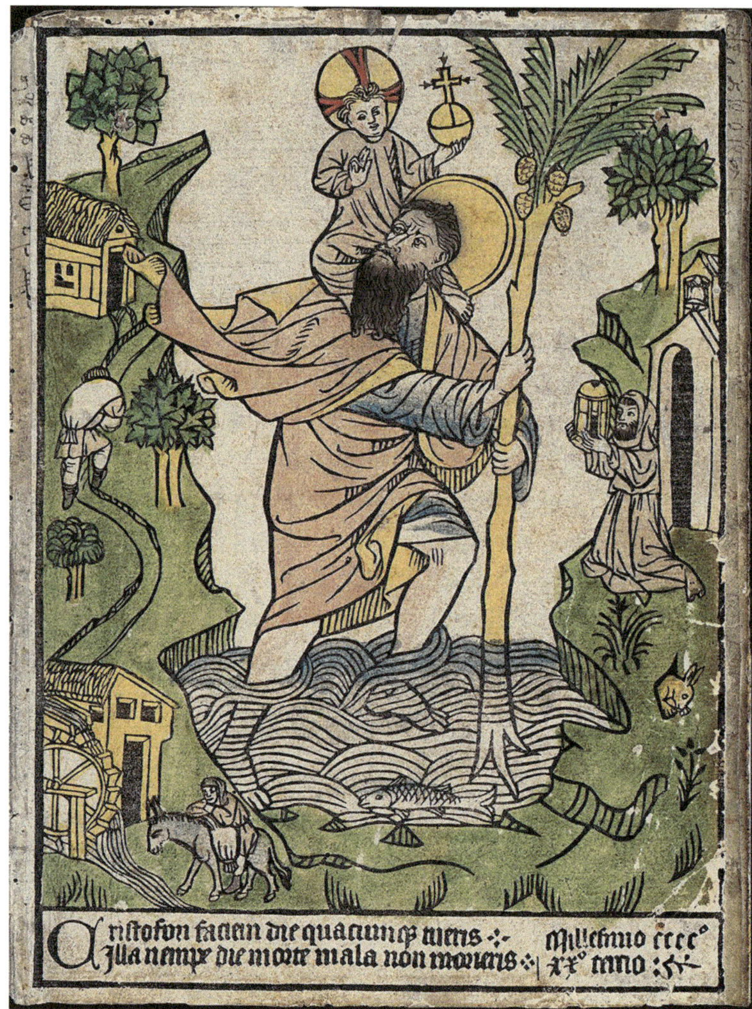

St. Christopher and Christ Crossing the Water, housed in the John Rylands Research Institute and Library

not been passed down to this day." Juan Gonzalez de Mendoza (1545–1618), a 16th-century Spanish historian, introduced China's artillery technology and printing techniques in his book *History of the Kingdom of China*. He believed that China used cannons earlier than Western countries, and printing techniques also predated Gutenberg in Germany. He said, "Now they (referring to China) still have many books printed 500 years before Germany began to invent printing techniques. I have a Chinese book, and I have also seen some others in Spain and Italy, as well as in the Indian Islands." Indeed, European woodblock printing absorbed the form of Chinese books, and everything from sample writing, engraving, and printing to binding was done according to Chinese craftsmanship.

Many people from Venice, the earliest city in Europe to know about printing cards in China, had visited China during the Yuan Dynasty. When cards were first introduced in Europe, card games had been popular in China for at least 200 years.

In the 13th century, after seeing the printed banknotes in China, Marco Polo and others from Italy were impressed. They recorded the shape, size, value, text printed on them, ink imprints, and exchange methods of banknotes with praise. Marco Polo detailed the situation of Chinese printed currency in his *The Travels of Marco Polo*, which indicates that there were no paper currencies in Africa and Europe at that time. His introductions made Europeans aware of the printing situation of the Chinese people.

In the late 14th and early 15th centuries, Europe began to see the emergence of woodblock engraved cards, religious paintings, religious books, and Latin grammar textbooks for elementary school students. Among them, cards were one of the earliest graphic prints to appear in Europe. At this time, Venice in Italy was also the center of printed portraits, with its printed cards flourishing for a time. By the mid-15th century, woodblock printing had become quite common in Europe.

On the basis of the popularization of woodblock printing in Europe, the German Gutenberg innovated movable type printing around 1450, over 400 years after Bi Sheng invented it. There is not much difference between the two persons' methods in the principle of movable type printing. Still, Gutenberg innovated two key processes, which are movable type production and printing, casting lead movable types in bulk and inventing the trigger printing machine, ushering in the era of industrial printing.

Not long after Gutenberg invented the printing press, movable type printing quickly became popular in various European countries. In Venice alone, by the late 15th century, there were about 100 newly established movable-type printing houses, and about 2 million books were published. Printing put an end to the monopoly of European monks on cultural education, promoting the European Renaissance. As Marx pointed out, "Printing has become a means of scientific rejuvenation and the most powerful lever for creating necessary prerequisites for spiritual development."

Spanish historian Mendoza mentioned in *History of the Kingdom of China* that Gutenberg was influenced by Chinese printing techniques. Chinese printing was introduced to Germany through two channels: one was through Russia, and the other was through Arab merchants carrying books to Germany. Gutenberg used these Chinese books as his printing blueprints. Mendoza's books were quickly translated into French, English, and Italian at that time, exerting a great influence in Europe. European scholars such as French writer Michel de Montaigne and historian Louis Leroy supported Mendoza's argument.

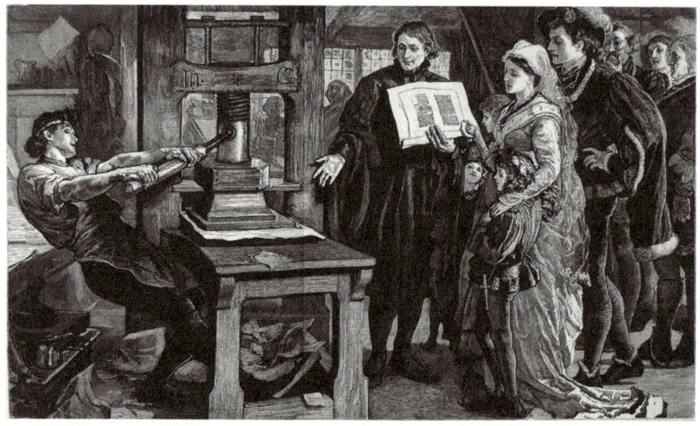

In 1476, William Caxton, the first British printer, presenting his printing machine and printed English books to King and Queen Edward IV

There are also some controversies in Western countries regarding the history of movable type printing in Europe. *The Encyclopedia Britannica* also mentioned that from 1423 to 1437, the Dutchman Laurens Janszoon Coster (1370–1440) successfully engraved wooden movable type to print Latin grammar and large title letters in Dutch, but the engraving quality of the main movable type did not surpass that of the woodblock, so it had not been promoted. This record is earlier than that of Gutenberg's invention of lead movable type printing.

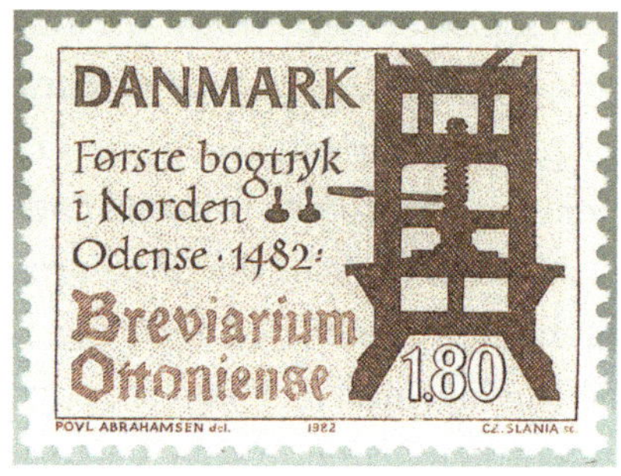

Early manual printing, Denmark issued a stamp in 1982 to commemorate the establishment of a printing shop in Odense in 1482

However, Gutenberg's movable type technique, which was revered as a deity by Westerners, did not attract Chinese people's attention because they had long been accustomed to movable type printing, and woodblock printing could almost fully meet the ancient society's demand for cultural products. The popularity of the lead movable type in China is closely related to the emergence of modern newspapers. When Western-style newspapers were first introduced into China in the 19th century, only traditional Chinese woodblock printing could be adopted for publication; as the saying goes, "Do as the Romans do." Because there was a natural, cultural conflict between the East and the West that ran before the printing press: the conflict of words, the typesetting, and plate-making processes between the Western and Chinese characters were vastly different. The printing press, which represents pressure and speed, was not a bottleneck problem for Chinese printing. What is difficult is the industrial production and repeated use of a large number of Chinese movable types.

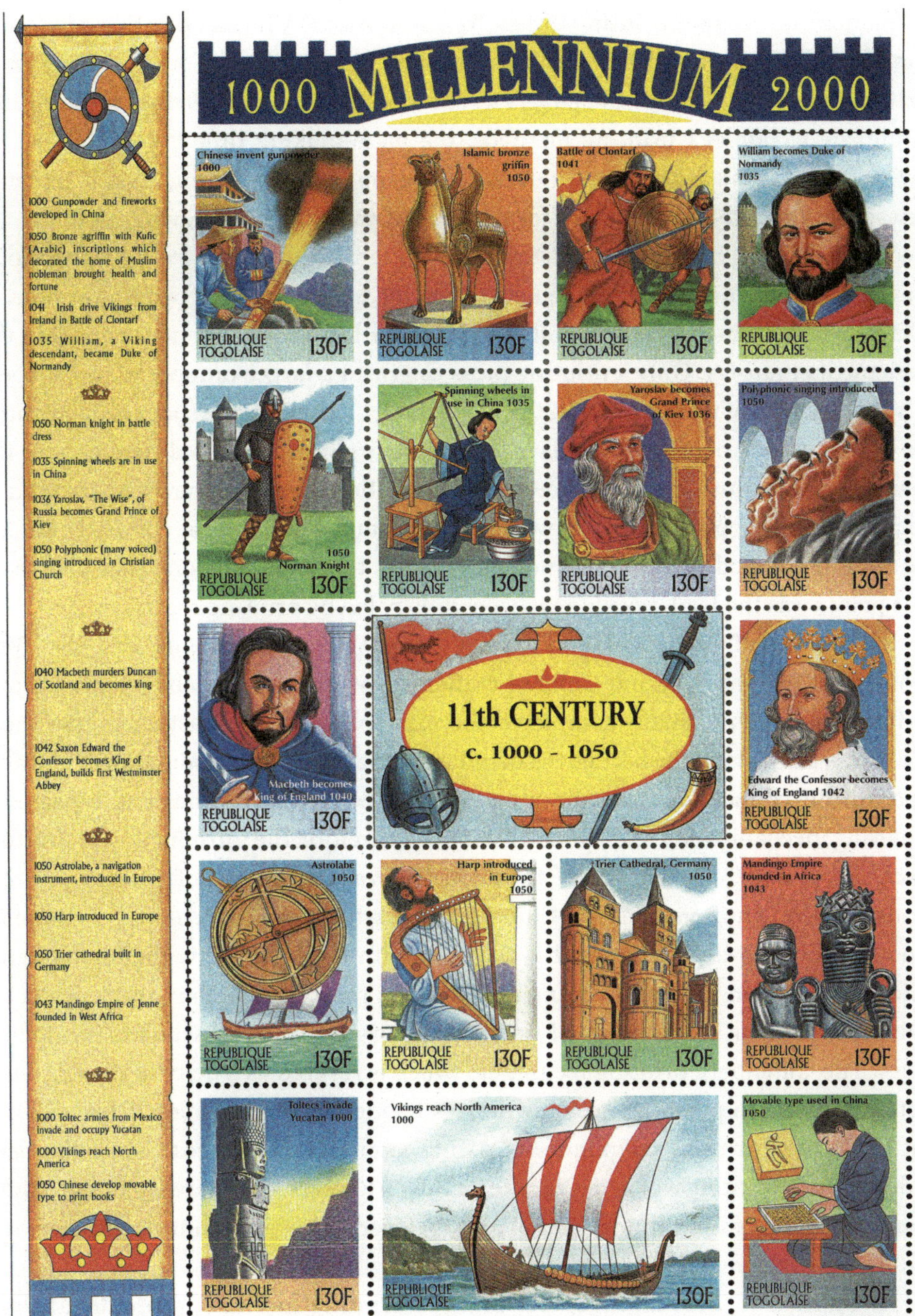

The millennium series stamps issued by the Republic of Togo in West Africa in 2000, showing the important events that affected the human process from 1000 to 1050, including the movable type printing invented by China

Modern newspaper printing differs from traditional Chinese printing models in that it has four unique and distinct characteristics. Firstly, it has strict requirements for plate-making speed. Early newspapers were called newsprint. If relying on traditional handmade woodblock printing methods, the plate-making time is too long, so it's obvious that news easily becomes outdated. Secondly, the printing craft is difficult. Newspapers usually have a large format, and if traditional engraving methods are used, it is difficult to guarantee the quality, while the use of flat lead plate printing press can ensure the quality of large format printing. Thirdly, the printing volume is relatively large, which is also a vital feature of the leading role of newspapers in the mass media industry. Only a printing press can print a larger number of newspapers in a short period of time. Fourthly, the newsworthy nature of newspapers determines the one-time feature of printing plates, while the woodblock printed classics have the possibility of reprinting and the need for preservation. However, newspapers need to frequently replace printing plates with similar layouts but different contents. Among the commonly used printing technologies at that time, the only one that met these four points was the lead movable type technology led by printing machines.

In the tide of exchanges and mutual learning between China and the West about printing, hardworking Chinese craftsmen, with unimaginable resilience and craftsmanship spirit, finally completed the massive project of "casting copper mold and lead type," solving the bottleneck of industrialization in the production of movable type. In this connection, lead movable type can be cast in batches and repeatedly, achieving mechanization and standardization. Therefore, the introduction of printing machines is not the only sign of the industrialization process of China's printing industry. The improvement of Chinese copper-type mold technology for mass production of movable-type mold is even more important. This is the fundamental difference between Chinese printing and Western printing, which is also a neglected research direction in the study of printing history by Western scholars in modern times. The Gutenberg printing technique, which is revered as a deity in the discourse system of Western printing, not only derives its movable type principle from China, but also its lead printing technique of "casting copper to make types," which has been widely used in printing works in Chinese for only 100 years. Compared with the 5,000-year civilization of the Chinese nation and the over 1000-year Chinese printing, it is just a snap of the finger.

In addition to Asia and Europe, Chinese printing had also gradually affected other countries and regions in the world. At the end of the 19th century, 50 woodblock prints were found in the ruins of an ancient city in Egypt, which were all the Islamic prayers, spells, and fragments of *The Koran* printed in ancient Arabic. They were said to have been printed from 900 to 1350, with printing methods similar to those of China. Therefore, some scholars believe that it may be that after the Mongolian army introduced printing to Arab countries during the Western expedition, it was then introduced to Egypt by travelers and businessmen in the early 14th century. In this way, Chinese printing was spread to Africa. Since then, printing had been introduced to the United States, Canada, and Australia. We can say with pride that Chinese printing has spread and impacted all over the world.

CHAPTER VI

The Contemporary Inheritance of Traditional Printing

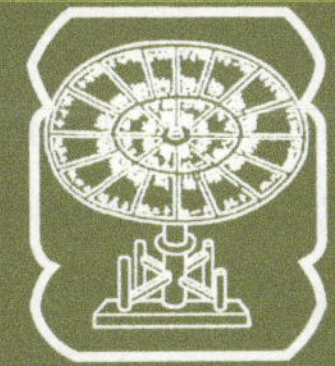

In today's era, when information technology develops rapidly, traditional woodblock printing and movable type printing techniques can no longer meet people's current needs. However, the cultural heritage contained in every stroke of traditional hand printing has been integrated into the cultural vein of the Chinese nation. As a carrier of excellent traditional Chinese culture, printing embodies the sentiment of the Chinese nation and contains the spirit of craftsmanship worth inheriting. Therefore, inheriting and promoting the spiritual and cultural connotations of traditional printing still hold great significance in the current era. In 1996, China Printing Museum was completed and opened, providing a national cultural palace for the inheritance and promotion of printing, where people can learn about printing history, appreciate printing culture, admire printing artifacts, and experience printing techniques. In the contemporary era, when excellent traditional Chinese culture is going through comprehensive rejuvenation, ancient traditional printing is undergoing creative transformation and innovative development: woodblock printing has achieved dynamic inheritance; movable type printing has incorporated the concept of filial piety, widely spread in the production of family genealogy; wood engraving water printing technique has integrated color painting technique to achieve the realistic replication of ancient paintings.

1. The Contemporary Inheritance of Engraved Block Printing Technique

In 2006, the engraved block printing technique was included in the first batch of the National Intangible Cultural Heritage List. Jinling Scriptural Press in Nanjing, Guangling Ancient Book Printing House in Yangzhou, Jiangsu Province, and Dege Sutra-Printing House in Sichuan Province are currently the top three units in China for preserving woodblock printing techniques. In 2009, the "Chinese Engraved Block Printing Technique" jointly applied by these three units was listed in the World Intangible Cultural Heritage List by the Intergovernmental Committee for the Safeguarding of Intangible Cultural Heritage of UNESCO.

In contemporary times, woodblock printing is still the mainstream printing technique for Buddhist scriptures. For example, Jinling Scriptural Press in Nanjing is a global publishing center for Chinese woodblock-printed Buddhist scriptures and a research center for Buddhist doctrine studies. Besides, It is a gathering place for Buddhist culture, historical culture, and intangible cultural heritage. The press not only circulates and prints Buddhist scriptures and Buddha statues, constantly expanding the catalog of circulating scriptures, but also further expands the practicality of traditional woodblock printing techniques. For instance, it uses different fonts, color processes, and other methods to produce block-printed classics of traditional culture and woodblock-printed works of some renowned painters.

Dege Sutra-Printing House in Sichuan Province is renowned as the world's most comprehensive, uniquely formatted, exquisitely engraved, beautifully typeset, meticulously proofread, and well-preserved Tibetan traditional woodblock printing institution. It has always adhered to the traditional method of printing scriptures. The literature and classics printed by the house have not only been disseminated in the vast Tibetan areas of China, but also collected by numerous Chinese museums and research institutions. They are also exported to India, Nepal, Bhutan, Japan, and Southeast Asian countries and regions, with some important scriptures even collected by libraries in Asia, America, and Europe.

In August 2003, with the approval of the State Council, Yangzhou City established the China Woodblock Printing Museum. It integrated the collection of 300,000 ancient bookplates by Yangzhou Guangling Publishing House into the new building of Yangzhou Museum, thus creating the "Yangzhou Double Museums"—Yangzhou Museum & China Woodblock Printing Museum. In 2019, Guangling Ancient Book Printing House in Yangzhou officially became one of the branches of the China Printing Museum. Yangzhou City has combined printing culture with tourism by creating a dynamic tourist area for woodblock printing techniques, promoting the vitality, utilization, and inheritance of Chinese woodblock printing techniques.

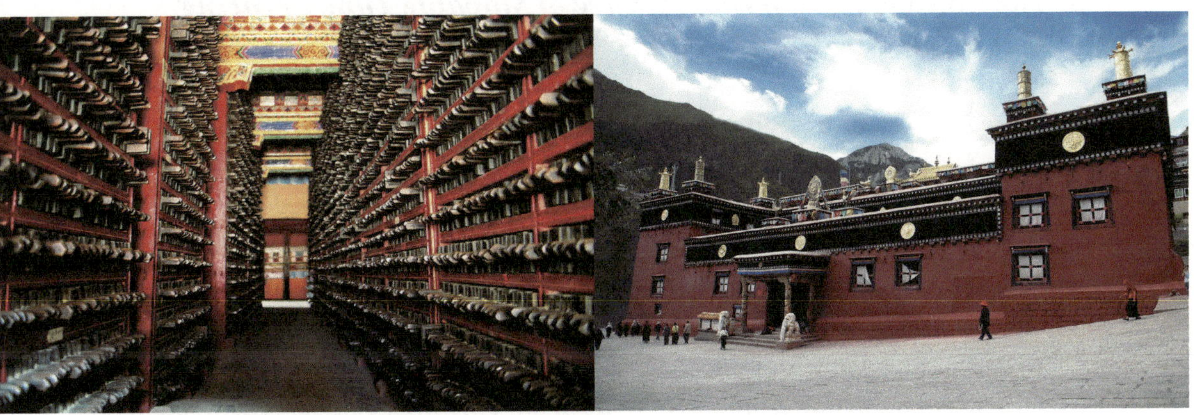

Dege Sutra-Printing House in Sichuan Province

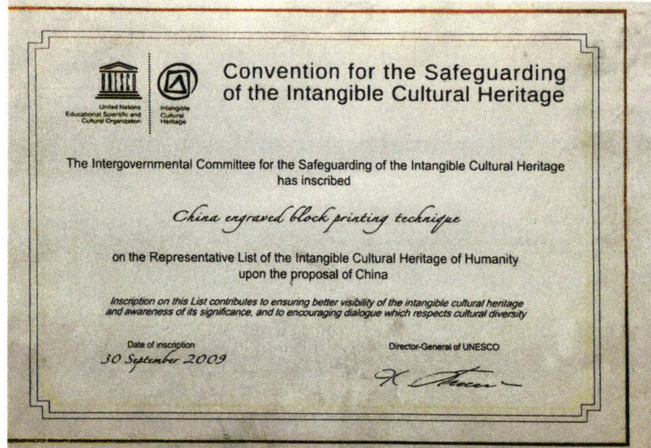

UNESCO
United Nations
Educational, Scientific and
Cultural Organization
Intangible
Cultural
Heritage

Convention for the Safeguarding
of the Intangible Cultural Heritage

The Intergovernmental Committee for the Safeguarding of the Intangible Cultural Heritage
has inscribed

China engraved block printing technique

on the Representative List of the Intangible Cultural Heritage of Humanity
upon the proposal of China

Inscription on this List contributes to ensuring better visibility of the intangible cultural heritage and awareness of its significance, and to encouraging dialogue which respects cultural diversity

Date of inscription
30 September 2009

Director-General of UNESCO

The English version of the certificate on the Representative List of the Intangible Cultural Heritage of Humanity for China engraved block printing technique, awarded by UNESCO in 2009

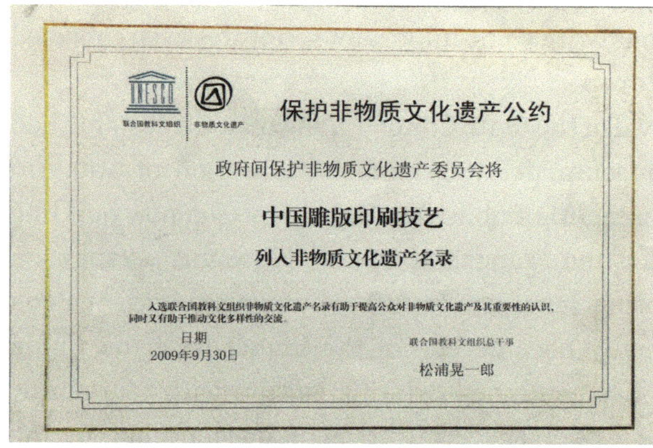

联合国教科文组织
非物质文化遗产

保护非物质文化遗产公约

政府间保护非物质文化遗产委员会将

中国雕版印刷技艺

列入非物质文化遗产名录

入选联合国教科文组织非物质文化遗产名录有助于提高公众对非物质文化遗产及其重要性的认识，同时又有助于推动文化多样性的交流。

日期
2009年9月30日

联合国教科文组织总干事
松浦晃一郎

The Chinese version of the certificate on the Representative List of the Intangible Cultural Heritage of Humanity for China engraved block printing technique, awarded by UNESCO in 2009

2. The Contemporary Inheritance of Movable Type Printing Technique

Whether clay, wood, or lead movable types, they all belong to both movable type printing techniques and letterpress printing techniques, sharing the same core principles. Since Bi Sheng invented movable type printing, Chinese people have used various materials to make movable types, such as lead, tin, and wood. Among the numerous movable type materials, wooden movable type was the most widely used in ancient China. As early as the Yuan Dynasty, Wang Zhen specifically attached "The Craft of Engraving Movable Type to Print" at the end of his *Book of Agriculture*, which detailed the printing process of wooden movable type. Compared to woodblock printing, movable type printing was less used in ancient Chinese character printing, but it has been used for thousands of years without interruption. In 2008, the wood movable type printing technique was included in the second batch of the National Intangible Cultural Heritage List. In 2010, the Chinese movable type printing technique was included in the list of Intangible Cultural Heritage that Needs Urgent Protection by UNESCO.

In Dongyuan Village, Gaolou Town (formerly Pingyangkeng Town), Rui'an City, Zhejiang Province, there stands an old house with a history of over 400 years. This was originally the old house of the Wang family, who had been dedicated to block printing for generations. Nine years ago, this place was purchased and repaired by the government, becoming the exhibition hall of China Wood Movable Type Printing Culture Village. For many residents in and around Dongyuan Village, wood movable type printing is not just a leisurely craft, but a necessity for daily life even today, because the woodblock printing technique has been passed down here due to the compilation and printing of genealogies which record the changes of a family lineage in the form of a genealogical chart, helping people to know their origins and consolidating the family ties.

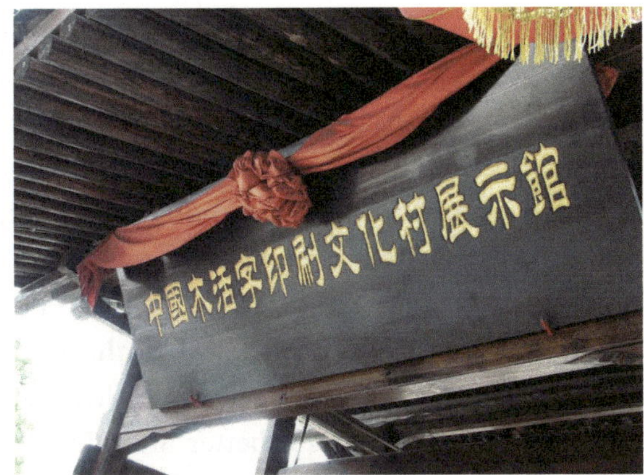

The exhibition hall of China Wood Movable Type Printing Culture Village in Rui'an, Zhejiang Province

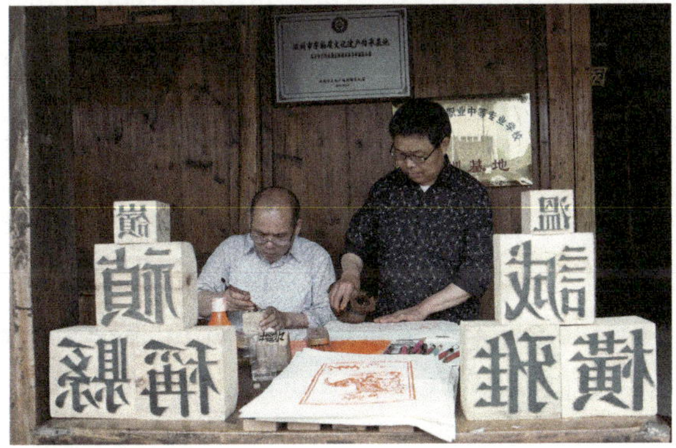

Inheritors of wooden movable type technique in the China Wood Movable Type Printing Culture Village, Rui'an, Zhejiang Province

Then, how did the Rui'an people solve the bottleneck of Chinese character movable type printing—the hard problem of picking up a large number of Chinese characters?

In this regard, the Wang family in Rui'an invented a unique and ingenious way of solving it. They created a "poem with five characters to a line" that rhyme with dialect tones as "word selection rules": "The king stands in the palace, the courtiers are all good. The common people follow the rules and rituals and peaceful borders. Meeting the messenger with plum blossoms, sending them to the people of Longtou. There is nothing special in Jiangnan but the beautiful branch of spring plum blossom. Only the toughest grass can stand strong winds, and only loyal officials can be tested through chaos. One man's principles are seen when he is in poverty, and one becomes ever firmer when his country is in ruins. The official historian ascends the golden palace, and the generals bow at the red steps. The sunlight rises through the window, and the moonlight shines on the screen. The mountains echo with the roar of apes, and the clouds carry the shadows of birds..." By arranging the wooden movable type in the order of the "word selection rules" and storing them in drawers of type cases, skilled technicians who have memorized the rhymes can easily select characters and typeset them.

Of course, there are still many inheritors and inheritance places of traditional movable type printing techniques across the country, such as the Hakka people in Ninghua, Sanming, Fujian Province, who still use wooden movable type to print family genealogies. As a result, the wooden movable type craftsmen there continue to pass down their skills from generation to generation. In 2015, the China Printing Museum established the Fujian Printing Cultural Protection Base in Ninghua, allowing inheritors to work in a stable place for the application of movable type printing.

In contemporary times, as people's living standards continue to improve, people have further pursuits for a better life. With the rejuvenation of traditional culture, cultural creative products incorporating movable type printing have become popular, such as movable type seals, movable type plates, and movable type accessories. Inheritors of movable type printing from various regions are also busy contributing to the cultural industry.

3. The Contemporary Inheritance of Process Printing Technique

The industrialization of civilization has led to the rapid development of printing techniques. At the same time, industrial printing has replaced manual printing in terms of the method of content dissemination. However, manual plate-making techniques are still used in art, and they continue to exist as a form of artistic expression. Over time, manual printing has evolved from a simple means of reproducing images to a medium of expression that artists have chosen and utilized. An example of this is the contemporary inheritance of the traditional printing techniques of Chinese New Year paintings.

Chinese folk woodblock New Year paintings were included in the first list of the "Chinese Folk Culture Heritage Rescue Project" in 2002. In 2006, woodblock New Year paintings were included in the first batch of the National Intangible Cultural Heritage List under the approval of the State Council. This list includes woodblock New Year paintings produced in 11 regions: Yangliuqing, Wuqiang, Taohuawu, Zhangzhou, Yangjiabu, Zhuxian Town, Tantou, Foshan, Liangping, Mianzhu, and Fengxiang. In 2008, the second batch of the National Intangible Cultural Heritage List added the woodblock New Year paintings produced in Pingyang, Dongchangfu, Zhangqiu, Huaxian, and Jiajiang. In 2011, the third batch of the National Intangible Cultural Heritage List included the woodblock New Year paintings produced in Laohekou as one of the expanded projects. These regions not only have established New Year painting museums to showcase the history of New Year paintings, but also have had artisans who continue to engrave and sell New Year paintings from generation to generation. In the contemporary era, when excellent traditional Chinese culture is undergoing rejuvenation across the board, many families still preserve the tradition of posting couplets, "Fu" characters, and New Year paintings during the Spring Festival. Therefore, the ancient technique of woodblock New Year paintings will continue to be inherited and developed in the new era.

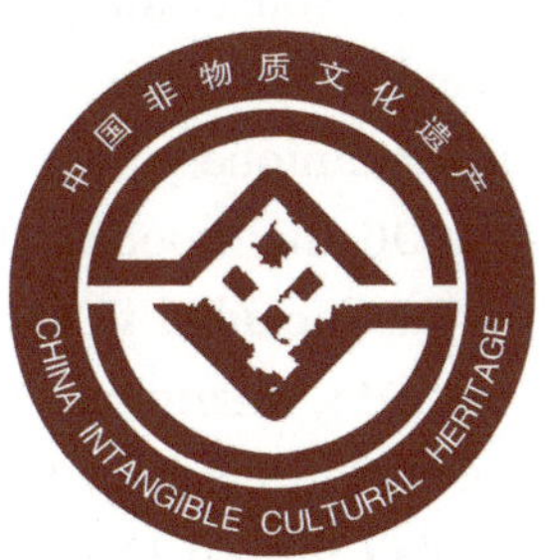

Symbol of China's Intangible Cultural Heritage

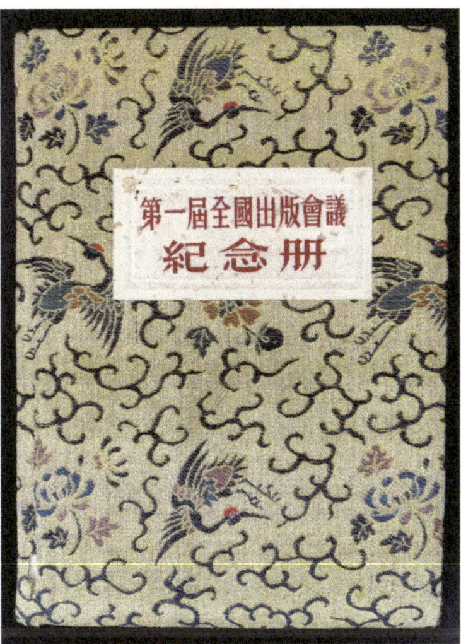

Commemorative Album of the First National Publishing Conference, woodblock watercolor printed by Rongbaozhai Studio in 1950

The term "woodblock watercolor printing" is naturally associated with traditional printing. In fact, while the woodblock watercolor printing technique has a long history, the term itself is relatively modern. In the early 1950s, artists introduced the traditional woodblock overprint technique inherited from the late Ming Dynasty into the replication of traditional Chinese painting and calligraphy, creating a new style of block-printed painting. They refined this technique into the accessible term "woodblock watercolor printing." Woodblock watercolor printing has achieved remarkable success in the field of high-fidelity reproduction of paintings and calligraphy, often creating a "true-to-life" effect. This is where the core value of woodblock watercolor printing lies. The paper and pigments used in woodblock watercolor printing are identical to those used in the original works, with the only difference being the use of wooden blocks instead of brushes. Nowadays, woodblock watercolor printing is also expanding into the fields of cultural and creative products and tourist souvenirs. Woodblock watercolor printing artworks that are closely connected to daily life will further promote the development of traditional process printing techniques.

In 2006, the "woodblock watercolor printing technique" invented by Rongbaozhai Studio was included in the first batch of the National Intangible Cultural Heritage List. In 2014, Shanghai Duoyunxuan Art Development Co., Ltd. was selected as a demonstration base for the productive protection of the second batch of National Intangible Cultural Heritage. In the same year, the "woodblock watercolor printing technique" declared by Hangzhou Shizhuzhai Art Museum was included in the fourth batch of the National Intangible Cultural Heritage Representative Project List.

Bibliography

Chen, Dengyuan. *The Chen's High School Chinese History*. World Books, 1933.

[Ming] Hu, Yinglin. *Shaoshi Shanfang Bicong*. Shanghai Bookstore Publishing House, 2001.

Li, Ying. *Chinese Color Printing for Two Thousand Years*. Jiangxi Science and Technology Publishing House, 2009.

[Spain] Mendoza, Juan Gonzalez de. *History of the Kingdom of China*. Translated by Sun Jiakun. Central Compilation and Translation Press, 2009.

Niu, Dasheng. *Study on Xixia Movable Type Printing*. Ningxia People's Press, 2004.

Qi, Zhifen. "Sino-Philippine Exchanges and the Introduction of Chinese Printing Technology into the Philippines. *Wen Xian*, no. 4 (1988).

[Northern Song] Shen, Kuo. *Dream Pool Essays*. Edited by Shi Shi. Shanghai Ancient Books Press, 2015.

[Japan] Shuei. *New Book of Buddhist Scriptures and Other Works*. Dalun Pinjia Jingshe, 1911–1920.

Sun, Xiangdong. *100 Classical Chinese Novels*. China Social Press, 1999.

Tang, Shaoming, and Editorial Committee. *Beijing Library Anthology of Literature, Volume 2*. Bibliographic Literature Press, 1992.

[Yuan] Tuitui et al. *History of the Song Dynasty*. Zhonghua Book Company, 1977.

World Book Editorial Department. *World Book 1981*. China National Publications Import Company, 1981.

Zhang, Shudong, Pang Duoyi, and Zheng Rusi. *General History of Chinese Printing*. Reviewed by Zheng Yongli and Li Xingcai. Printing Industry Press, 1999.

Zhang, Xiumin. *The History of Chinese Printing: First Volume. Revised and Enlarged Edition of Illustrated Collections*. Reviewed by Han Qi. Zhejiang Ancient Books Publishing House, 2006.

ABOUT THE EDITORS

HUA JUEMING, a researcher and former associate director of the Institute for the History of Natural Sciences at the Chinese Academy of Sciences, is a renowned expert in the history of science and technology in China. His main research areas include ancient bronze metallurgy, steel technology, the history of machinery, and the philosophy of technology. In recent years, he has been devoted to the research and preservation of traditional crafts. He is the author of several works, including *Essays on the History of Chinese Metallurgy, Ancient Chinese Metal Technology, Five Thousand Years of Chinese Science and Technology,* and *Ancient Chinese Metal Technology.*

FENG LISHENG, a researcher and director of the Institute for the History of Science and Ancient Documents at Tsinghua University, is mainly engaged in research on the history of mathematics in China and abroad, the history of Chinese machinery, the history of metrology, the history of physics, and the history of science and technology among Chinese ethnic minorities. He is the author of works such as *The History of Ancient Chinese Surveying* and *The History of Sino-Japanese Mathematical Relations.*

ABOUT THE AUTHOR

LI YING is the Deputy Director of the National Library of China, Vice President and Secretary-General of the Chinese Printing History Research Association, and a member of the Chinese Popular Science Writers Association. He is the author of works such as *The Printing Cultural Heritage of the Sui, Tang, and Five Dynasties* and *2000 Years of Color Printing in China.*

ABOUT THE TRANSLATOR

CHEN WEI: PhD, English professor of Jiangnan University, Wuxi, Jiangsu Province, PRC.